Learning Data Mining with Python

Harness the power of Python to analyze data and create insightful predictive models

Robert Layton

BIRMINGHAM - MUMBAI

Learning Data Mining with Python

First published: July 2015

Production reference: 1230715

Published by Packt Publishing Ltd.
Livery Place
35 Livery Street
Birmingham B3 2PB, UK.

ISBN 978-1-78439-605-3

www.packtpub.com

Credits

Author
Robert Layton

Reviewers
Asad Ahamad
P Ashwin
Christophe Van Gysel
Edward C. Delaporte V

Commissioning Editor
Taron Pereira

Acquisition Editor
James Jones

Content Development Editor
Siddhesh Salvi

Technical Editor
Naveenkumar Jain

Copy Editors
Roshni Banerjee
Trishya Hajare

Project Coordinator
Nidhi Joshi

Proofreader
Safis Editing

Indexer
Priya Sane

Graphics
Sheetal Aute

Production Coordinator
Nitesh Thakur

Cover Work
Nitesh Thakur

About the Author

Robert Layton has a PhD in computer science and has been an avid Python programmer for many years. He has worked closely with some of the largest companies in the world on data mining applications for real-world data and has also been published extensively in international journals and conferences. He has extensive experience in cybercrime and text-based data analytics, with a focus on behavioral modeling, authorship analysis, and automated open source intelligence. He has contributed code to a number of open source libraries, including the scikit-learn library used in this book, and was a Google Summer of Code mentor in 2014. Robert runs a data mining consultancy company called dataPipeline, providing data mining and analytics solutions to businesses in a variety of industries.

About the Reviewers

Asad Ahamad is a data enthusiast and loves to work on data to solve challenging problems.

He did his master's degree in industrial mathematics with computer application at Jamia Millia Islamia, New Delhi. He admires mathematics a lot and always tries to use it to gain maximum profit for businesses.

He has good experience working in data mining, machine learning, and data science and has worked for various multinationals in India. He mainly uses R and Python to perform data wrangling and modeling. He is fond of using open source tools for data analysis.

He is an active social media user. Feel free to connect with him on Twitter at `@asadtaj88`.

P Ashwin is a Bangalore-based engineer who wears many different hats depending on the occasion. He graduated from IIIT, Hyderabad at in 2012 with an M Tech in computer science and engineering. He has a total of 5 years of experience in the software industry, where he has worked in different domains such as testing, data warehousing, replication, and automation. He is very well versed in DB concepts, SQL, and scripting with Bash and Python. He has earned professional certifications in products from Oracle, IBM, Informatica, and Teradata. He's also an ISTQB-certified tester.

In his free time, he volunteers in different technical hackathons or social service activities. He was introduced to Raspberry Pi in one of the hackathons and he's been hooked on it ever since. He writes a lot of code in Python, C, C++, and Shell on his Raspberry Pi B+ cluster. He's currently working on creating his own Beowulf cluster of 64 Raspberry Pi 2s.

Christophe Van Gysel is pursuing a doctorate degree in computer science at the University of Amsterdam under the supervision of Maarten de Rijke and Marcel Worring. He has interned at Google, where he worked on large-scale machine learning and automated speech recognition. During his internship in Facebook's security infrastructure team, he worked on information security and implemented measures against compression side-channel attacks. In the past, he was active as a security researcher. He discovered and reported security vulnerabilities in the web services of Google, Facebook, Dropbox, and PayPal, among others.

Edward C. Delaporte V leads a software development group at the University of Illinois, and he has contributed to the documentation of the Kivy framework. He is thankful to all those whose contributions to the open source community made his career possible, and he hopes this book helps continue to attract enthusiasts to software development.

www.PacktPub.com

Support files, eBooks, discount offers, and more

For support files and downloads related to your book, please visit www.PacktPub.com.

Did you know that Packt offers eBook versions of every book published, with PDF and ePub files available? You can upgrade to the eBook version at www.PacktPub.com and as a print book customer, you are entitled to a discount on the eBook copy. Get in touch with us at service@packtpub.com for more details.

At www.PacktPub.com, you can also read a collection of free technical articles, sign up for a range of free newsletters and receive exclusive discounts and offers on Packt books and eBooks.

https://www2.packtpub.com/books/subscription/packtlib

Do you need instant solutions to your IT questions? PacktLib is Packt's online digital book library. Here, you can search, access, and read Packt's entire library of books.

Why subscribe?

- Fully searchable across every book published by Packt
- Copy and paste, print, and bookmark content
- On demand and accessible via a web browser

Free access for Packt account holders

If you have an account with Packt at www.PacktPub.com, you can use this to access PacktLib today and view 9 entirely free books. Simply use your login credentials for immediate access.

Table of Contents

Preface

If you have ever wanted to get into data mining, but didn't know where to start, I've written this book with you in mind.

Many data mining books are highly mathematical, which is great when you are coming from such a background, but I feel they often miss the forest for the trees—that is, they focus so much on how the algorithms work, that we forget about why we are using these algorithms.

In this book, my aim has been to create a book for those who can program and want to learn data mining. By the end of this book, my aim is that you have a good understanding of the basics, some best practices to jump into solving problems with data mining, and some pointers on the next steps you can take.

Each chapter in this book introduces a new topic, algorithm, and dataset. For this reason, it can be a bit of a whirlwind tour, moving quickly from topic to topic. However, for each of the chapters, think about how you can improve upon the results presented in the chapter. Then, take a shot at implementing it!

One of my favorite quotes is from Shakespeare's Henry IV:

> *But will they come when you do call for them?*

Before this quote, a character is claiming to be able to call spirits. In response, Hotspur points out that anyone can call spirits, but what matters is whether they actually come when they are called.

In much the same way, learning data mining is about performing experiments and getting the result. Anyone can come up with an idea to create a new data mining algorithm or improve upon an experiment's results. However, what matters is: can you build it and does it work?

What this book covers

Chapter 1, Getting Started with Data Mining, introduces the technologies we will be using, along with implementing two basic algorithms to get started.

Chapter 2, Classifying with scikit-learn Estimators, covers classification, which is a key form of data mining. You'll also learn about some structures to make your data mining experimentation easier to perform..

Chapter 3, Predicting Sports Winners with Decision Trees, introduces two new algorithms, *Decision Trees and Random Forests*, and uses them to predict sports winners by creating useful features.

Chapter 4, Recommending Movies Using Affinity Analysis, looks at the problem of recommending products based on past experience and introduces the Apriori algorithm.

Chapter 5, Extracting Features with Transformers, introduces different types of features you can create and how to work with different datasets.

Chapter 6, Social Media Insight Using Naive Bayes, uses the Naive Bayes algorithm to automatically parse text-based information from the social media website, Twitter.

Chapter 7, Discovering Accounts to Follow Using Graph Mining, applies cluster and network analysis to find good people to follow on social media.

Chapter 8, Beating CAPTCHAs with Neural Networks, looks at extracting information from images and then training neural networks to find words and letters in those images.

Chapter 9, Authorship Attribution, looks at determining who wrote a given document, by extracting text-based features and using support vector machines.

Chapter 10, Clustering News Articles, uses the k-means clustering algorithm to group together news articles based on their content.

Chapter 11, Classifying Objects in Images Using Deep Learning, determines what type of object is being shown in an image, by applying deep neural networks.

Chapter 12, Working with Big Data, looks at workflows for applying algorithms to big data and how to get insight from it.

Appendix, Next Steps…, goes through each chapter, giving hints on where to go next for a deeper understanding of the concepts introduced.

What you need for this book

It should come as no surprise that you'll need a computer, or access to one, to complete this book. The computer should be reasonably modern, but it doesn't need to be overpowered. Any modern processor (from about 2010 onwards) and 4 GB of RAM will suffice, and you can probably run almost all of the code on a slower system too.

The exception here is with the final two chapters. In these chapters, I step through using Amazon Web Services (AWS) to run the code. This will probably cost you some money, but the advantage is less system setup than running the code locally. If you don't want to pay for those services, the tools used can all be set up on a local computer, but you will definitely need a modern system to run it. A processor built in at least 2012 and with more than 4 GB of RAM is necessary.

I recommend the Ubuntu operating system, but the code should work well on Windows, Macs, or any other Linux variant. You may need to consult the documentation for your system to get some things installed, though.

In this book, I use pip to install code, which is a command-line tool for installing Python libraries. Another option is to use Anaconda, which can be found online here: `http://continuum.io/downloads`.

I have also tested all code using Python 3. Most of the code examples work on Python 2, with no changes. If you run into any problems and can't get around them, send an email and we can offer a solution.

Who this book is for

This book is for programmers who want to get started in data mining in an application-focused manner.

If you haven't programmed before, I strongly recommend that you learn at least the basics before you get started. This book doesn't introduce programming, nor does it give too much time to explain the actual implementation (in code) of how to type out the instructions. That said, once you go through the basics, you should be able to come back to this book fairly quickly—there is no need to be an expert programmer first!

I highly recommend that you have some Python programming experience. If you don't, feel free to jump in, but you might want to take a look at some Python code first, possibly focusing on tutorials using the IPython Notebook. Writing programs in the IPython Notebook works a little differently than other methods such as writing a Java program in a fully fledged IDE.

Conventions

In this book, you will find a number of text styles that distinguish between different kinds of information. Here are some examples of these styles and an explanation of their meaning.

The most important is code. Code that you need to enter is displayed separate from the text, in a box like this one:

```
if True:
    print("Welcome to the book")
```

Keep a careful eye on indentation. Python cares about how much lines are indented. In this book, I've used four spaces for indentation. You can use a different number (or tabs), but you need to be consistent. If you get a bit lost counting indentation levels, reference the code bundle that comes with the book.

Where I refer to code in text, `I'll use this format`. You don't need to type this in your IPython Notebooks, unless the text specifically states otherwise.

Any command-line input or output is written as follows:

```
# cp file1.txt file2.txt
```

New terms and **important words** are shown in bold. Words that you see on the screen, for example, in menus or dialog boxes, appear in the text like this: "Click on the **Export** link."

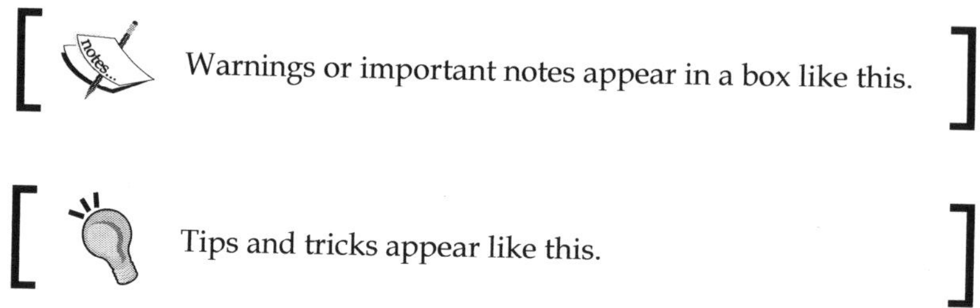

Warnings or important notes appear in a box like this.

Tips and tricks appear like this.

Reader feedback

Feedback from our readers is always welcome. Let us know what you think about this book—what you liked or disliked. Reader feedback is important for us as it helps us develop titles that you will really get the most out of.

To send us general feedback, simply e-mail feedback@packtpub.com, and mention the book's title in the subject of your message.

If there is a topic that you have expertise in and you are interested in either writing or contributing to a book, see our author guide at www.packtpub.com/authors.

Customer support

Now that you are the proud owner of a Packt book, we have a number of things to help you to get the most from your purchase.

Downloading the example code

You can download the example code files from your account at http://www.packtpub.com for all the Packt Publishing books you have purchased. If you purchased this book elsewhere, you can visit http://www.packtpub.com/support and register to have the files e-mailed directly to you.

Downloading the color images of this book

We also provide you with a PDF file that has color images of the screenshots/diagrams used in this book. The color images will help you better understand the changes in the output. You can download this file from https://www.packtpub.com/sites/default/files/downloads/6053OS_ColorImages.pdf.

Errata

Although we have taken every care to ensure the accuracy of our content, mistakes do happen. If you find a mistake in one of our books—maybe a mistake in the text or the code—we would be grateful if you could report this to us. By doing so, you can save other readers from frustration and help us improve subsequent versions of this book. If you find any errata, please report them by visiting `http://www.packtpub.com/submit-errata`, selecting your book, clicking on the **Errata Submission Form** link, and entering the details of your errata. Once your errata are verified, your submission will be accepted and the errata will be uploaded to our website or added to any list of existing errata under the Errata section of that title.

To view the previously submitted errata, go to `https://www.packtpub.com/books/content/support` and enter the name of the book in the search field. The required information will appear under the **Errata** section.

Piracy

Piracy of copyrighted material on the Internet is an ongoing problem across all media. At Packt, we take the protection of our copyright and licenses very seriously. If you come across any illegal copies of our works in any form on the Internet, please provide us with the location address or website name immediately so that we can pursue a remedy.

Please contact us at `copyright@packtpub.com` with a link to the suspected pirated material.

We appreciate your help in protecting our authors and our ability to bring you valuable content.

Questions

If you have a problem with any aspect of this book, you can contact us at `questions@packtpub.com`, and we will do our best to address the problem.

1
Getting Started with Data Mining

We are collecting information at a scale that has never been seen before in the history of mankind and placing more day-to-day importance on the use of this information in everyday life. We expect our computers to translate Web pages into other languages, predict the weather, suggest books we would like, and diagnose our health issues. These expectations will grow, both in the number of applications and also in the efficacy we expect. Data mining is a methodology that we can employ to train computers to make decisions with data and forms the backbone of many high-tech systems of today.

The Python language is fast growing in popularity, for a good reason. It gives the programmer a lot of flexibility; it has a large number of modules to perform different tasks; and Python code is usually more readable and concise than in any other languages. There is a large and an active community of researchers, practitioners, and beginners using Python for data mining.

In this chapter, we will introduce data mining with Python. We will cover the following topics:

- What is data mining and where can it be used?
- Setting up a Python-based environment to perform data mining
- An example of affinity analysis, recommending products based on purchasing habits
- An example of (a classic) classification problem, predicting the plant species based on its measurement

Introducing data mining

Data mining provides a way for a computer to learn how to make decisions with data. This decision could be predicting tomorrow's weather, blocking a spam email from entering your inbox, detecting the language of a website, or finding a new romance on a dating site. There are many different applications of data mining, with new applications being discovered all the time.

Data mining is part of algorithms, statistics, engineering, optimization, and computer science. We also use concepts and knowledge from other fields such as linguistics, neuroscience, or town planning. Applying it effectively usually requires this domain-specific knowledge to be integrated with the algorithms.

Most data mining applications work with the same high-level view, although the details often change quite considerably. We start our data mining process by creating a dataset, describing an aspect of the real world. Datasets comprise of two aspects:

- Samples that are objects in the real world. This can be a book, photograph, animal, person, or any other object.
- Features that are descriptions of the samples in our dataset. Features could be the length, frequency of a given word, number of legs, date it was created, and so on.

The next step is tuning the data mining algorithm. Each data mining algorithm has parameters, either within the algorithm or supplied by the user. This tuning allows the algorithm to learn how to make decisions about the data.

As a simple example, we may wish the computer to be able to categorize people as "short" or "tall". We start by collecting our dataset, which includes the heights of different people and whether they are considered short or tall:

Person	Height	Short or tall?
1	155cm	Short
2	165cm	Short
3	175cm	Tall
4	185cm	Tall

The next step involves tuning our algorithm. As a simple algorithm; if the height is more than x, the person is tall, otherwise they are short. Our training algorithm will then look at the data and decide on a good value for x. For the preceding dataset, a reasonable value would be 170 cm. Anyone taller than 170 cm is considered tall by the algorithm. Anyone else is considered short.

In the preceding dataset, we had an obvious feature type. We wanted to know if people are short or tall, so we collected their heights. This engineering feature is an important problem in data mining. In later chapters, we will discuss methods for choosing good features to collect in your dataset. Ultimately, this step often requires some expert domain knowledge or at least some trial and error.

In this book, we will introduce data mining through Python. In some cases, we choose clarity of code and workflows, rather than the most optimized way to do this. This sometimes involves skipping some details that can improve the algorithm's speed or effectiveness.

Using Python and the IPython Notebook

In this section, we will cover installing Python and the environment that we will use for most of the book, the IPython Notebook. Furthermore, we will install the `numpy` module, which we will use for the first set of examples.

Installing Python

The Python language is a fantastic, versatile, and an easy to use language.

For this book, we will be using Python 3.4, which is available for your system from the Python Organization's website: `https://www.python.org/downloads/`.

There will be two major versions to choose from, Python 3.4 and Python 2.7. Remember to download and install **Python 3.4**, which is the version tested throughout this book.

In this book, we will be assuming that you have some knowledge of programming and Python itself. You do not need to be an expert with Python to complete this book, although a good level of knowledge will help.

If you do not have any experience with programming, I recommend that you pick up the *Learning Python* book from.

The Python organization also maintains a list of two online tutorials for those new to Python:

- For nonprogrammers who want to learn programming through the Python language: `https://wiki.python.org/moin/BeginnersGuide/NonProgrammers`
- For programmers who already know how to program, but need to learn Python specifically: `https://wiki.python.org/moin/BeginnersGuide/Programmers`

Windows users will need to set an environment variable in order to use Python from the command line. First, find where Python 3 is installed; the default location is `C:\Python34`. Next, enter this command into the command line (cmd program): set the enviornment to `PYTHONPATH=%PYTHONPATH%;C:\Python34`. Remember to change the `C:\Python34` if Python is installed into a different directory.

Once you have Python running on your system, you should be able to open a command prompt and run the following code:

```
$ python3
Python 3.4.0 (default, Apr 11 2014, 13:05:11)
[GCC 4.8.2] on Linux
Type "help", "copyright", "credits" or "license" for more information.
>>> print("Hello, world!")
Hello, world!
>>> exit()
```

Note that we will be using the dollar sign ($) to denote that a command is to be typed into the terminal (also called a shell or `cmd` on Windows). You do not need to type this character (or the space that follows it). Just type in the rest of the line and press *Enter*.

After you have the above `"Hello, world!"` example running, exit the program and move on to installing a more advanced environment to run Python code, the IPython Notebook.

> Python 3.4 will include a program called **pip**, which is a package manager that helps to install new libraries on your system. You can verify that `pip` is working on your system by running the `$ pip3 freeze` command, which tells you which packages you have installed on your system.

Installing IPython

IPython is a platform for Python development that contains a number of tools and environments for running Python and has more features than the standard interpreter. It contains the powerful IPython Notebook, which allows you to write programs in a web browser. It also formats your code, shows output, and allows you to annotate your scripts. It is a great tool for exploring datasets and we will be using it as our main environment for the code in this book.

To install IPython on your computer, you can type the following into a command line prompt (not into Python):

```
$ pip install ipython[all]
```

You will need administrator privileges to install this system-wide. If you do not want to (or can't) make system-wide changes, you can install it for just the current user by running this command:

```
$ pip install --user ipython[all]
```

This will install the IPython package into a user-specific location—you will be able to use it, but nobody else on your computer can. If you are having difficulty with the installation, check the official documentation for more detailed installation instructions: `http://ipython.org/install.html`.

With the IPython Notebook installed, you can launch it with the following:

```
$ ipython3 notebook
```

This will do two things. First, it will create an IPython Notebook instance that will run in the command prompt you just used. Second, it will launch your web browser and connect to this instance, allowing you to create a new notebook. It will look something similar to the following screenshot (where home/bob will be replaced by your current working directory):

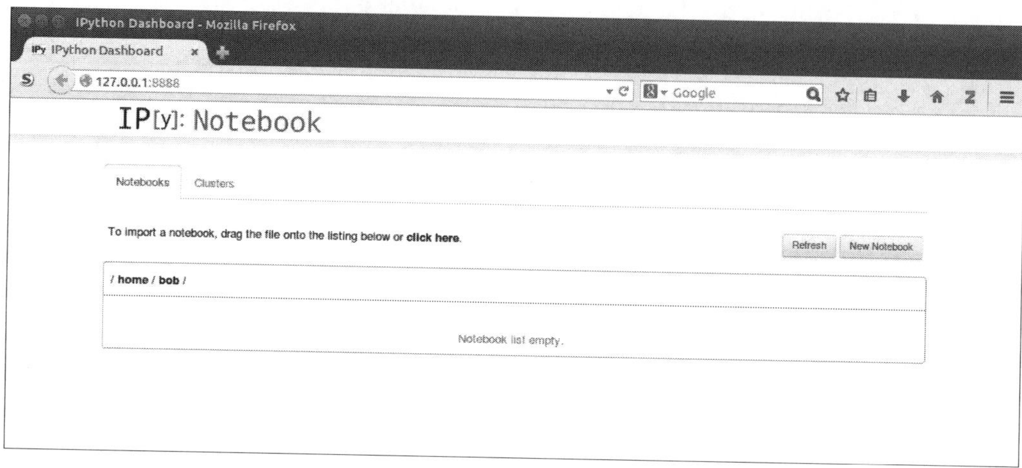

To stop the IPython Notebook from running, open the command prompt that has the instance running (the one you used earlier to run the `IPython` command). Then, press *Ctrl* + *C* and you will be prompted `Shutdown this notebook server (y/[n])?`. Type *y* and press *Enter* and the IPython Notebook will shutdown.

Installing scikit-learn

The `scikit-learn` package is a machine learning library, written in Python. It contains numerous algorithms, datasets, utilities, and frameworks for performing machine learning. Built upon the scientific python stack, scikit-learn users such as the `numpy` and `scipy` libraries are often optimized for speed. This makes scikit-learn fast and scalable in many instances and also useful for all skill ranges from beginners to advanced research users. We will cover more details of scikit-learn in *Chapter 2, Classifying with scikit-learn Estimators*.

To install `scikit-learn`, you can use the `pip` utility that comes with Python 3, which will also install the `numpy` and `scipy` libraries if you do not already have them. Open a terminal with administrator/root privileges and enter the following command:

```
$ pip3 install -U scikit-learn
```

Windows users may need to install the `numpy` and `scipy` libraries before installing scikit-learn. Installation instructions are available at `www.scipy.org/install.html` for those users.

Users of major Linux distributions such as Ubuntu or Red Hat may wish to install the official package from their package manager. Not all distributions have the latest versions of scikit-learn, so check the version before installing it. The minimum version needed for this book is 0.14.

Those wishing to install the latest version by compiling the source, or view more detailed installation instructions, can go to `http://scikit-learn.org/stable/install.html` to view the official documentation on installing scikit-learn.

A simple affinity analysis example

In this section, we jump into our first example. A common use case for data mining is to improve sales by asking a customer who is buying a product if he/she would like another similar product as well. This can be done through affinity analysis, which is the study of when things exist together.

What is affinity analysis?

Affinity analysis is a type of data mining that gives similarity between samples (objects). This could be the similarity between the following:

- users on a website, in order to provide varied services or targeted advertising
- items to sell to those users, in order to provide recommended movies or products
- human genes, in order to find people that share the same ancestors

We can measure affinity in a number of ways. For instance, we can record how frequently two products are purchased together. We can also record the accuracy of the statement when a person buys object 1 and also when they buy object 2. Other ways to measure affinity include computing the similarity between samples, which we will cover in later chapters.

Product recommendations

One of the issues with moving a traditional business online, such as commerce, is that tasks that used to be done by humans need to be automated in order for the online business to scale. One example of this is up-selling, or selling an extra item to a customer who is already buying. Automated product recommendations through data mining are one of the driving forces behind the e-commerce revolution that is turning billions of dollars per year into revenue.

In this example, we are going to focus on a basic product recommendation service. We design this based on the following idea: when two items are historically purchased together, they are more likely to be purchased together in the future. This sort of thinking is behind many product recommendation services, in both online and offline businesses.

A very simple algorithm for this type of product recommendation algorithm is to simply find any historical case where a user has brought an item and to recommend other items that the historical user brought. In practice, simple algorithms such as this can do well, at least better than choosing random items to recommend. However, they can be improved upon significantly, which is where data mining comes in.

To simplify the coding, we will consider only two items at a time. As an example, people may buy bread and milk at the same time at the supermarket. In this early example, we wish to find simple rules of the form:

If a person buys product X, then they are likely to purchase product Y

More complex rules involving multiple items will not be covered such as people buying sausages and burgers being more likely to buy tomato sauce.

Loading the dataset with NumPy

The dataset can be downloaded from the code package supplied with the book. Download this file and save it on your computer, noting the path to the dataset. For this example, I recommend that you create a new folder on your computer to put your dataset and code in. From here, open your IPython Notebook, navigate to this folder, and create a new notebook.

The dataset we are going to use for this example is a NumPy two-dimensional array, which is a format that underlies most of the examples in the rest of the book. The array looks like a table, with rows representing different samples and columns representing different features.

The cells represent the value of a particular feature of a particular sample. To illustrate, we can load the dataset with the following code:

```
import numpy as np
dataset_filename = "affinity_dataset.txt"
X = np.loadtxt(dataset_filename)
```

For this example, run the IPython Notebook and create an IPython Notebook. Enter the above code into the first cell of your Notebook. You can then run the code by pressing *Shift* + *Enter* (which will also add a new cell for the next lot of code). After the code is run, the square brackets to the left-hand side of the first cell will be assigned an incrementing number, letting you know that this cell has been completed. The first cell should look like the following:

```
In [1]: import numpy as np
        dataset_filename = "affinity_dataset.txt"
        X = np.loadtxt(dataset_filename)
```

For later code that will take more time to run, an asterisk will be placed here to denote that this code is either running or scheduled to be run. This asterisk will be replaced by a number when the code has completed running.

You will need to save the dataset into the same directory as the IPython Notebook. If you choose to store it somewhere else, you will need to change the `dataset_filename` value to the new location.

Next, we can show some of the rows of the dataset to get a sense of what the dataset looks like. Enter the following line of code into the next cell and run it, in order to print the first five lines of the dataset:

```
print(X[:5])
```

Downloading the example code

You can download the example code files from your account at `http://www.packtpub.com` for all the Packt Publishing books you have purchased. If you purchased this book elsewhere, you can visit `http://www.packtpub.com/support` and register to have the files e-mailed directly to you.

The result will show you which items were bought in the first five transactions listed:

```
In [2]: print(X[:5])

        [[ 0.  0.  1.  1.  1.]
         [ 1.  1.  0.  1.  0.]
         [ 1.  0.  1.  1.  0.]
         [ 0.  0.  1.  1.  1.]
         [ 0.  1.  0.  0.  1.]]
```

The dataset can be read by looking at each row (horizontal line) at a time. The first row `(0, 0, 1, 1, 1)` shows the items purchased in the first transaction. Each column (vertical row) represents each of the items. They are bread, milk, cheese, apples, and bananas, respectively. Therefore, in the first transaction, the person bought cheese, apples, and bananas, but not bread or milk.

Each of these features contain binary values, stating only whether the items were purchased and not how many of them were purchased. A 1 indicates that "at least 1" item was bought of this type, while a 0 indicates that absolutely none of that item was purchased.

Implementing a simple ranking of rules

We wish to find rules of the type *If a person buys product X, then they are likely to purchase product Y*. We can quite easily create a list of all of the rules in our dataset by simply finding all occasions when two products were purchased together. However, we then need a way to determine good rules from bad ones. This will allow us to choose specific products to recommend.

Rules of this type can be measured in many ways, of which we will focus on two: **support** and **confidence**.

Support is the number of times that a rule occurs in a dataset, which is computed by simply counting the number of samples that the rule is valid for. It can sometimes be normalized by dividing by the total number of times the premise of the rule is valid, but we will simply count the total for this implementation.

While the support measures how often a rule exists, confidence measures how accurate they are when they can be used. It can be computed by determining the percentage of times the rule applies when the premise applies. We first count how many times a rule applies in our dataset and divide it by the number of samples where the premise (the `if` statement) occurs.

As an example, we will compute the support and confidence for the rule *if a person buys apples, they also buy bananas*.

As the following example shows, we can tell whether someone bought apples in a transaction by checking the value of `sample[3]`, where a sample is assigned to a row of our matrix:

```
In [9]: # First, how many rows contain our premise: that a person is buying apples
        num_apple_purchases = 0
        for sample in X:
            if sample[3] == 1:  # This person bought Apples
                num_apple_purchases += 1
        print("{0} people bought Apples".format(num_apple_purchases))

        36 people bought Apples
```

Similarly, we can check if bananas were bought in a transaction by seeing if the value for `sample[4]` is equal to 1 (and so on). We can now compute the number of times our rule exists in our dataset and, from that, the confidence and support.

Now we need to compute these statistics for all rules in our database. We will do this by creating a dictionary for both *valid rules* and *invalid rules*. The key to this dictionary will be a tuple (premise and conclusion). We will store the indices, rather than the actual feature names. Therefore, we would store (3 and 4) to signify the previous rule *If a person buys Apples, they will also buy Bananas*. If the premise and conclusion are given, the rule is considered valid. While if the premise is given but the conclusion is not, the rule is considered invalid for that sample.

To compute the confidence and support for all possible rules, we first set up some dictionaries to store the results. We will use `defaultdict` for this, which sets a default value if a key is accessed that doesn't yet exist. We record the number of valid rules, invalid rules, and occurrences of each premise:

```
from collections import defaultdict
valid_rules = defaultdict(int)
invalid_rules = defaultdict(int)
num_occurances = defaultdict(int)
```

Next we compute these values in a large loop. We iterate over each sample and feature in our dataset. This first feature forms the premise of the rule—if a person buys a product premise:

```
for sample in X:
  for premise in range(4):
```

We check whether the premise exists for this sample. If not, we do not have any more processing to do on this sample/premise combination, and move to the next iteration of the loop:

```
if sample[premise] == 0: continue
```

If the premise is valid for this sample (it has a value of 1), then we record this and check each conclusion of our rule. We skip over any conclusion that is the same as the premise—this would give us rules such as If a person buys Apples, then they buy Apples, which obviously doesn't help us much;

```
num_occurances[premise] += 1
for conclusion in range(n_features):
    if premise == conclusion: continue
```

If the conclusion exists for this sample, we increment our valid count for this rule. If not, we increment our invalid count for this rule:

```
if sample[conclusion] == 1:
    valid_rules[(premise, conclusion)] += 1
    else:
    invalid_rules[(premise, conclusion)] += 1
```

We have now completed computing the necessary statistics and can now compute the *support* and *confidence* for each rule. As before, the support is simply our `valid_rules` value:

```
support = valid_rules
```

The confidence is computed in the same way, but we must loop over each rule to compute this:

```
confidence = defaultdict(float)
for premise, conclusion in valid_rules.keys():
    rule = (premise, conclusion)
    confidence[rule] = valid_rules[rule] / num_occurances[premise]
```

We now have a dictionary with the support and confidence for each rule. We can create a function that will print out the rules in a readable format. The signature of the rule takes the premise and conclusion indices, the support and confidence dictionaries we just computed, and the features array that tells us what the features mean:

```
def print_rule(premise, conclusion,
               support, confidence, features):
```

We get the names of the features for the premise and conclusion and print out the rule in a readable format:

```
premise_name = features[premise]
conclusion_name = features[conclusion]
print("Rule: If a person buys {0} they will also buy
  {1}".format(premise_name, conclusion_name))
```

Then we print out the `Support` and `Confidence` of this rule:

```
print(" - Support: {0}".format(support[(premise,
                                        conclusion)]))
print(" - Confidence: {0:.3f}".format(confidence[(premise,
                                                  conclusion)]))
```

We can test the code by calling it in the following way—feel free to experiment with different premises and conclusions:

```
In [31]: premise = 1
         conclusion = 3
         print_rule(premise, conclusion, support, confidence, features)

         Rule: If a person buys milk they will also buy apples
          - Confidence: 0.196
          - Support: 9
```

Ranking to find the best rules

Now that we can compute the support and confidence of all rules, we want to be able to find the *best* rules. To do this, we perform a ranking and print the ones with the highest values. We can do this for both the support and confidence values.

To find the rules with the highest support, we first sort the support dictionary. Dictionaries do not support ordering by default; the `items()` function gives us a list containing the data in the dictionary. We can sort this list using the `itemgetter` class as our key, which allows for the sorting of nested lists such as this one. Using `itemgetter(1)` allows us to sort based on the values. Setting `reverse=True` gives us the highest values first:

```
from operator import itemgetter
sorted_support = sorted(support.items(), key=itemgetter(1), re
verse=True)
```

We can then print out the top five rules:

```
for index in range(5):
    print("Rule #{0}".format(index + 1))
    premise, conclusion = sorted_support[index][0]
    print_rule(premise, conclusion, support, confidence, features)
```

The result will look like the following:

```
In [40]: for index in range(5):
             print("Rule #{0}".format(index + 1))
             (premise, conclusion) = sorted_support[index][0]
             print_rule(premise, conclusion, support, confidence, features)
         Rule #1
         Rule: If a person buys cheese they will also buy bananas
          - Confidence: 0.659
          - Support: 27

         Rule #2
         Rule: If a person buys bananas they will also buy cheese
          - Confidence: 0.458
          - Support: 27

         Rule #3
         Rule: If a person buys apples they will also buy cheese
          - Confidence: 0.694
          - Support: 25

         Rule #4
         Rule: If a person buys cheese they will also buy apples
          - Confidence: 0.610
          - Support: 25

         Rule #5
         Rule: If a person buys bananas they will also buy apples
          - Confidence: 0.356
          - Support: 21
```

Similarly, we can print the top rules based on confidence. First, compute the sorted confidence list:

```
sorted_confidence = sorted(confidence.items(), key=itemgetter(1),
reverse=True)
```

Next, print them out using the same method as before. Note the change to `sorted_confidence` on the third line;

```
for index in range(5):
    print("Rule #{0}".format(index + 1))
    premise, conclusion = sorted_confidence[index][0]
    print_rule(premise, conclusion, support, confidence, features)
```

```
In [42]: for index in range(5):
             print("Rule #{0}".format(index + 1))
             (premise, conclusion) = sorted_confidence[index][0]
             print_rule(premise, conclusion, support, confidence, features)

         Rule #1
         Rule: If a person buys apples they will also buy cheese
          - Confidence: 0.694
          - Support: 25

         Rule #2
         Rule: If a person buys cheese they will also buy bananas
          - Confidence: 0.659
          - Support: 27

         Rule #3
         Rule: If a person buys bread they will also buy bananas
          - Confidence: 0.630
          - Support: 17

         Rule #4
         Rule: If a person buys cheese they will also buy apples
          - Confidence: 0.610
          - Support: 25

         Rule #5
         Rule: If a person buys apples they will also buy bananas
          - Confidence: 0.583
          - Support: 21
```

Two rules are near the top of both lists. The first is **If a person buys apples, they will also buy cheese**, and the second is **If a person buys cheese, they will also buy bananas**. A store manager can use rules like these to organize their store. For example, if apples are on sale this week, put a display of cheeses nearby. Similarly, it would make little sense to put both bananas on sale at the same time as cheese, as nearly 66 percent of people buying cheese will buy bananas anyway—our sale won't increase banana purchases all that much.

Data mining has great exploratory power in examples like this. A person can use data mining techniques to explore relationships within their datasets to find new insights. In the next section, we will use data mining for a different purpose: prediction.

A simple classification example

In the affinity analysis example, we looked for correlations between different variables in our dataset. In classification, we instead have a single variable that we are interested in and that we call the **class** (also called the target). If, in the previous example, we were interested in how to make people buy more apples, we could set that variable to be the class and look for classification rules that obtain that goal. We would then look only for rules that relate to that goal.

What is classification?

Classification is one of the largest uses of data mining, both in practical use and in research. As before, we have a set of samples that represents objects or things we are interested in classifying. We also have a new array, the class values. These class values give us a categorization of the samples. Some examples are as follows:

- Determining the species of a plant by looking at its measurements. The class value here would be *Which species is this?*.
- Determining if an image contains a dog. The class would be *Is there a dog in this image?*.
- Determining if a patient has cancer based on the test results. The class would be *Does this patient have cancer?*.

While many of the examples above are binary (yes/no) questions, they do not have to be, as in the case of plant species classification in this section.

The goal of classification applications is to train a model on a set of samples with known classes, and then apply that model to new unseen samples with unknown classes. For example, we want to train a spam classifier on my past e-mails, which I have labeled as spam or not spam. I then want to use that classifier to determine whether my next email is spam, without me needing to classify it myself.

Loading and preparing the dataset

The dataset we are going to use for this example is the famous Iris database of plant classification. In this dataset, we have 150 plant samples and four measurements of each: **sepal length**, **sepal width**, **petal length**, and **petal width** (all in centimeters). This classic dataset (first used in 1936!) is one of the classic datasets for data mining. There are three classes: **Iris Setosa**, **Iris Versicolour**, and **Iris Virginica**. The aim is to determine which type of plant a sample is, by examining its measurements.

The `scikit-learn` library contains this dataset built-in, making the loading of the dataset straightforward:

```
from sklearn.datasets import load_iris
dataset = load_iris()
X = dataset.data
y = dataset.target
```

You can also print(`dataset.DESCR`) to see an outline of the dataset, including some details about the features.

The features in this dataset are continuous values, meaning they can take any range of values. Measurements are a good example of this type of feature, where a measurement can take the value of 1, 1.2, or 1.25 and so on. Another aspect about continuous features is that feature values that are close to each other indicate similarity. A plant with a sepal length of 1.2 cm is like a plant with sepal width of 1.25 cm.

In contrast are categorical features. These features, while often represented as numbers, cannot be compared in the same way. In the Iris dataset, the class values are an example of a categorical feature. The class 0 represents Iris Setosa, class 1 represents Iris Versicolour, and class 2 represents Iris Virginica. This doesn't mean that Iris Setosa is more similar to Iris Versicolour than it is to Iris Virginica—despite the class value being more similar. The numbers here represent categories. All we can say is whether categories are the same or different.

There are other types of features too, some of which will be covered in later chapters.

While the features in this dataset are continuous, the algorithm we will use in this example requires categorical features. Turning a continuous feature into a categorical feature is a process called discretization.

A simple discretization algorithm is to choose some threshold and any values below this threshold are given a value 0. Meanwhile any above this are given the value 1. For our threshold, we will compute the mean (average) value for that feature. To start with, we compute the mean for each feature:

```
attribute_means = X.mean(axis=0)
```

This will give us an array of length 4, which is the number of features we have. The first value is the mean of the values for the first feature and so on. Next, we use this to transform our dataset from one with continuous features to one with discrete categorical features:

```
X_d = np.array(X >= attribute_means, dtype='int')
```

We will use this new `X_d` dataset (for *X discretized*) for our training and testing, rather than the original dataset (*X*).

Implementing the OneR algorithm

OneR is a simple algorithm that simply predicts the class of a sample by finding the most frequent class for the feature values. OneR is a shorthand for *One Rule*, indicating we only use a single rule for this classification by choosing the feature with the best performance. While some of the later algorithms are significantly more complex, this simple algorithm has been shown to have good performance in a number of real-world datasets.

The algorithm starts by iterating over every value of every feature. For that value, count the number of samples from each class that have that feature value. Record the most frequent class for the feature value, and the error of that prediction.

For example, if a feature has two values, *0* and *1*, we first check all samples that have the value *0*. For that value, we may have 20 in class *A*, 60 in class *B*, and a further 20 in class *C*. The most frequent class for this value is *B*, and there are 40 instances that have difference classes. The prediction for this feature value is *B* with an error of 40, as there are 40 samples that have a different class from the prediction. We then do the same procedure for the value *1* for this feature, and then for all other feature value combinations.

Once all of these combinations are computed, we compute the error for each feature by summing up the errors for all values for that feature. The feature with the lowest total error is chosen as the *One Rule* and then used to classify other instances.

In code, we will first create a function that computes the class prediction and error for a specific feature value. We have two necessary imports, `defaultdict` and `itemgetter`, that we used in earlier code:

```
from collections import defaultdict
from operator import itemgetter
```

Next, we create the function definition, which needs the dataset, classes, the index of the feature we are interested in, and the value we are computing:

```
def train_feature_value(X, y_true, feature_index, value):
```

We then iterate over all the samples in our dataset, counting the actual classes for each sample with that feature value:

```
class_counts = defaultdict(int)
for sample, y in zip(X, y_true):
    if sample[feature_index] == value:
        class_counts[y] += 1
```

We then find the most frequently assigned class by sorting the `class_counts` dictionary and finding the highest value:

```
sorted_class_counts = sorted(class_counts.items(),
  key=itemgetter(1), reverse=True)
    most_frequent_class = sorted_class_counts[0][0]
```

Finally, we compute the error of this rule. In the OneR algorithm, any sample with this feature value would be predicted as being the most frequent class. Therefore, we compute the error by summing up the counts for the other classes (not the most frequent). These represent training samples that this rule does not work on:

```
incorrect_predictions = [class_count for class_value, class_count
in class_counts.items()
if class_value != most_frequent_class]
error = sum(incorrect_predictions)
```

Finally, we return both the predicted class for this feature value and the number of incorrectly classified training samples, the error, of this rule:

```
return most_frequent_class, error
```

With this function, we can now compute the error for an entire feature by looping over all the values for that feature, summing the errors, and recording the predicted classes for each value.

The function header needs the dataset, classes, and feature index we are interested in:

```
def train_on_feature(X, y_true, feature_index):
```

Next, we find all of the unique values that the given feature takes. The indexing in the next line looks at the whole column for the given feature and returns it as an array. We then use the set function to find only the unique values:

```
values = set(X[:,feature_index])
```

Next, we create our dictionary that will store the predictors. This dictionary will have feature values as the keys and classification as the value. An entry with key 1.5 and value 2 would mean that, when the feature has value set to 1.5, classify it as belonging to class 2. We also create a list storing the errors for each feature value:

```
predictors = {}
errors = []
```

As the main section of this function, we iterate over all the unique values for this feature and use our previously defined `train_feature_value()` function to find the most frequent class and the error for a given feature value. We store the results as outlined above:

```
for current_value in values:
  most_frequent_class, error = train_feature_value(X,
    y_true, feature_index, current_value)
  predictors[current_value] = most_frequent_class
  errors.append(error)
```

Finally, we compute the total errors of this rule and return the predictors along with this value:

```
total_error = sum(errors)
return predictors, total_error
```

Testing the algorithm

When we evaluated the affinity analysis algorithm of the last section, our aim was to explore the current dataset. With this classification, our problem is different. We want to build a model that will allow us to classify previously unseen samples by comparing them to what we know about the problem.

For this reason, we split our machine-learning workflow into two stages: training and testing. In training, we take a portion of the dataset and create our model. In testing, we apply that model and evaluate how effectively it worked on the dataset. As our goal is to create a model that is able to classify previously unseen samples, we cannot use our testing data for training the model. If we do, we run the risk of overfitting.

Overfitting is the problem of creating a model that classifies our training dataset very well, but performs poorly on new samples. The solution is quite simple: never use training data to test your algorithm. This simple rule has some complex variants, which we will cover in later chapters; but, for now, we can evaluate our OneR implementation by simply splitting our dataset into two small datasets: a training one and a testing one. This workflow is given in this section.

The `scikit-learn` library contains a function to split data into training and testing components:

```
from sklearn.cross_validation import train_test_split
```

This function will split the dataset into two subdatasets, according to a given ratio (which by default uses 25 percent of the dataset for testing). It does this randomly, which improves the confidence that the algorithm is being appropriately tested:

```
Xd_train, Xd_test, y_train, y_test = train_test_split(X_d, y, random_
state=14)
```

We now have two smaller datasets: `Xd_train` contains our data for training and `Xd_test` contains our data for testing. `y_train` and `y_test` give the corresponding class values for these datasets.

We also specify a specific `random_state`. Setting the random state will give the same split every time the same value is entered. It will *look* random, but the algorithm used is deterministic and the output will be consistent. For this book, I recommend setting the random state to the same value that I do, as it will give you the same results that I get, allowing you to verify your results. To get truly random results that change every time you run it, set `random_state` to `none`.

Next, we compute the predictors for all the features for our dataset. Remember to only use the training data for this process. We iterate over all the features in the dataset and use our previously defined functions to train the predictors and compute the errors:

```
all_predictors = {}
errors = {}
for feature_index in range(Xd_train.shape[1]):
  predictors, total_error = train_on_feature(Xd_train, y_train,
    feature_index)
  all_predictors[feature_index] = predictors
  errors[feature_index] = total_error
```

Next, we find the best feature to use as our "One Rule", by finding the feature with the lowest error:

```
best_feature, best_error = sorted(errors.items(), key=itemgetter(1))
[0]
```

We then create our `model` by storing the predictors for the best feature:

```
model = {'feature': best_feature,
  'predictor': all_predictors[best_feature][0]}
```

Our model is a dictionary that tells us which feature to use for our *One Rule* and the predictions that are made based on the values it has. Given this model, we can predict the class of a previously unseen sample by finding the value of the specific feature and using the appropriate predictor. The following code does this for a given sample:

```
variable = model['variable']
predictor = model['predictor']
prediction = predictor[int(sample[variable])]
```

Often we want to predict a number of new samples at one time, which we can do using the following function; we use the above code, but iterate over all the samples in a dataset, obtaining the prediction for each sample:

```
def predict(X_test, model):
    variable = model['variable']
    predictor = model['predictor']
    y_predicted = np.array([predictor[int(sample[variable])] for
      sample in X_test])
    return y_predicted
```

For our `testing` dataset, we get the predictions by calling the following function:

```
y_predicted = predict(X_test, model)
```

We can then compute the accuracy of this by comparing it to the known classes:

```
accuracy = np.mean(y_predicted == y_test) * 100
print("The test accuracy is {:.1f}%".format(accuracy))
```

This gives an accuracy of 68 percent, which is not bad for a single rule!

Summary

In this chapter, we introduced data mining using Python. If you were able to run the code in this section (note that the full code is available in the supplied code package), then your computer is set up for much of the rest of the book. Other Python libraries will be introduced in later chapters to perform more specialized tasks.

We used the IPython Notebook to run our code, which allows us to immediately view the results of a small section of the code. This is a useful framework that will be used throughout the book.

We introduced a simple affinity analysis, finding products that are purchased together. This type of exploratory analysis gives an insight into a business process, an environment, or a scenario. The information from these types of analysis can assist in business processes, finding the next big medical breakthrough, or creating the next artificial intelligence.

Also, in this chapter, there was a simple classification example using the OneR algorithm. This simple algorithm simply finds the best feature and predicts the class that most frequently had this value in the training dataset.

Over the next few chapters, we will expand on the concepts of classification and affinity analysis. We will also introduce the scikit-learn package and the algorithms it includes.

2

Classifying with scikit-learn Estimators

The `scikit-learn` library is a collection of data mining algorithms, written in Python and using a common programming interface. This allows users to easily try different algorithms as well as utilize standard tools for doing effective testing and parameter searching. There are a large number of algorithms and utilities in scikit-learn.

In this chapter, we focus on setting up a good framework for running data mining procedures. This will be used in later chapters, which are all focused on applications and techniques to use in those situations.

The key concepts introduced in this chapter are as follows:

- **Estimators**: This is to perform classification, clustering, and regression
- **Transformers**: This is to perform preprocessing and data alterations
- **Pipelines**: This is to put together your workflow into a replicable format

scikit-learn estimators

Estimators are `scikit-learn's` abstraction, allowing for the standardized implementation of a large number of classification algorithms. Estimators are used for classification. Estimators have the following two main functions:

- `fit()`: This performs the training of the algorithm and sets internal parameters. It takes two inputs, the training sample dataset and the corresponding classes for those samples.
- `predict()`: This predicts the class of the testing samples that is given as input. This function returns an array with the predictions of each input testing sample.

Most `scikit-learn` estimators use the `NumPy` arrays or a related format for input and output.

There are a large number of estimators in scikit-learn. These include **support vector machines (SVM)**, **random forests**, and **neural networks**. Many of these algorithms will be used in later chapters. In this chapter, we will use a different estimator from `scikit-learn`: **nearest neighbor**.

For this chapter, you will need to install a new library called `matplotlib`. The easiest way to install it is to use `pip3`, as you did in *Chapter 1, Getting Started with Data Mining*, to install `scikit-learn`:

```
$pip3 install matplotlib
```

If you have any difficulty installing `matplotlib`, seek the official installation instructions at `http://matplotlib.org/users/installing.html`.

Nearest neighbors

Nearest neighbors is perhaps one of the most intuitive algorithms in the set of standard data mining algorithms. To predict the class of a new sample, we look through the training dataset for the samples that are most similar to our new sample. We take the most similar sample and predict the class that the majority of those samples have.

As an example, we wish to predict the class of the triangle, based on which class it is more similar to (represented here by having similar objects closer together). We seek the three nearest neighbors, which are two diamonds and one square. There are more diamonds than circles, and the predicted class for the triangle is, therefore, a diamond:

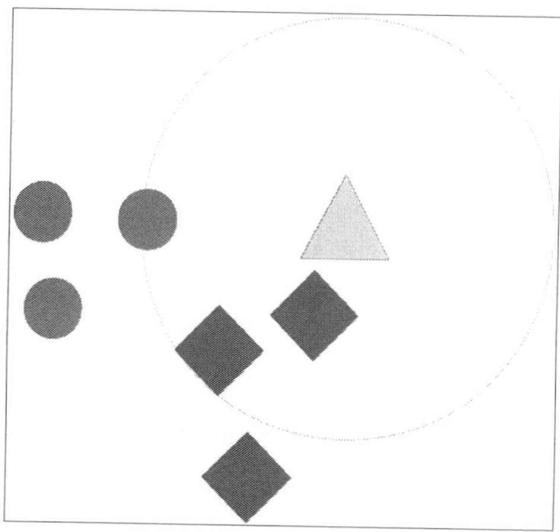

Nearest neighbors can be used for nearly any dataset-however, it can be very computationally expensive to compute the distance between all pairs of samples. For example if there are 10 samples in the dataset, there are 45 unique distances to compute. However, if there are 1000 samples, there are nearly 500,000! Various methods exist for improving this speed dramatically; some of which are covered in the later chapters of this book.

It can also do poorly in categorical-based datasets, and another algorithm should be used for these instead.

Distance metrics

A key underlying concept in data mining is that of distance. If we have two samples, we need to know how close they are to each other. Further more, we need to answer questions such as are these two samples more similar than the other two? Answering questions like these is important to the outcome of the case.

The most common distance metric that the people are aware of is **Euclidean** distance, which is the *real-world* distance. If you were to plot the points on a graph and measure the distance with a straight ruler, the result would be the Euclidean distance. A little more formally, it is the square root of the sum of the squared distances for each feature.

Euclidean distance is intuitive, but provides poor accuracy if some features have larger values than others. It also gives poor results when lots of features have a value of 0, known as a sparse matrix. There are other distance metrics in use; two commonly employed ones are the Manhattan and Cosine distance.

The **Manhattan** distance is the sum of the absolute differences in each feature (with no use of square distances). Intuitively, it can be thought of as the number of moves a rook piece (or castle) in chess would take to move between the points, if it were limited to moving one square at a time. While the Manhattan distance does suffer if some features have larger values than others, the effect is not as dramatic as in the case of Euclidean.

The **Cosine** distance is better suited to cases where some features are larger than others and when there are lots of zeros in the dataset. Intuitively, we draw a line from the origin to each of the samples, and measure the angle between those lines. This can be seen in the following diagram:

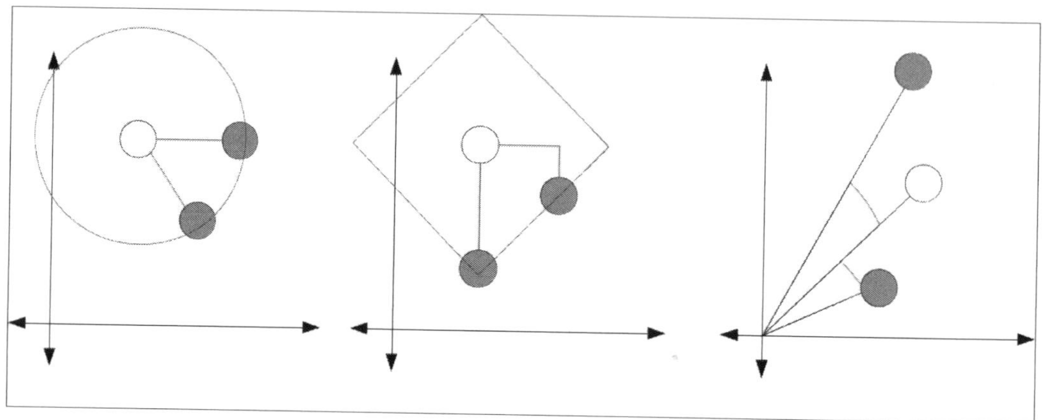

In this example, each of the grey circles are in the same distance from the white circle. In (a), the distances are Euclidean, and therefore, similar distances fit around a circle. This distance can be measured using a ruler. In (b), the distances are Manhattan, also called City Block. We compute the distance by moving across rows and columns, similar to how a Rook (Castle) in Chess moves. Finally, in (c), we have the Cosine distance that is measured by computing the angle between the lines drawn from the sample to the vector, and ignore the actual length of the line.

The distance metric chosen can have a large impact on the final performance. For example, if you have many features, the Euclidean distance between random samples approaches the same value. This makes it hard to compare samples as the distances are the same! Manhattan distance can be more stable in some circumstances, but if some features have very large values, this can *overrule* lots of similarities in other features. Finally, Cosine distance is a good metric for comparing items with a large number of features, but it discards some information about the length of the vector, which is useful in some circumstances.

For this chapter, we will stay with Euclidean distance, using other metrics in later chapters.

Loading the dataset

The dataset we are going to use is called *Ionosphere*, which is the recording of many high-frequency antennas. The aim of the antennas is to determine whether there is a structure in the ionosphere and a region in the upper atmosphere. Those that have a structure are deemed good, while those that do not are deemed bad. The aim of this application is to build a data mining classifier that can determine whether an image is good or bad.

(Image Credit: `https://www.flickr.com/photos/geckzilla/16149273389/`)

This can be downloaded from the UCL Machine Learning data repository, which contains a large number of datasets for different data mining applications. Go to `http://archive.ics.uci.edu/ml/datasets/Ionosphere` and click on **Data Folder**. Download the `ionosphere.data` and `ionosphere.names` files to a folder on your computer. For this example, I'll assume that you have put the dataset in a directory called Data in your home folder.

The location of your home folder depends on your operating system. For Windows, it is usually at `C:\Documents and Settings\username`. For Mac or Linux machines, it is usually at `/home/username`. You can get your home folder by running this python code:

```
import os
print(os.path.expanduser("~"))
```

For each row in the dataset, there are 35 values. The first 34 are measurements taken from the 17 antennas (two values for each antenna). The last is either 'g' or 'b'; that stands for good and bad, respectively.

Start the IPython Notebook server and create a new notebook called **Ionosphere Nearest Neighbors** for this chapter.

First, we load up the `NumPy` and `csv` libraries that we will need for our code:

```
import numpy as np
import csv
```

To load the dataset, we first get the filename of the dataset. First, get the folder the dataset is stored in from your data folder:

```
data_filename = os.path.join(data_folder, "Ionosphere",
"ionosphere.data")
```

We then create the `X` and `y` NumPy arrays to store the dataset in. The sizes of these arrays are known from the dataset. Don't worry if you don't know the size of future datasets—we will use other methods to load the dataset in future chapters and you won't need to know this size beforehand:

```
X = np.zeros((351, 34), dtype='float')
y = np.zeros((351,), dtype='bool')
```

The dataset is in a **Comma-Separated Values (CSV)** format, which is a commonly used format for datasets. We are going to use the `csv` module to load this file. Import it and set up a `csv` reader object:

```
with open(data_filename, 'r') as input_file:
    reader = csv.reader(input_file)
```

Next, we loop over the lines in the file. Each line represents a new set of measurements, which is a sample in this dataset. We use the enumerate function to get the line's index as well, so we can update the appropriate sample in the dataset (`X`):

```
        for i, row in enumerate(reader):
```

We take the first 34 values from this sample, turn each into a float, and save that to our dataset:

```
        data = [float(datum) for datum in row[:-1]]
        X[i] = data
```

Finally, we take the last value of the row and set the class. We set it to 1 (or `True`) if it is a good sample, and 0 if it is not:

```
y[i] = row[-1] == 'g'
```

We now have a dataset of samples and features in `X`, and the corresponding classes in `y`, as we did in the classification example in *Chapter 1, Getting Started with Data Mining*.

Moving towards a standard workflow

Estimators in `scikit-learn` have two main functions: `fit()` and `predict()`. We train the algorithm using the `fit` method and our training set. We evaluate it using the `predict` method on our testing set.

First, we need to create these training and testing sets. As before, import and run the `train_test_split` function:

```
from sklearn.cross_validation import train_test_split
X_train, X_test, y_train, y_test = train_test_split(X, y, random_
state=14)
```

Then, we import the nearest neighbor class and create an instance for it. We leave the parameters as defaults for now, and will choose good parameters later in this chapter. By default, the algorithm will choose the five nearest neighbors to predict the class of a testing sample:

```
from sklearn.neighbors import KNeighborsClassifier
estimator = KNeighborsClassifier()
```

After creating our estimator, we must then fit it on our training dataset. For the nearest neighbor class, this records our dataset, allowing us to find the nearest neighbor for a new data point, by comparing that point to the training dataset:

```
estimator.fit(X_train, y_train)
```

We then train the algorithm with our test set and evaluate with our testing set:

```
y_predicted = estimator.predict(X_test)
accuracy = np.mean(y_test == y_predicted) * 100
print("The accuracy is {0:.1f}%".format(accuracy))
```

This scores 86.4 percent accuracy, which is impressive for a default algorithm and just a few lines of code! Most `scikit-learn` default parameters are chosen explicitly to work well with a range of datasets. However, you should always aim to choose parameters based on knowledge of the application experiment.

Running the algorithm

In our earlier experiments, we set aside a portion of the dataset as a testing set, with the rest being the training set. We train our algorithm on the training set and evaluate how effective it will be based on the testing set. However, what happens if we get lucky and choose an easy testing set? Alternatively, what if it was particularly troublesome? We can discard a good model due to poor results resulting from such an "unlucky" split of our data.

The cross-fold validation framework is a way to address the problem of choosing a testing set and a standard methodology in data mining. The process works by doing a number of experiments with different training and testing splits, but using each sample in a testing set only once. The procedure is as follows:

1. Split the entire dataset into a number of sections called folds.
2. For each fold in the dataset, execute the following steps:
    - Set that fold aside as the current testing set
    - Train the algorithm on the remaining folds
    - Evaluate on the current testing set
3. Report on all the evaluation scores, including the average score.
4. In this process, each sample is used in the testing set only once. This reduces (but doesn't completely eliminate) the likelihood of choosing lucky testing sets.

Throughout this book, the code examples build upon each other within a chapter. Each chapter's code should be entered into the same `IPython` Notebook, unless otherwise specified.

The `scikit-learn` library contains a number of cross fold validation methods. A `helper` function is given that performs the preceding procedure. We can import it now in our IPython Notebook:

```
from sklearn.cross_validation import cross_val_score
```

By default, `cross_val_score` uses a specific methodology called **Stratified K Fold** to split the dataset into folds. This creates folds that have approximately the same proportion of classes in each fold, again reducing the likelihood of choosing poor folds. This is a great default, so we won't mess with it right now.

Next, we use this function, passing the original (full) dataset and classes:

```
scores = cross_val_score(estimator, X, y, scoring='accuracy')
average_accuracy = np.mean(scores) * 100
print("The average accuracy is {0:.1f}%".format(average_accuracy))
```

This gives a slightly more modest result of 82.3 percent, but it is still quite good considering we have not yet tried setting better parameters. In the next section, we will see how we would go about changing the parameters to achieve a better outcome.

Setting parameters

Almost all data mining algorithms have parameters that the user can set. This is often a cause of generalizing an algorithm to allow it to be applicable in a wide variety of circumstances. Setting these parameters can be quite difficult, as choosing good parameter values is often highly reliant on features of the dataset.

The nearest neighbor algorithm has several parameters, but the most important one is that of the number of nearest neighbors to use when predicting the class of an unseen attribution. In `scikit-learn`, this parameter is called `n_neighbors`. In the following figure, we show that when this number is too low, a randomly labeled sample can cause an error. In contrast, when it is too high, the actual nearest neighbors have a lower effect on the result:

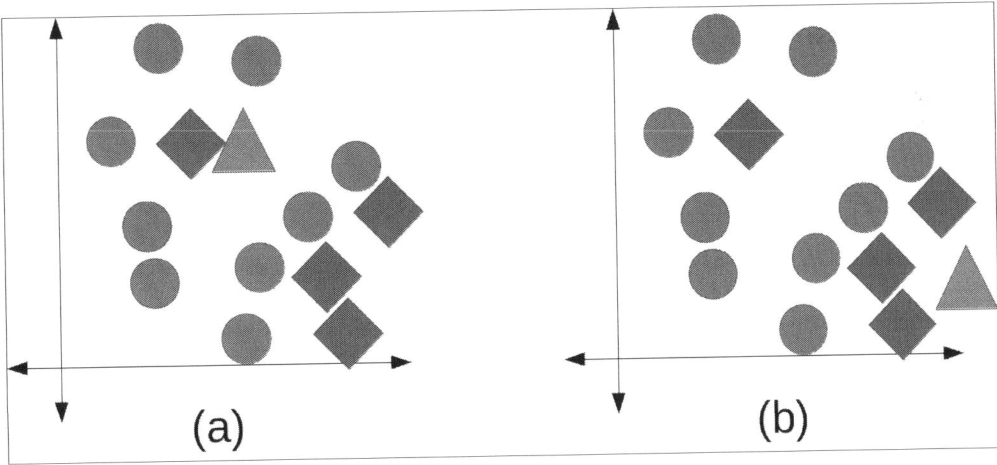

In the figure (a), on the left-hand side, we would usually expect the test sample (the triangle) to be classified as a circle. However, if `n_neighbors` is 1, the single red diamond in this area (likely a noisy sample) causes the sample to be predicted as being a diamond, while it appears to be in a red area. In the figure (b), on the right-hand side, we would usually expect the test sample to be classified as a diamond. However, if `n_neighbors` is 7, the three nearest neighbors (which are all diamonds) are overridden by the large number of circle samples.

If we want to test a number of values for the `n_neighbors` parameter, for example, each of the values from 1 to 20, we can rerun the experiment many times by setting `n_neighbors` and observing the result:

```
avg_scores = []
all_scores = []
parameter_values = list(range(1, 21))  # Include 20
for n_neighbors in parameter_values:
    estimator = KNeighborsClassifier(n_neighbors=n_neighbors)
    scores = cross_val_score(estimator, X, y, scoring='accuracy')
```

Compute and store the average in our list of scores. We also store the full set of scores for later analysis:

```
    avg_scores.append(np.mean(scores))
    all_scores.append(scores)
```

We can then plot the relationship between the value of `n_neighbors` and the accuracy. First, we tell the IPython Notebook that we want to show plots inline in the notebook itself:

```
%matplotlib inline
```

We then import `pyplot` from the `matplotlib` library and plot the parameter values alongside average scores:

```
from matplotlib import pyplot as plt plt.plot(parameter_values,
avg_scores, '-o')
```

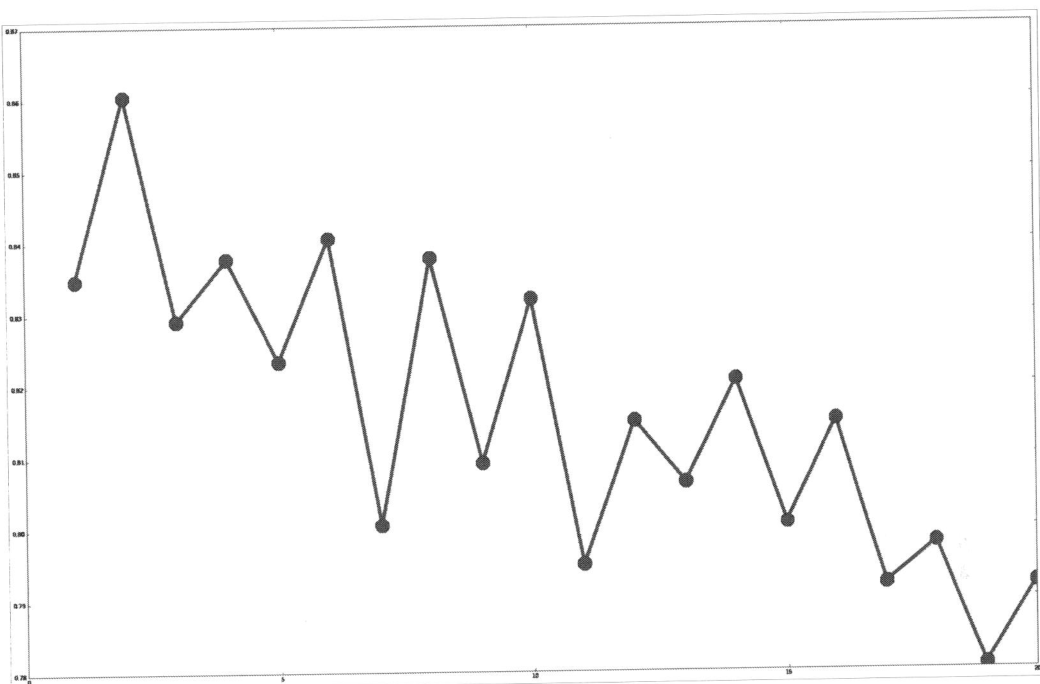

While there is a lot of variance, the plot shows a decreasing trend as the number of neighbors increases.

Preprocessing using pipelines

When taking measurements of real-world objects, we can often get features in very different ranges. For instance, if we are measuring the qualities of an animal, we might have several features, as follows:

- **Number of legs**: This is between the range of 0-8 for most animals, while some have many more!
- **Weight**: This is between the range of only a few micrograms, all the way to a blue whale with a weight of 190,000 kilograms!
- **Number of hearts**: This can be between zero to five, in the case of the earthworm.

For a mathematical-based algorithm to compare each of these features, the differences in the scale, range, and units can be difficult to interpret. If we used the above features in many algorithms, the weight would probably be the most influential feature due to only the larger numbers and not anything to do with the actual effectiveness of the feature.

One of the methods to overcome this is to use a process called preprocessing to *normalize* the features so that they all have the same range, or are put into categories like *small*, *medium* and *large*. Suddenly, the large difference in the types of features has less of an impact on the algorithm, and can lead to large increases in the accuracy.

Preprocessing can also be used to choose only the more effective features, create new features, and so on. Preprocessing in `scikit-learn` is done through `Transformer` objects, which take a dataset in one form and return an altered dataset after some transformation of the data. These don't have to be numerical, as Transformers are also used to extract features-however, in this section, we will stick with preprocessing.

An example

We can show an example of the problem by *breaking* the `Ionosphere` dataset. While this is only an example, many real-world datasets have problems of this form. First, we create a copy of the array so that we do not alter the original dataset:

```
X_broken = np.array(X)
```

Next, we *break* the dataset by dividing every second feature by `10`:

```
X_broken[:,::2] /= 10
```

In theory, this should not have a great effect on the result. After all, the values for these features are still relatively the same. The major issue is that the scale has changed and the odd features are now *larger* than the even features. We can see the effect of this by computing the accuracy:

```
estimator = KNeighborsClassifier()
original_scores = cross_val_score(estimator, X, y,
  scoring='accuracy')
print("The original average accuracy for is
{0:.1f}%".format(np.mean(original_scores) * 100))
broken_scores = cross_val_score(estimator, X_broken, y,
  scoring='accuracy')
print("The 'broken' average accuracy for is
  {0:.1f}%".format(np.mean(broken_scores) * 100))
```

This gives a score of 82.3 percent for the original dataset, which drops down to 71.5 percent on the broken dataset. We can fix this by scaling all the features to the range `0` to `1`.

Standard preprocessing

The preprocessing we will perform for this experiment is called feature-based normalization through the `MinMaxScaler` class. Continuing with the IPython notebook from the rest of this chapter, first, we import this class:

```
from sklearn.preprocessing import MinMaxScaler
```

This class takes each feature and scales it to the range `0` to `1`. The minimum value is replaced with `0`, the maximum with `1`, and the other values somewhere in between.

To apply our preprocessor, we run the transform function on it. While `MinMaxScaler` doesn't, some transformers need to be trained first in the same way that the classifiers do. We can combine these steps by running the `fit_transform` function instead:

```
X_transformed = MinMaxScaler().fit_transform(X)
```

Here, `X_transformed` will have the same shape as *X*. However, each column will have a maximum of 1 and a minimum of 0.

There are various other forms of normalizing in this way, which is effective for other applications and feature types:

- Ensure the sum of the values for each sample equals to 1, using `sklearn.preprocessing.Normalizer`
- Force each feature to have a zero mean and a variance of 1, using `sklearn.preprocessing.StandardScaler`, which is a commonly used starting point for normalization
- Turn numerical features into binary features, where any value above a threshold is 1 and any below is 0, using `sklearn.preprocessing.Binarizer`

We will use combinations of these preprocessors in later chapters, along with other types of `Transformers` object.

Putting it all together

We can now create a workflow by combining the code from the previous sections, using the broken dataset previously calculated:

```
X_transformed = MinMaxScaler().fit_transform(X_broken)
estimator = KNeighborsClassifier()
transformed_scores = cross_val_score(estimator, X_transformed, y,
  scoring='accuracy')
print("The average accuracy for is
  {0:.1f}%".format(np.mean(transformed_scores) * 100))
```

This gives us back our score of 82.3 percent accuracy. The `MinMaxScaler` resulted in features of the same scale, meaning that no features overpowered others by simply being bigger values. While the Nearest Neighbor algorithm can be confused with larger features, some algorithms handle scale differences better. In contrast, some are much worse!

Pipelines

As experiments grow, so does the complexity of the operations. We may split up our dataset, binarize features, perform feature-based scaling, perform sample-based scaling, and many more operations.

Keeping track of all of these operations can get quite confusing and can result in being unable to replicate the result. Problems include forgetting a step, incorrectly applying a transformation, or adding a transformation that wasn't needed.

Another issue is the order of the code. In the previous section, we created our `X_transformed` dataset and then created a new estimator for the cross validation. If we had multiple steps, we would need to track all of these changes to the dataset in the code.

Pipelines are a construct that addresses these problems (and others, which we will see in the next chapter). Pipelines store the steps in your data mining workflow. They can take your raw data in, perform all the necessary transformations, and then create a prediction. This allows us to use pipelines in functions such as `cross_val_score`, where they expect an estimator. First, import the `Pipeline` object:

```
from sklearn.pipeline import Pipeline
```

Pipelines take a list of steps as input, representing the chain of the data mining application. The last step needs to be an `Estimator`, while all previous steps are `Transformers`. The input dataset is altered by each `Transformer`, with the output of one step being the input of the next step. Finally, the samples are classified by the last step's estimator. In our pipeline, we have two steps:

1. Use `MinMaxScaler` to scale the feature values from 0 to 1
2. Use `KNeighborsClassifier` as the classification algorithms

Each step is then represented by a tuple `('name', step)`. We can then create our pipeline:

```
scaling_pipeline = Pipeline([('scale', MinMaxScaler()),
                             ('predict', KNeighborsClassifier())])
```

The key here is the list of tuples. The first tuple is our scaling step and the second tuple is the predicting step. We give each step a name: the first we call `scale` and the second we call `predict`, but you can choose your own names. The second part of the tuple is the actual Transformer or estimator object.

Running this pipeline is now very easy, using the cross validation code from before:

```
scores = cross_val_score(scaling_pipeline, X_broken, y,
scoring='accuracy')
print("The pipeline scored an average accuracy for is {0:.1f}%".
format(np.mean(transformed_scores) * 100))
```

This gives us the same score as before (82.3 percent), which is expected, as we are effectively running the same steps.

In later chapters, we will use more advanced testing methods, and setting up pipelines is a great way to ensure that the code complexity does not grow unmanageably.

Summary

In this chapter, we used several of `scikit-learn's` methods for building a standard workflow to run and evaluate data mining models. We introduced the Nearest Neighbors algorithm, which is already implemented in `scikit-learn` as an estimator. Using this class is quite easy; first, we call the `fit` function on our training data, and second, we use the `predict` function to predict the class of testing samples.

We then looked at preprocessing by fixing poor feature scaling. This was done using a `Transformer` object and the `MinMaxScaler` class. These functions also have a `fit` method and then a transform, which takes a dataset as an input and returns a transformed dataset as an output.

In the next chapter, we will use these concepts in a larger example, predicting the outcome of sports matches using real-world data.

3

Predicting Sports Winners with Decision Trees

In this chapter, we will look at predicting the winner of sports matches using a different type of classification algorithm: decision trees. These algorithms have a number of advantages over other algorithms. One of the main advantages is that they are readable by humans. In this way, decision trees can be used to learn a procedure, which could then be given to a human to perform if needed. Another advantage is that they work with a variety of features, which we will see in this chapter.

We will cover the following topics in this chapter:

- Using the pandas library for loading and manipulating data
- Decision trees
- Random forests
- Using real-world datasets in data mining
- Creating new features and testing them in a robust framework

Loading the dataset

In this chapter, we will look at predicting the winner of games of the **National Basketball Association** (**NBA**). Matches in the NBA are often close and can be decided in the last minute, making predicting the winner quite difficult. Many sports share this characteristic, whereby the *expected winner* could be beaten by another team on the right day.

Various research into predicting the winner suggests that there may be an upper limit to sports outcome prediction accuracy which, depending on the sport, is between 70 percent and 80 percent accuracy. There is a significant amount of research being performed into sports prediction, often through data mining or statistics-based methods.

Collecting the data

The data we will be using is the match history data for the NBA for the 2013-2014 season. The website `http://Basketball-Reference.com` contains a significant number of resources and statistics collected from the NBA and other leagues. To download the dataset, perform the following steps:

1. Navigate to `http://www.basketball-reference.com/leagues/NBA_2014_games.html` in your web browser.
2. Click on the **Export** button next to the **Regular Season** heading.
3. Download the file to your data folder and make a note of the path.

This will download a **CSV** (short for **Comma Separated Values**) file containing the results of the 1,230 games in the regular season for the NBA.

CSV files are simply text files where each line contains a new row and each value is separated by a comma (hence the name). CSV files can be created manually by simply typing into a text editor and saving with a `.csv` extension. They can also be opened in any program that can read text files, but can also be opened in Excel as a spreadsheet.

We will load the file with the **pandas** (short for **Python Data Analysis**) library, which is an incredibly useful library for manipulating data. Python also contains a built-in library called `csv` that supports reading and writing CSV files. However, we will use pandas, which provides more powerful functions that we will use later in the chapter for creating new features.

For this chapter, you will need to install pandas. The easiest way to install it is to use `pip3`, as you did in *Chapter 1, Getting Started with Data Mining* to install `scikit-learn`:

```
$pip3 install pandas
```

If you have difficulty in installing pandas, head to their website at `http://pandas.pydata.org/getpandas.html` and read the installation instructions for your system.

Using pandas to load the dataset

The pandas library is a library for loading, managing, and manipulating data. It handles data structures behind-the-scenes and supports analysis methods, such as computing the mean.

When doing multiple data mining experiments, you will find that you write many of the same functions again and again, such as reading files and extracting features. Each time this reimplementation happens, you run the risk of introducing bugs. Using a high-class library such as pandas significantly reduces the amount of work needed to do these functions and also gives you more confidence in using well tested code.

Throughout this book, we will be using pandas quite significantly, introducing use cases as we go.

We can load the dataset using the `read_csv` function:

```
import pandas as pd
dataset = pd.read_csv(data_filename)
```

The result of this is a pandas **Dataframe**, and it has some useful functions that we will use later on. Looking at the resulting dataset, we can see some issues. Type the following and run the code to see the first five rows of the dataset:

```
dataset.ix[:5]
```

Here's the output:

Out[47]:

Date	NaN	Visitor/Neutral	PTS	Home/Neutral	PTS	NaN	Notes
Tue Oct 29 2013	Box Score	Orlando Magic	87	Indiana Pacers	97	NaN	NaN
		Los Angeles Clippers	103	Los Angeles Lakers	116	NaN	NaN
		Chicago Bulls	95	Miami Heat	107	NaN	NaN
Wed Oct 30 2013	Box Score	Brooklyn Nets	94	Cleveland Cavaliers	98	NaN	NaN

This is actually a usable dataset, but it contains some problems that we will fix up soon.

Cleaning up the dataset

After looking at the output, we can see a number of problems:

- The date is just a string and not a date object
- The first row is blank
- From visually inspecting the results, the headings aren't complete or correct

These issues come from the data, and we could fix this by altering the data itself. However, in doing this, we could forget the steps we took or misapply them; that is, we can't replicate our results. As with the previous section where we used pipelines to track the transformations we made to a dataset, we will use pandas to apply transformations to the raw data itself.

The `pandas.read_csv` function has parameters to fix each of these issues, which we can specify when loading the file. We can also change the headings after loading the file, as shown in the following code:

```
dataset = pd.read_csv(data_filename, parse_dates=["Date"],
  skiprows=[0,])
dataset.columns = ["Date", "Score Type", "Visitor Team",
  "VisitorPts", "Home Team", "HomePts", "OT?", "Notes"]
```

The results have significantly improved, as we can see if we print out the resulting data frame:

```
dataset.ix[:5]
```

The output is as follows:

Out[48]:

	Date	Score Type	Visitor Team	VisitorPts	Home Team	HomePts	OT?	Notes
0	2013-10-29	Box Score	Orlando Magic	87	Indiana Pacers	97	NaN	NaN
1	2013-10-29	Box Score	Los Angeles Clippers	103	Los Angeles Lakers	116	NaN	NaN
2	2013-10-29	Box Score	Chicago Bulls	95	Miami Heat	107	NaN	NaN
3	2013-10-30	Box Score	Brooklyn Nets	94	Cleveland Cavaliers	98	NaN	NaN
4	2013-10-30	Box Score	Atlanta Hawks	109	Dallas Mavericks	118	NaN	NaN
5	2013-10-30	Box Score	Washington Wizards	102	Detroit Pistons	113	NaN	NaN

Even in well-compiled data sources such as this one, you need to make some adjustments. Different systems have different nuances, resulting in data files that are not quite compatible with each other.

Now that we have our dataset, we can compute a baseline. A baseline is an accuracy that indicates an easy way to get a good accuracy. Any data mining solution should beat this.

In each match, we have two teams: a home team and a visitor team. An obvious baseline, called the chance rate, is 50 percent. Choosing randomly will (over time) result in an accuracy of 50 percent.

Extracting new features

We can now extract our features from this dataset by combining and comparing the existing data. First up, we need to specify our class value, which will give our classification algorithm something to compare against to see if its prediction is correct or not. This could be encoded in a number of ways; however, for this application, we will specify our class as 1 if the home team wins and 0 if the visitor team wins. In basketball, the team with the most points wins. So, while the data set doesn't specify who wins, we can compute it easily.

We can specify the data set by the following:

```
dataset["HomeWin"] = dataset["VisitorPts"] < dataset["HomePts"]
```

We then copy those values into a `NumPy` array to use later for our `scikit-learn` classifiers. There is not currently a clean integration between pandas and scikit-learn, but they work nicely together through the use of `NumPy` arrays. While we will use pandas to extract features, we will need to extract the values to use them with scikit-learn:

```
y_true = dataset["HomeWin"].values
```

The preceding array now holds our class values in a format that scikit-learn can read.

We can also start creating some features to use in our data mining. While sometimes we just throw the raw data into our classifier, we often need to derive continuous numerical or categorical features.

The first two features we want to create to help us predict which team will win are whether either of those two teams won their last game. This would roughly approximate which team is playing well.

We will compute this feature by iterating through the rows in order and recording which team won. When we get to a new row, we look up whether the team won the last time we saw them.

We first create a (default) dictionary to store the team's last result:

```
from collections import defaultdict
won_last = defaultdict(int)
```

The key of this dictionary will be the team and the value will be whether they won their previous game. We can then iterate over all the rows and update the current row with the team's last result:

```
for index, row in dataset.iterrows():
    home_team = row["Home Team"]
    visitor_team = row["Visitor Team"]
    row["HomeLastWin"] = won_last[home_team]
    row["VisitorLastWin"] = won_last[visitor_team]
    dataset.ix[index] = row
```

Note that the preceding code relies on our dataset being in chronological order. Our dataset is in order; however, if you are using a dataset that is not in order, you will need to replace `dataset.iterrows()` with `dataset.sort("Date").iterrows()`.

We then set our dictionary with the each team's result (from this row) for the next time we see these teams. The code is as follows:

```
    won_last[home_team] = row["HomeWin"]
    won_last[visitor_team] = not row["HomeWin"]
```

After the preceding code runs, we will have two new features: `HomeLastWin` and `VisitorLastWin`. We can have a look at the dataset. There isn't much point in looking at the first five games though. Due to the way our code runs, we didn't have data for them at that point. Therefore, until a team's second game of the season, we won't know their current form. We can instead look at different places in the list. The following code will show the 20th to the 25th games of the season:

```
dataset.ix[20:25]
```

Here's the output:

Out[52]:

	Date	Score Type	Visitor Team	VisitorPts	Home Team	HomePts	OT?	Notes	HomeWin	HomeLastWin	VisitorLastWin
20	2013-11-01	Box Score	Milwaukee Bucks	105	Boston Celtics	98	NaN	NaN	False	False	False
21	2013-11-01	Box Score	Miami Heat	100	Brooklyn Nets	101	NaN	NaN	True	False	False
22	2013-11-01	Box Score	Cleveland Cavaliers	84	Charlotte Bobcats	90	NaN	NaN	True	False	True
23	2013-11-01	Box Score	Portland Trail Blazers	113	Denver Nuggets	98	NaN	NaN	False	False	False
24	2013-11-01	Box Score	Dallas Mavericks	105	Houston Rockets	113	NaN	NaN	True	True	True
25	2013-11-01	Box Score	San Antonio Spurs	91	Los Angeles Lakers	85	NaN	NaN	False	False	True

You can change those indices to look at other parts of the data, as there are over 1000 games in our dataset!

Currently, this gives a false value to all teams (including the previous year's champion!) when they are first seen. We could improve this feature using the previous year's data, but will not do that in this chapter.

Decision trees

Decision trees are a class of supervised learning algorithm like a flow chart that consists of a sequence of nodes, where the values for a sample are used to make a decision on the next node to go to.

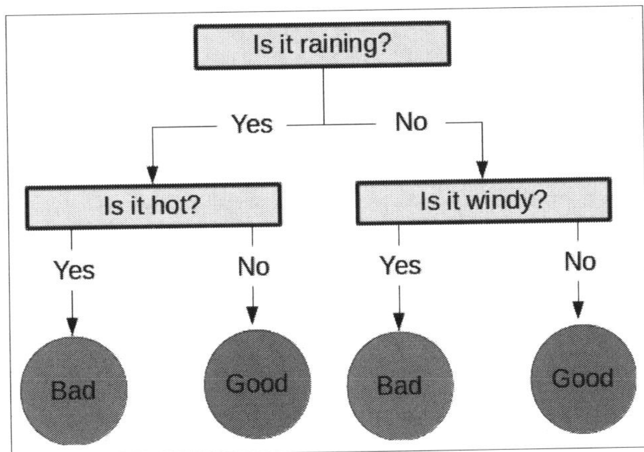

As with most classification algorithms, there are two components:

- The first is the training stage, where a tree is built using training data. While the nearest neighbor algorithm from the previous chapter did not have a training phase, it is needed for decision trees. In this way, the nearest neighbor algorithm is a lazy learner, only doing any work when it needs to make a prediction. In contrast, decision trees, like most classification methods, are eager learners, undertaking work at the training stage.
- The second is the predicting stage, where the trained tree is used to predict the classification of new samples. Using the previous example tree, a data point of `["is raining", "very windy"]` would be classed as `"bad weather"`.

There are many algorithms for creating decision trees. Many of these algorithms are iterative. They start at the base node and decide the best feature to use for the first decision, then go to each node and choose the next best feature, and so on. This process is stopped at a certain point, when it is decided that nothing more can be gained from extending the tree further.

The `scikit-learn` package implements the **CART (Classification and Regression Trees)** algorithm as its default decision tree class, which can use both categorical and continuous features.

Parameters in decision trees

One of the most important features for a decision tree is the stopping criterion. As a tree is built, the final few decisions can often be somewhat arbitrary and rely on only a small number of samples to make their decision. Using such specific nodes can results in trees that significantly overfit the training data. Instead, a stopping criterion can be used to ensure that the decision tree does not reach this exactness.

Instead of using a stopping criterion, the tree could be created in full and then trimmed. This trimming process removes nodes that do not provide much information to the overall process. This is known as pruning.

The decision tree implementation in scikit-learn provides a method to stop the building of a tree using the following options:

- `min_samples_split`: This specifies how many samples are needed in order to create a new node in the decision tree
- `min_samples_leaf`: This specifies how many samples must be resulting from a node for it to stay

The first dictates whether a decision node will be created, while the second dictates whether a decision node will be kept.

Another parameter for decision tress is the criterion for creating a decision. Gini impurity and Information gain are two popular ones:

- **Gini impurity**: This is a measure of how often a decision node would incorrectly predict a sample's class
- **Information gain**: This uses information-theory-based entropy to indicate how much extra information is gained by the decision node

Using decision trees

We can import the `DecisionTreeClassifier` class and create a decision tree using scikit-learn:

```
from sklearn.tree import DecisionTreeClassifier
clf = DecisionTreeClassifier(random_state=14)
```

> We used 14 for our `random_state` again and will do so for most of the book. Using the same random seed allows for replication of experiments. However, with your experiments, you should mix up the random state to ensure that the algorithm's performance is not tied to the specific value.

We now need to extract the dataset from our pandas data frame in order to use it with our `scikit-learn` classifier. We do this by specifying the columns we wish to use and using the `values` parameter of a view of the data frame. The following code creates a dataset using our last win values for both the home team and the visitor team:

```
X_previouswins = dataset[["HomeLastWin", "VisitorLastWin"]].values
```

Decision trees are estimators, as introduced in *Chapter 2, Classifying with scikit-learn Estimators*, and therefore have `fit` and `predict` methods. We can also use the `cross_val_score` method to get the average score (as we did previously):

```
scores = cross_val_score(clf, X_previouswins, y_true,
scoring='accuracy')
print("Accuracy: {0:.1f}%".format(np.mean(scores) * 100))
```

This scores 56.1 percent: we are better than choosing randomly! We should be able to do better. Feature engineering is one of the most difficult tasks in data mining, and choosing good features is key to getting good outcomes—more so than choosing the right algorithm!

Sports outcome prediction

We may be able to do better by trying other features. We have a method for testing how accurate our models are. The `cross_val_score` method allows us to try new features.

There are many possible features we could use, but we will try the following questions:

- Which team is considered better generally?
- Which team won their last encounter?

We will also try putting the raw teams into the algorithm to check whether the algorithm can learn a model that checks how different teams play against each other.

Putting it all together

For the first feature, we will create a feature that tells us if the home team is generally *better* than the visitors. To do this, we will load the standings (also called a ladder in some sports) from the NBA in the previous season. A team will be considered better if it ranked higher in 2013 than the other team.

To obtain the standings data, perform the following steps:

1. Navigate to `http://www.basketball-reference.com/leagues/NBA_2013_standings.html` in your web browser.
2. Select **Expanded Standings** to get a single list for the entire league.
3. Click on the **Export** link.
4. Save the downloaded file in your data folder.

Back in your IPython Notebook, enter the following lines into a new cell. You'll need to ensure that the file was saved into the location pointed to by the `data_folder` variable. The code is as follows:

```
standings_filename = os.path.join(data_folder,
"leagues_NBA_2013_standings_expanded-standings.csv")
standings = pd.read_csv(standings_filename, skiprows=[0,1])
```

You can view the ladder by just typing `standings` into a new cell and running the code:

```
Standings
```

The output is as follows:

Out[57]:

	Rk	Team	Overall	Home	Road	E	W	A	C	SE	...	Post	≤3	≥10	Oct	Nov	Dec	Jan	Feb	Mar	Apr
0	1	Miami Heat	66-16	37-4	29-12	41-11	25-5	14-4	12-6	15-1	...	30-2	9-3	39-8	1-0	10-3	10-5	8-5	12-1	17-1	8-1
1	2	Oklahoma City Thunder	60-22	34-7	26-15	21-9	39-13	7-3	8-2	6-4	...	21-8	3-6	44-6	NaN	13-4	11-2	11-5	7-4	12-5	6-2
2	3	San Antonio Spurs	58-24	35-6	23-18	25-5	33-19	8-2	9-1	8-2	...	16-12	9-5	31-10	1-0	12-4	12-4	12-3	8-3	10-4	3-6
3	4	Denver Nuggets	57-25	38-3	19-22	19-11	38-14	5-5	10-0	4-6	...	24-4	11-7	28-8	0-1	8-8	9-6	12-3	8-4	13-2	7-1
4	5	Los Angeles Clippers	56-26	32-9	24-17	21-9	35-17	7-3	8-2	6-4	...	17-9	3-5	38-12	1-0	8-6	16-0	9-7	8-5	7-7	7-1
5	6	Memphis Grizzlies	56-26	32-9	24-17	22-8	34-18	8-2	8-2	6-4	...	23-8	6-4	28-9	0-1	12-1	7-7	10-7	9-2	11-6	7-2
6	7	New York Knicks	54-28	31-10	23-18	37-15	17-13	10-6	12-6	15-3	...	22-10	7-5	31-12	NaN	11-4	10-5	7-6	6-5	12-6	8-2
7	8	Brooklyn Nets	49-33	26-15	23-18	36-16	13-17	11-5	13-5	12-6	...	18-11	9-4	23-17	NaN	11-4	5-11	11-4	7-5	8-7	7-2
8	9	Indiana Pacers	49-32	30-11	19-21	31-20	18-12	6-11	13-3	12-6	...	17-11	4-9	27-14	1-0	7-8	10-5	9-6	9-3	11-5	2-5
9	10	Golden State Warriors	47-35	28-13	19-22	19-11	28-24	7-3	5-5	7-3	...	17-13	5-3	20-18	1-0	8-6	12-4	8-7	4-8	9-7	5-3

Next, we create a new feature using a similar pattern to the previous feature. We iterate over the rows, looking up the standings for the home team and visitor team. The code is as follows:

```
dataset["HomeTeamRanksHigher"] = 0
for index, row in dataset.iterrows():
    home_team = row["Home Team"]
    visitor_team = row["Visitor Team"]
```

As an important adjustment to the data, a team was renamed between the 2013 and 2014 seasons (but it was still the same team). This is an example of one of the many different things that can happen when trying to integrate data! We will need to adjust the team lookup, ensuring we get the correct team's ranking:

```
    if home_team == "New Orleans Pelicans":
        home_team = "New Orleans Hornets"
    elif visitor_team == "New Orleans Pelicans":
        visitor_team = "New Orleans Hornets"
```

Now we can get the rankings for each team. We then compare them and update the feature in the row:

```
    home_rank = standings[standings["Team"] ==
        home_team]["Rk"].values[0]
        visitor_rank = standings[standings["Team"] ==
        visitor_team]["Rk"].values[0]
        row["HomeTeamRanksHigher"] = int(home_rank > visitor_rank)
        dataset.ix[index] = row
```

Next, we use the `cross_val_score` function to test the result. First, we extract the dataset:

```
X_homehigher =  dataset[["HomeLastWin", "VisitorLastWin",
  "HomeTeamRanksHigher"]].values
```

Then, we create a new `DecisionTreeClassifier` and run the evaluation:

```
clf = DecisionTreeClassifier(random_state=14)
scores = cross_val_score(clf, X_homehigher, y_true,
  scoring='accuracy')
print("Accuracy: {0:.1f}%".format(np.mean(scores) * 100))
```

This now scores 60.3 percent—even better than our previous result. Can we do better?

Next, let's test which of the two teams won their last match. While rankings can give some hints on who won (the higher ranked team is more likely to win), sometimes teams play better against other teams. There are many reasons for this – for example, some teams may have strategies that work against other teams really well. Following our previous pattern, we create a dictionary to store the winner of the past game and create a new feature in our data frame. The code is as follows:

```
last_match_winner = defaultdict(int)
dataset["HomeTeamWonLast"] = 0
```

Then, we iterate over each row and get the home team and visitor team:

```
for index, row in dataset.iterrows():
    home_team = row["Home Team"]
    visitor_team = row["Visitor Team"]
```

We want to see who won the last game between these two teams regardless of which team was playing *at home*. Therefore, we sort the team names alphabetically, giving us a consistent key for those two teams:

```
        teams = tuple(sorted([home_team, visitor_team]))
```

We look up in our dictionary to see who won the last encounter between the two teams. Then, we update the row in the dataset data frame:

```
        row["HomeTeamWonLast"] = 1 if last_match_winner[teams] ==
          row["Home Team"] else 0
          dataset.ix[index] = row
```

Finally, we update our dictionary with the winner of this game in order to compute the feature for the next time these two teams meet:

```
winner = row["Home Team"] if row["HomeWin"] else row
["Visitor Team"]
last_match_winner[teams] = winner
```

Next, we will create a dataset with just our two features. You could try different combinations of features to see if they obtain different results. The code is as follows:

```
X_lastwinner =  dataset[["HomeTeamRanksHigher", "HomeTeam
  WonLast"]].values
clf = DecisionTreeClassifier(random_state=14)
scores = cross_val_score(clf, X_lastwinner, y_true,
  scoring='accuracy')
print("Accuracy: {0:.1f}%".format(np.mean(scores) * 100))
```

This scores 60.6 percent . Our results are getting better and better.

Finally, we will check what happens if we throw a lot of data at the decision tree, and see if it can learn an effective model anyway. We will enter the teams into the tree and check whether a decision tree can learn to incorporate that information.

While decision trees are capable of learning from categorical features, the implementation in scikit-learn requires those features to be encoded first. We can use the `LabelEncoder` transformer to convert between the string-based team names into integers. The code is as follows:

```
from sklearn.preprocessing import LabelEncoder
encoding = LabelEncoder()
```

We will fit this transformer to the home teams so that it learns an integer representation for each team:

```
encoding.fit(dataset["Home Team"].values)
```

We extract all of the labels for the home teams and visitor teams, and then join them (called *stacking* in `NumPy`) to create a matrix encoding both the home team and the visitor team for each game. The code is as follows:

```
home_teams = encoding.transform(dataset["Home Team"].values)
visitor_teams = encoding.transform(dataset["Visitor Team"].values)
X_teams = np.vstack([home_teams, visitor_teams]).T
```

These integers can be fed into the decision tree, but they will still be interpreted as continuous features by `DecisionTreeClassifier`. For example, teams may be allocated integers 0 to 16. The algorithm will see teams 1 and 2 as being similar, while teams 4 and 10 will be different—but this makes no sense as all. All of the teams are different from each other—two teams are either the same or they are not!

To fix this inconsistency, we use the `OneHotEncoder` transformer to encode these integers into a number of binary features. Each binary feature will be a single value for the feature. For example, if the NBA team Chicago Bulls is allocated as integer 7 by the `LabelEncoder`, then the seventh feature returned by the `OneHotEncoder` will be a 1 if the team is *Chicago Bulls* and 0 for all other teams. This is done for every possible value, resulting in a much larger dataset. The code is as follows:

```
from sklearn.preprocessing import OneHotEncoder
onehot = OneHotEncoder()
```

We fit and transform on the same dataset, saving the results:

```
X_teams_expanded = onehot.fit_transform(X_teams).todense()
```

Next, we run the decision tree as before on the new dataset:

```
clf = DecisionTreeClassifier(random_state=14)
scores = cross_val_score(clf, X_teams_expanded, y_true,
  scoring='accuracy')
print("Accuracy: {0:.1f}%".format(np.mean(scores) * 100))
```

This scores an accuracy of 60 percent. The score is better than the baseline, but not as good as before. It is possible that the larger number of features were not handled properly by the decision trees. For this reason, we will try changing the algorithm and see if that helps. Data mining can be an iterative process of trying new algorithms and features.

Random forests

A single decision tree can learn quite complex functions. However, in many ways it will be prone to overfitting—learning rules that work only for the training set. One of the ways that we can adjust for this is to limit the number of rules that it learns. For instance, we could limit the depth of the tree to just three layers. Such a tree will learn the best rules for splitting the dataset at a global level, but won't learn highly specific rules that separate the dataset into highly accurate groups. This trade-off results in trees that may have a good generalization, but overall slightly poorer performance.

To compensate for this, we could create many decision trees and then ask each to predict the class value. We could take a majority vote and use that answer as our overall prediction. Random forests work on this principle.

There are two problems with the aforementioned procedure. The first problem is that building decision trees is largely deterministic—using the same input will result in the same output each time. We only have one training dataset, which means our input (and therefore the output) will be the same if we try build multiple trees. We can address this by choosing a random subsample of our dataset, effectively creating `new` training sets. This process is called **bagging**.

The second problem is that the features that are used for the first few decision nodes in our tree will be quite good. Even if we choose random subsamples of our training data, it is still quite possible that the decision trees built will be largely the same. To compensate for this, we also choose a random subset of the features to perform our data splits on.

Then, we have randomly built trees using randomly chosen samples, using (nearly) randomly chosen features. This is a Random Forest and, perhaps *unintuitively*, this algorithm is very effective on many datasets.

How do ensembles work?

The randomness inherent in Random forests may make it seem like we are leaving the results of the algorithm up to chance. However, we apply the benefits of averaging to nearly randomly built decision trees, resulting in an algorithm that reduces the variance of the result.

Variance is the error introduced by variations in the training dataset on the algorithm. Algorithms with a high variance (such as decision trees) can be greatly affected by variations to the training dataset. This results in models that have the problem of overfitting.

In contrast, **bias** is the error introduced by assumptions in the algorithm rather than anything to do with the dataset, that is, if we had an algorithm that presumed that all features would be normally distributed then our algorithm may have a high error if the features were not. Negative impacts from bias can be reduced by analyzing the data to see if the classifier's data model matches that of the actual data.

By averaging a large number of decision trees, this variance is greatly reduced. This results in a model with a higher overall accuracy.

In general, ensembles work on the assumption that errors in prediction are effectively random and that those errors are quite different from classifier to classifier. By averaging the results across many models, these random errors are canceled out—leaving the true prediction. We will see many more ensembles in action throughout the rest of the book.

Parameters in Random forests

The Random forest implementation in scikit-learn is called `RandomForestClassifier`, and it has a number of parameters. As Random forests use many instances of `DecisionTreeClassifier`, they share many of the same parameters such as the criterion (Gini Impurity or Entropy/Information Gain), `max_features`, and `min_samples_split`.

Also, there are some new parameters that are used in the ensemble process:

- `n_estimators`: This dictates how many decision trees should be built. A higher value will take longer to run, but will (probably) result in a higher accuracy.
- `oob_score`: If true, the method is tested using samples that aren't in the random subsamples chosen for training the decision trees.
- `n_jobs`: This specifies the number of cores to use when training the decision trees in parallel.

The `scikit-learn` package uses a library called `Joblib` for in-built parallelization. This parameter dictates how many cores to use. By default, only a single core is used—if you have more cores, you can increase this, or set it to -1 to use all cores.

Applying Random forests

Random forests in scikit-learn use the estimator interface, allowing us to use almost the exact same code as before to do cross fold validation:

```
from sklearn.ensemble import RandomForestClassifier
clf = RandomForestClassifier(random_state=14)
scores = cross_val_score(clf, X_teams, y_true, scoring='accuracy')
print("Accuracy: {0:.1f}%".format(np.mean(scores) * 100))
```

This results in an immediate benefit of 60.6 percent, up by 0.6 points by just swapping the classifier.

Random forests, using subsets of the features, should be able to learn more effectively with more features than normal decision trees. We can test this by throwing more features at the algorithm and seeing how it goes:

```
X_all = np.hstack([X_home_higher, X_teams])
clf = RandomForestClassifier(random_state=14)
scores = cross_val_score(clf, X_all, y_true, scoring='accuracy')
print("Accuracy: {0:.1f}%".format(np.mean(scores) * 100))
```

This results in 61.1 percent —even better! We can also try some other parameters using the `GridSearchCV` class as we introduced in *Chapter 2, Classifying with scikit-learn Estimators*:

```
parameter_space = {
  "max_features": [2, 10, 'auto'],
  "n_estimators": [100,],
  "criterion": ["gini", "entropy"],
  "min_samples_leaf": [2, 4, 6],
}
clf = RandomForestClassifier(random_state=14)
grid = GridSearchCV(clf, parameter_space)
grid.fit(X_all, y_true)
print("Accuracy: {0:.1f}%".format(grid.best_score_ * 100))
```

This has a much better accuracy of 64.2 percent!

If we wanted to see the parameters used, we can print out the best model that was found in the grid search. The code is as follows:

```
print(grid.best_estimator_)
```

The result shows the parameters that were used in the best scoring model:

```
RandomForestClassifier(bootstrap=True, compute_importances=None,
  criterion='entropy', max_depth=None, max_features=2,
    max_leaf_nodes=None, min_density=None, min_samples_leaf=6,
      min_samples_split=2, n_estimators=100, n_jobs=1,
        oob_score=False, random_state=14, verbose=0)
```

Engineering new features

In the previous few examples, we saw that changing the features can have quite a large impact on the performance of the algorithm. Through our small amount of testing, we had more than 10 percent variance just from the features.

You can create features that come from a simple function in pandas by doing something like this:

```
dataset["New Feature"] = feature_creator()
```

The `feature_creator` function must return a list of the feature's value for each sample in the dataset. A common pattern is to use the dataset as a parameter:

```
dataset["New Feature"] = feature_creator(dataset)
```

You can create those features more directly by setting all the values to a single "default" value, like 0 in the next line:

```
dataset["My New Feature"] = 0
```

You can then iterate over the dataset, computing the features as you go. We used this format in this chapter to create many of our features:

```
for index, row in dataset.iterrows():
    home_team = row["Home Team"]
    visitor_team = row["Visitor Team"]
    # Some calculation here to alter row
    dataset.ix[index] = row
```

Keep in mind that this pattern isn't very efficient. If you are going to do this, try all of your features at once. A common "best practice" is to touch every sample as little as possible, preferably only once.

Some example features that you could try and implement are as follows:

- How many days has it been since each team's previous match? Teams may be tired if they play too many games in a short time frame.
- How many games of the last five did each team win? This will give a more stable form of the `HomeLastWin` and `VisitorLastWin` features we extracted earlier (and can be extracted in a very similar way).
- Do teams have a good record when visiting certain other teams? For instance, one team may play well in a particular stadium, even if they are the visitors.

If you are facing trouble extracting features of these types, check the pandas documentation at `http://pandas.pydata.org/pandas-docs/stable/` for help. Alternatively, you can try an online forum such as Stack Overflow for assistance.

More extreme examples could use player data to estimate the strength of each team's sides to predict who won. These types of complex features are used every day by gamblers and sports betting agencies to try to turn a profit by predicting the outcome of sports matches.

Summary

In this chapter, we extended our use of scikit-learn's classifiers to perform classification and introduced the pandas library to manage our data. We analyzed real-world data on basketball results from the NBA, saw some of the problems that even well-curated data introduces, and created new features for our analysis.

We saw the effect that good features have on performance and used an ensemble algorithm, Random forests, to further improve the accuracy.

In the next chapter, we will extend the affinity analysis that we performed in the first chapter to create a program to find similar books. We will see how to use algorithms for ranking and also use approximation to improve the scalability of data mining.

4
Recommending Movies Using Affinity Analysis

In this chapter, we will look at affinity analysis that determines when objects occur frequently together. This is colloquially called market basket analysis, after one of the use cases of determining when items are purchased together frequently.

In *Chapter 3, Predicting Sports Winners with Decision Trees*, we looked at an object as a focus and used features to describe that object. In this chapter, the data has a different form. We have transactions where the objects of interest (movies, in this chapter) are used within those transactions in some way. The aim is to discover when objects occur simultaneously. In this example, we wish to work out when two movies are recommended by the same reviewers.

The key concepts of this chapter are as follows:

- Affinity analysis
- Feature association mining using the Apriori algorithm
- Movie recommendations
- Sparse data formats

Affinity analysis

Affinity analysis is the task of determining when objects are used in similar ways. In the previous chapter, we focused on whether the objects themselves are similar. The data for affinity analysis is often described in the form of a transaction. Intuitively, this comes from a transaction at a store—determining when objects are purchased together.

However, it can be applied to many processes:

- Fraud detection
- Customer segmentation
- Software optimization
- Product recommendations

Affinity analysis is usually much more exploratory than classification. We often don't have the complete dataset we expect for many classification tasks. For instance, in movie recommendation, we have reviews from different people on different movies. However, it is unlikely we have each reviewer review all of the movies in our dataset. This leaves an important and difficult question in affinity analysis. If a reviewer hasn't reviewed a movie, is that an indication that they aren't interested in the movie (and therefore wouldn't recommend it) or simply that they haven't reviewed it yet?

We won't answer that question in this chapter, but thinking about gaps in your datasets can lead to questions like this. In turn, that can lead to answers that may help improve the efficacy of your approach.

Algorithms for affinity analysis

We introduced a basic method for affinity analysis in *Chapter 1, Getting Started with Data Mining*, which tested all of the possible rule combinations. We computed the confidence and support for each rule, which in turn allowed us to rank them to find the best rules.

However, this approach is not efficient. Our dataset in *Chapter 1, Getting Started with Data Mining*, had just five items for sale. We could expect even a small store to have hundreds of items for sale, while many online stores would have thousands (or millions!). With a naive rule creation, such as our previous algorithm, the growth in time needed to compute these rules increases exponentially. As we add more items, the time it takes to compute all rules increases significantly faster. Specifically, the total possible number of rules is $2n - 1$. For our five-item dataset, there are 31 possible rules. For 10 items, it is 1023. For just 100 items, the number has 30 digits. Even the drastic increase in computing power couldn't possibly keep up with the increases in the number of items stored online. Therefore, we need algorithms that work smarter, as opposed to computers that work harder.

The classic algorithm for affinity analysis is called the Apriori algorithm. It addresses the exponential problem of creating sets of items that occur frequently within a database, called **frequent itemsets**. Once these frequent itemsets are discovered, creating association rules is straightforward.

The intuition behind Apriori is both simple and clever. First, we ensure that a rule has sufficient *support* within the dataset. Defining a minimum support level is the key parameter for Apriori. To build a frequent itemset, for an itemset (A, B) to have a support of at least 30, both A and B must occur at least 30 times in the database. This property extends to larger sets as well. For an itemset (A, B, C, D) to be considered frequent, the set (A, B, C) must also be frequent (as must D).

These *frequent itemsets* can be built up and possible itemsets that are not frequent (of which there are many) will never be tested. This saves significant time in testing new rules.

Other example algorithms for affinity analysis include the **Eclat** and **FP-growth** algorithms. There are many improvements to these algorithms in the data mining literature that further improve the efficiency of the method. In this chapter, we will focus on the basic Apriori algorithm.

Choosing parameters

To perform association rule mining for affinity analysis, we first use the Apriori to generate frequent itemsets. Next, we create association rules (for example, if a person recommended movie *X*, they would also recommend movie *Y*) by testing combinations of premises and conclusions within those frequent itemsets.

For the first stage, the Apriori algorithm needs a value for the minimum support that an itemset needs to be considered frequent. Any itemsets with less support will not be considered. Setting this minimum support too low will cause Apriori to test a larger number of itemsets, slowing the algorithm down. Setting it too high will result in fewer itemsets being considered frequent.

In the second stage, after the frequent itemsets have been discovered, association rules are tested based on their confidence. We could choose a minimum confidence level, a number of rules to return, or simply return all of them and let the user decide what to do with them.

In this chapter, we will return only rules above a given confidence level. Therefore, we need to set our minimum confidence level. Setting this too low will result in rules that have a high support, but are not very accurate. Setting this higher will result in only more accurate rules being returned, but with fewer rules being discovered.

The movie recommendation problem

Product recommendation is big business. Online stores use it to up-sell to customers by recommending other products that they could buy. Making better recommendations leads to better sales. When online shopping is selling to millions of customers every year, there is a lot of potential money to be made by selling more items to these customers.

Product recommendations have been researched for many years; however, the field gained a significant boost when Netflix ran their Netflix Prize between 2007 and 2009. This competition aimed to determine if anyone can predict a user's rating of a film better than Netflix was currently doing. The prize went to a team that was just over 10 percent better than the current solution. While this may not seem like a large improvement, such an improvement would net millions to Netflix in revenue from better movie recommendations.

Obtaining the dataset

Since the inception of the Netflix Prize, Grouplens, a research group at the University of Minnesota, has released several datasets that are often used for testing algorithms in this area. They have released several versions of a movie rating dataset, which have different sizes. There is a version with 100,000 reviews, one with 1 million reviews and one with 10 million reviews.

The datasets are available from `http://grouplens.org/datasets/movielens/` and the dataset we are going to use in this chapter is the MovieLens 1 million dataset. Download this dataset and unzip it in your data folder. Start a new IPython Notebook and type the following code:

```
import os
import pandas as pd
data_folder = os.path.join(os.path.expanduser("~"), "Data",
  "ml-100k")
ratings_filename = os.path.join(data_folder, "u.data")
```

Ensure that `ratings_filename` points to the `u.data` file in the unzipped folder.

Loading with pandas

The MovieLens dataset is in a good shape; however, there are some changes from the default options in `pandas.read_csv` that we need to make. To start with, the data is separated by tabs, not commas. Next, there is no heading line. This means the first line in the file is actually data and we need to manually set the column names.

When loading the file, we set the delimiter parameter to the tab character, tell pandas not to read the first row as the header (with `header=None`), and set the column names. Let's look at the following code:

```
all_ratings = pd.read_csv(ratings_filename, delimiter="\t",
    header=None, names = ["UserID", "MovieID", "Rating", "Datetime"])
```

While we won't use it in this chapter, you can properly parse the date timestamp using the following line:

```
all_ratings["Datetime"] = pd.to_datetime(all_ratings['Datetime'],
  unit='s')
```

You can view the first few records by running the following in a new cell:

```
all_ratings[:5]
```

The result will come out looking something like this:

	UserID	MovieID	Rating	Datetime
0	196	242	3	1997-12-04 15:55:49
1	186	302	3	1998-04-04 19:22:22
2	22	377	1	1997-11-07 07:18:36
3	244	51	2	1997-11-27 05:02:03
4	166	346	1	1998-02-02 05:33:16

Sparse data formats

This dataset is in a sparse format. Each row can be thought of as a cell in a large feature matrix of the type used in previous chapters, where rows are users and columns are individual movies. The first column would be each user's review of the first movie, the second column would be each user's review of the second movie, and so on.

There are 1,000 users and 1,700 movies in this dataset, which means that the full matrix would be quite large. We may run into issues storing the whole matrix in memory and computing on it would be troublesome. However, this matrix has the property that most cells are empty, that is, there is no review for most movies for most users. There is no review of movie `#675` for user `#213` though, and not for most other combinations of user and movie.

The format given here represents the full matrix, but in a more compact way. The first row indicates that user `#196` reviewed movie `#242`, giving it a ranking of 3 (out of five) on the December 4, 1997.

Any combination of user and movie that isn't in this database is assumed to not exist. This saves significant space, as opposed to storing a bunch of zeroes in memory. This type of format is called a **sparse matrix** format. As a rule of thumb, if you expect about 60 percent or more of your dataset to be empty or zero, a sparse format will take less space to store.

When computing on sparse matrices, the focus isn't usually on the data we don't have—comparing all of the zeroes. We usually focus on the data we have and compare those.

The Apriori implementation

The goal of this chapter is to produce rules of the following form: *if a person recommends these movies, they will also recommend this movie*. We will also discuss extensions where a person recommends a set of movies is likely to recommend another particular movie.

To do this, we first need to determine if a person recommends a movie. We can do this by creating a new feature `Favorable`, which is `True` if the person gave a favorable review to a movie:

```
all_ratings["Favorable"] = all_ratings["Rating"] > 3
```

We can see the new feature by viewing the dataset:

```
all_ratings[10:15]
```

	UserID	MovieID	Rating	Datetime	Favorable
10	62	257	2	1997-11-12 22:07:14	False
11	286	1014	5	1997-11-17 15:38:45	True
12	200	222	5	1997-10-05 09:05:40	True
13	210	40	3	1998-03-27 21:59:54	False
14	224	29	3	1998-02-21 23:40:57	False

We will sample our dataset to form a training dataset. This also helps reduce the size of the dataset that will be searched, making the Apriori algorithm run faster. We obtain all reviews from the first 200 users:

```
ratings = all_ratings[all_ratings['UserID'].isin(range(200))]
```

Next, we can create a dataset of only the favorable reviews in our sample:

```
favorable_ratings = ratings[ratings["Favorable"]]
```

We will be searching the user's favorable reviews for our itemsets. So, the next thing we need is the movies which each user has given a favorable. We can compute this by grouping the dataset by the User ID and iterating over the movies in each group:

```
favorable_reviews_by_users = dict((k, frozenset(v.values))
                                  for k, v in favorable_ratings
                                  groupby("UserID")["MovieID"])
```

In the preceding code, we stored the values as a `frozenset`, allowing us to quickly check if a movie has been rated by a user. Sets are much faster than lists for this type of operation, and we will use them in a later code.

Finally, we can create a DataFrame that tells us how frequently each movie has been given a favorable review:

```
num_favorable_by_movie = ratings[["MovieID", "Favorable"]].
  groupby("MovieID").sum()
```

We can see the top five movies by running the following code:

```
num_favorable_by_movie.sort("Favorable", ascending=False)[:5]
```

Let's see the top five movies list:

MovieID	Favorable
50	100
100	89
258	83
181	79
174	74

The Apriori algorithm

The Apriori algorithm is part of our affinity analysis and deals specifically with finding frequent itemsets within the data. The basic procedure of Apriori builds up new candidate itemsets from previously discovered frequent itemsets. These candidates are tested to see if they are frequent, and then the algorithm iterates as explained here:

1. Create initial frequent itemsets by placing each item in its own itemset. Only items with at least the minimum support are used in this step.
2. New candidate itemsets are created from the most recently discovered frequent itemsets by finding supersets of the existing frequent itemsets.
3. All candidate itemsets are tested to see if they are frequent. If a candidate is not frequent then it is discarded. If there are no new frequent itemsets from this step, go to the last step.
4. Store the newly discovered frequent itemsets and go to the second step.
5. Return all of the discovered frequent itemsets.

This process is outlined in the following workflow:

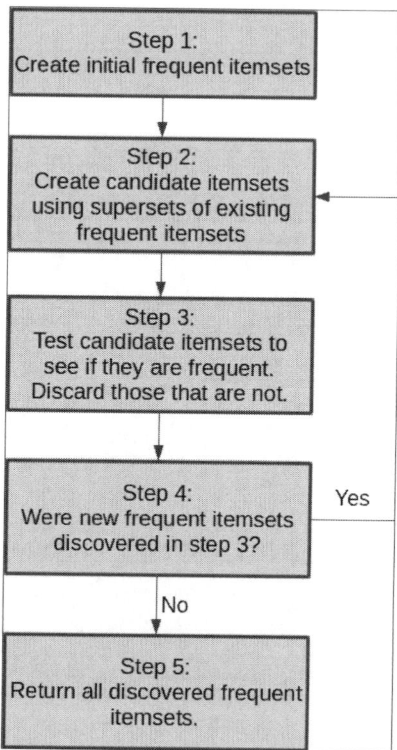

Implementation

On the first iteration of Apriori, the newly discovered itemsets will have a length of 2, as they will be supersets of the initial itemsets created in the first step. On the second iteration (after applying the fourth step), the newly discovered itemsets will have a length of 3. This allows us to quickly identify the newly discovered itemsets, as needed in second step.

We can store our discovered frequent itemsets in a dictionary, where the key is the length of the itemsets. This allows us to quickly access the itemsets of a given length, and therefore the most recently discovered frequent itemsets, with the help of the following code:

```
frequent_itemsets = {}
```

We also need to define the minimum support needed for an itemset to be considered frequent. This value is chosen based on the dataset but feel free to try different values. I recommend only changing it by 10 percent at a time though, as the time the algorithm takes to run will be significantly different! Let's apply minimum support:

```
min_support = 50
```

To implement the first step of the Apriori algorithm, we create an itemset with each movie individually and test if the itemset is frequent. We use `frozenset`, as they allow us to perform set operations later on, and they can also be used as keys in our counting dictionary (normal sets cannot). Let's look at the following code:

```
frequent_itemsets[1] = dict((frozenset((movie_id,)),
                            row["Favorable"])
                            for movie_id, row in num_favorable_
                              by_movie.iterrows()
                            if row["Favorable"] > min_support)
```

We implement the second and third steps together for efficiency by creating a function that takes the newly discovered frequent itemsets, creates the supersets, and then tests if they are frequent. First, we set up the function and the counting dictionary:

```
from collections import defaultdict
def find_frequent_itemsets(favorable_reviews_by_users, k_1_itemsets,
min_support):
    counts = defaultdict(int)
```

In keeping with our rule of thumb of reading through the data as little as possible, we iterate over the dataset once per call to this function. While this doesn't matter too much in this implementation (our dataset is relatively small), it is a good practice to get into for larger applications. We iterate over all of the users and their reviews:

```
    for user, reviews in favorable_reviews_by_users.items():
```

Next, we go through each of the previously discovered itemsets and see if it is a subset of the current set of reviews. If it is, this means that the user has reviewed each movie in the itemset. Let's look at the code:

```
        for itemset in k_1_itemsets:
            if itemset.issubset(reviews):
```

We can then go through each individual movie that the user has reviewed that isn't in the itemset, create a superset from it, and record in our counting dictionary that we saw this particular itemset. Let's look at the code:

```
                for other_reviewed_movie in reviews - itemset:
                    current_superset = itemset | frozenset((other_
                                        reviewed_movie,))
                    counts[current_superset] += 1
```

We end our function by testing which of the candidate itemsets have enough support to be considered frequent and return only those:

```
    return dict([(itemset, frequency) for itemset, frequency in
counts.items() if frequency >= min_support])
```

To run our code, we now create a loop that iterates over the steps of the Apriori algorithm, storing the new itemsets as we go. In this loop, *k* represents the length of the soon-to-be discovered frequent itemsets, allowing us to access the previously most discovered ones by looking in our `frequent_itemsets` dictionary using the key *k - 1*. We create the frequent itemsets and store them in our dictionary by their length. Let's look at the code:

```
for k in range(2, 20):
    cur_frequent_itemsets =
      find_frequent_itemsets(favorable_reviews_by_users,
        frequent_itemsets[k-1],
          min_support)
     frequent_itemsets[k] = cur_frequent_itemsets
```

We want to break out the preceding loop if we didn't find any new frequent itemsets (and also to print a message to let us know what is going on):

```
if len(cur_frequent_itemsets) == 0:
    print("Did not find any frequent itemsets of length {}".
      format(k))
    sys.stdout.flush()
    break
```

We use `sys.stdout.flush()` to ensure that the printouts happen while the code is still running. Sometimes, in large loops in particular cells, the printouts will not happen until the code has completed. Flushing the output in this way ensures that the printout happens when we want. Don't do it too much though—the flush operation carries a computational cost (as does printing) and this will slow down the program.

If we do find frequent itemsets, we print out a message to let us know the loop will be running again. This algorithm can take a while to run, so it is helpful to know that the code is still running while you wait for it to complete! Let's look at the code:

```
else:
    print("I found {} frequent itemsets of length
    {}".format(len(cur_frequent_itemsets), k))
    sys.stdout.flush()
```

Finally, after the end of the loop, we are no longer interested in the first set of itemsets anymore—these are itemsets of length one, which won't help us create association rules - we need at least two items to create association rules. Let's delete them:

```
del frequent_itemsets[1]
```

You can now run this code. It may take a few minutes, more if you have older hardware. If you find you are having trouble running any of the code samples, take a look at using an online cloud provider for additional speed. Details about using the cloud to do the work are given in *Appendix, Next Steps*.

The preceding code returns 1,718 frequent itemsets of varying lengths. You'll notice that the number of itemsets grows as the length increases before it shrinks. It grows because of the increasing number of possible rules. After a while, the large number of combinations no longer has the support necessary to be considered frequent. This results in the number shrinking. This shrinking is the benefit of the Apriori algorithm. If we search all possible itemsets (not just the supersets of frequent ones), we would be searching thousands of times more itemsets to see if they are frequent.

Extracting association rules

After the Apriori algorithm has completed, we have a list of frequent itemsets. These aren't exactly association rules, but they are similar to it. A frequent itemset is a set of items with a minimum support, while an association rule has a premise and a conclusion.

We can make an association rule from a frequent itemset by taking one of the movies in the itemset and denoting it as the conclusion. The other movies in the itemset will be the premise. This will form rules of the following form: *if a reviewer recommends all of the movies in the premise, they will also recommend the conclusion.*

For each itemset, we can generate a number of association rules by setting each movie to be the conclusion and the remaining movies as the premise.

In code, we first generate a list of all of the rules from each of the frequent itemsets, by iterating over each of the discovered frequent itemsets of each length:

```
candidate_rules = []
for itemset_length, itemset_counts in frequent_itemsets.items():
    for itemset in itemset_counts.keys():
```

We then iterate over every movie in this itemset, using it as our conclusion. The remaining movies in the itemset are the premise. We save the premise and conclusion as our candidate rule:

```
        for conclusion in itemset:
            premise = itemset - set((conclusion,))
            candidate_rules.append((premise, conclusion))
```

This returns a very large number of candidate rules. We can see some by printing out the first few rules in the list:

```
print(candidate_rules[:5])
```

The resulting output shows the rules that were obtained:

```
[(frozenset({79}), 258), (frozenset({258}), 79), (frozenset({50}),
  64), (frozenset({64}), 50), (frozenset({127}), 181)]
```

In these *rules*, the first part (the `frozenset`) is the list of movies in the premise, while the number after it is the conclusion. In the first case, if a reviewer recommends movie 79, they are also likely to recommend movie 258.

Next, we compute the confidence of each of these rules. This is performed much like in *Chapter 1, Getting Started with Data Mining*, with the only changes being those necessary for computing using the new data format.

The process starts by creating dictionaries to store how many times we see the premise leading to the conclusion (a *correct* example of the rule) and how many times it doesn't (an *incorrect* example). Let's look at the code:

```
correct_counts = defaultdict(int)
incorrect_counts = defaultdict(int)
```

We iterate over all of the users, their favorable reviews, and over each candidate association rule:

```
for user, reviews in favorable_reviews_by_users.items():
    for candidate_rule in candidate_rules:
        premise, conclusion = candidate_rule
```

We then test to see if the premise is applicable to this user. In other words, did the user favorably review all of the movies in the premise? Let's look at the code:

```
        if premise.issubset(reviews):
```

If the premise applies, we see if the conclusion movie was also rated favorably. If so, the rule is correct in this instance. If not, it is incorrect. Let's look at the code:

```
        if premise.issubset(reviews):
            if conclusion in reviews:
                correct_counts[candidate_rule] += 1
            else:
                incorrect_counts[candidate_rule] += 1
```

We then compute the confidence for each rule by dividing the correct count by the total number of times the rule was seen:

```
rule_confidence = {candidate_rule: correct_counts[candidate_rule]
  / float(correct_counts[candidate_rule] +
    incorrect_counts[candidate_rule])
              for candidate_rule in candidate_rules}
```

Now we can print the top five rules by sorting this confidence dictionary and printing the results:

```
from operator import itemgetter
sorted_confidence = sorted(rule_confidence.items(),
  key=itemgetter(1), reverse=True)
for index in range(5):
    print("Rule #{0}".format(index + 1))
    (premise, conclusion) = sorted_confidence[index][0]
```

```
    print("Rule: If a person recommends {0} they will also
      recommend {1}".format(premise, conclusion))
    print(" - Confidence:
      {0:.3f}".format(rule_confidence[(premise, conclusion)]))
    print("")
```

The result is as follows:

```
Rule #1
Rule: If a person recommends frozenset({64, 56, 98, 50, 7}) they will
also recommend 174
 - Confidence: 1.000

Rule #2
Rule: If a person recommends frozenset({98, 100, 172, 79, 50, 56})
they will also recommend 7
 - Confidence: 1.000

Rule #3
Rule: If a person recommends frozenset({98, 172, 181, 174, 7}) they
will also recommend 50
 - Confidence: 1.000

Rule #4
Rule: If a person recommends frozenset({64, 98, 100, 7, 172, 50}) they
will also recommend 174
 - Confidence: 1.000

Rule #5
Rule: If a person recommends frozenset({64, 1, 7, 172, 79, 50}) they
will also recommend 181
 - Confidence: 1.000
```

The resulting printout shows only the movie IDs, which isn't very helpful without the names of the movies also. The dataset came with a file called `u.items`, which stores the movie names and their corresponding `MovieID` (as well as other information, such as the genre).

We can load the titles from this file using pandas. Additional information about the file and categories is available in the **README** that came with the dataset. The data in the files is in CSV format, but with data separated by the | symbol; it has no header and the encoding is important to set. The column names were found in the `README` file.

```
movie_name_filename = os.path.join(data_folder, "u.item")
movie_name_data = pd.read_csv(movie_name_filename, delimiter="|",
  header=None, encoding = "mac-roman")
```

```
movie_name_data.columns = ["MovieID", "Title", "Release Date",
  "Video Release", "IMDB", "<UNK>", "Action", "Adventure",
    "Animation", "Children's", "Comedy", "Crime", "Documentary",
      "Drama", "Fantasy", "Film-Noir",
  "Horror", "Musical", "Mystery", "Romance", "Sci-Fi", "Thriller",
     "War", "Western"]
```

Getting the movie title is important, so we will create a function that will return a movie's title from its `MovieID`, saving us the trouble of looking it up each time. Let's look at the code:

```
def get_movie_name(movie_id):
```

We look up the `movie_name_data` DataFrame for the given `MovieID` and return only the title column:

```
    title_object = movie_name_data[movie_name_data["MovieID"] ==
      movie_id]["Title"]
```

We use the values parameter to get the actual value (and not the pandas `Series` object that is currently stored in `title_object`). We are only interested in the first value—there should only be one title for a given `MovieID` anyway!

```
    title = title_object.values[0]
```

We end the function by returning the title as needed. Let's look at the code:

```
    return title
```

In a new IPython Notebook cell, we adjust our previous code for printing out the top rules to also include the titles:

```
for index in range(5):
    print("Rule #{0}".format(index + 1))
    (premise, conclusion) = sorted_confidence[index][0]
    premise_names = ", ".join(get_movie_name(idx) for idx
      in premise)
    conclusion_name = get_movie_name(conclusion)
    print("Rule: If a person recommends {0} they will
      also recommend {1}".format(premise_names, conclusion_name))
    print(" - Confidence: {0:.3f}".format(confidence[(premise,
      conclusion)]))
    print("")
```

The result is much more readable (there are still some issues, but we can ignore them for now):

```
Rule #1
Rule: If a person recommends Shawshank Redemption, The (1994), Pulp
Fiction (1994), Silence of the Lambs, The (1991), Star Wars (1977),
Twelve Monkeys (1995) they will also recommend Raiders of the Lost Ark
(1981)
 - Confidence: 1.000

Rule #2
Rule: If a person recommends Silence of the Lambs, The (1991), Fargo
(1996), Empire Strikes Back, The (1980), Fugitive, The (1993), Star
Wars (1977), Pulp Fiction (1994) they will also recommend Twelve
Monkeys (1995)
 - Confidence: 1.000

Rule #3
Rule: If a person recommends Silence of the Lambs, The (1991), Empire
Strikes Back, The (1980), Return of the Jedi (1983), Raiders of the
Lost Ark (1981), Twelve Monkeys (1995) they will also recommend Star
Wars (1977)
 - Confidence: 1.000

Rule #4
Rule: If a person recommends Shawshank Redemption, The (1994), Silence
of the Lambs, The (1991), Fargo (1996), Twelve Monkeys (1995), Empire
Strikes Back, The (1980), Star Wars (1977) they will also recommend
Raiders of the Lost Ark (1981)
 - Confidence: 1.000

Rule #5
Rule: If a person recommends Shawshank Redemption, The (1994), Toy
Story (1995), Twelve Monkeys (1995), Empire Strikes Back, The (1980),
Fugitive, The (1993), Star Wars (1977) they will also recommend Return
of the Jedi (1983)
 - Confidence: 1.000
```

Evaluation

In a broad sense, we can evaluate the association rules using the same concept as for classification. We use a test set of data that was not used for training, and evaluate our discovered rules based on their performance in this test set.

To do this, we will compute the test set confidence, that is, the confidence of each rule on the testing set.

We won't apply a formal evaluation metric in this case; we simply examine the rules and look for good examples.

First, we extract the test dataset, which is all of the records we didn't use in the training set. We used the first 200 users (by ID value) for the training set, and we will use all of the rest for the testing dataset. As with the training set, we will also get the favorable reviews for each of the users in this dataset as well. Let's look at the code:

```
test_dataset =
all_ratings[~all_ratings['UserID'].isin(range(200))]
test_favorable = test_dataset[test_dataset["Favorable"]]
test_favorable_by_users = dict((k, frozenset(v.values)) for k, v
  in test_favorable.groupby("UserID")["MovieID"])
```

We then count the correct instances where the premise leads to the conclusion, in the same way we did before. The only change here is the use of the test data instead of the training data. Let's look at the code:

```
correct_counts = defaultdict(int)
incorrect_counts = defaultdict(int)
for user, reviews in test_favorable_by_users.items():
    for candidate_rule in candidate_rules:
        premise, conclusion = candidate_rule
        if premise.issubset(reviews):
            if conclusion in reviews:
                correct_counts[candidate_rule] += 1
            else:
                incorrect_counts[candidate_rule] += 1
```

Next, we compute the confidence of each rule from the correct counts. Let's look at the code:

```
test_confidence = {candidate_rule: correct_counts[candidate_rule]
  / float(correct_counts[candidate_rule] + incorrect_counts
    [candidate_rule])
  for candidate_rule in rule_confidence}
```

Finally, we print out the best association rules with the titles instead of the movie IDs.

```
for index in range(5):
    print("Rule #{0}".format(index + 1))
```

```
    (premise, conclusion) = sorted_confidence[index][0]
    premise_names = ", ".join(get_movie_name(idx) for idx in
      premise)
    conclusion_name = get_movie_name(conclusion)
    print("Rule: If a person recommends {0} they will also
      recommend {1}".format(premise_names, conclusion_name))
    print(" - Train Confidence:
      {0:.3f}".format(rule_confidence.get((premise, conclusion),
        -1)))
    print(" - Test Confidence:
      {0:.3f}".format(test_confidence.get((premise, conclusion),
        -1)))
    print("")
```

We can now see which rules are most applicable in new unseen data:

```
Rule #1
Rule: If a person recommends Shawshank Redemption, The (1994), Pulp
Fiction (1994), Silence of the Lambs, The (1991), Star Wars (1977),
Twelve Monkeys (1995) they will also recommend Raiders of the Lost Ark
(1981)
 - Train Confidence: 1.000
 - Test Confidence: 0.909

Rule #2
Rule: If a person recommends Silence of the Lambs, The (1991), Fargo
(1996), Empire Strikes Back, The (1980), Fugitive, The (1993), Star
Wars (1977), Pulp Fiction (1994) they will also recommend Twelve
Monkeys (1995)
 - Train Confidence: 1.000
 - Test Confidence: 0.609

Rule #3
Rule: If a person recommends Silence of the Lambs, The (1991), Empire
Strikes Back, The (1980), Return of the Jedi (1983), Raiders of the
Lost Ark (1981), Twelve Monkeys (1995) they will also recommend Star
Wars (1977)
 - Train Confidence: 1.000
 - Test Confidence: 0.946

Rule #4
Rule: If a person recommends Shawshank Redemption, The (1994), Silence
of the Lambs, The (1991), Fargo (1996), Twelve Monkeys (1995), Empire
Strikes Back, The (1980), Star Wars (1977) they will also recommend
Raiders of the Lost Ark (1981)
```

```
  - Train Confidence: 1.000
  - Test Confidence: 0.971

Rule #5
Rule: If a person recommends Shawshank Redemption, The (1994), Toy
Story (1995), Twelve Monkeys (1995), Empire Strikes Back, The (1980),
Fugitive, The (1993), Star Wars (1977) they will also recommend Return
of the Jedi (1983)
 - Train Confidence: 1.000
 - Test Confidence: 0.900
```

The second rule, for instance, has a perfect confidence in the training data, but it is only accurate in 60 percent of cases for the test data. Many of the other rules in the top 10 have high confidences in test data though, making them good rules for making recommendations.

If you are looking through the rest of the rules, some will have a test confidence of -1. Confidence values are always between 0 and 1. This value indicates that the particular rule wasn't found in the test dataset at all.

Summary

In this chapter, we performed affinity analysis in order to recommend movies based on a large set of reviewers. We did this in two stages. First, we found frequent itemsets in the data using the Apriori algorithm. Then, we created association rules from those itemsets.

The use of the Apriori algorithm was necessary due to the size of the dataset. While in *Chapter 1, Getting Started With Data Mining*, we used a brute-force approach, the exponential growth in the time needed to compute those rules required a smarter approach. This is a common pattern for data mining: we can solve many problems in a brute force manner, but smarter algorithms allow us to apply the concepts to larger datasets.

We performed training on a subset of our data in order to find the association rules, and then tested those rules on the rest of the data—a testing set. From what we discussed in the previous chapters, we could extend this concept to use cross-fold validation to better evaluate the rules. This would lead to a more robust evaluation of the quality of each rule.

So far, all of our datasets have been in terms of features. However, not all datasets are "pre-defined" in this way. In the next chapter, we will look at scikit-learn's transformers (they were introduced in *Chapter 3, Predicting Sports Winners with Decision Trees*) as a way to extract features from data. We will discuss how to implement our own transformers, extend existing ones, and concepts we can implement using them.

5
Extracting Features with Transformers

The datasets we have used so far have been described in terms of features. In the previous chapter, we used a transaction-centric dataset. However, ultimately this was just a different format for representing feature-based data.

There are many other types of datasets, including text, images, sounds, movies, or even real objects. Most data mining algorithms, however, rely on having numerical or categorical features. This means we need a way to represent these types before we input them into the data mining algorithm.

In this chapter, we will discuss how to extract numerical and categorical features, and choose the best features when we do have them. We will discuss some common patterns and techniques for extracting features.

The key concepts introduced in this chapter include:

- Extracting features from datasets
- Creating new features
- Selecting good features
- Creating your own transformer for custom datasets

Feature extraction

Extracting features is one of the most critical tasks in data mining, and it generally affects your end result more than the choice of data mining algorithm. Unfortunately, there are no hard and fast rules for choosing features that will result in high performance data mining. In many ways, this is where the science of data mining becomes more of an art. Creating good features relies on intuition, domain expertise, data mining experience, trial and error, and sometimes a little luck.

Representing reality in models

Not all datasets are presented in terms of features. Sometimes, a dataset consists of nothing more than all of the books that have been written by a given author. Sometimes, it is the film of each of the movies released in 1979. At other times, it is a library collection of interesting historical artifacts.

From these datasets, we may want to perform a data mining task. For the books, we may want to know the different categories that the author writes. In the films, we may wish to see how women are portrayed. In the historical artifacts, we may want to know whether they are from one country or another. It isn't possible to just pass these raw datasets into a decision tree and see what the result is.

For a data mining algorithm to assist us here, we need to represent these as features. Features are a way to create a model and the model provides an approximation of reality in a way that data mining algorithms can understand. Therefore, a model is just a simplified version of some aspect of the real world. As an example, the game of chess is a simplified model for historical warfare.

Selecting features has another advantage: they reduce the complexity of the real world into a more manageable model. Imagine how much information it would take to properly, accurately, and fully describe a real-world object to someone that has no background knowledge of the item. You would need to describe the size, weight, texture, composition, age, flaws, purpose, origin, and so on.

The complexity of real objects is too much for current algorithms, so we use these simpler models instead.

This simplification also focuses our intent in the data mining application. In later chapters, we will look at clustering and where it is critically important. If you put random features in, you will get random results out.

However, there is a downside as this simplification reduces the detail, or may remove good indicators of the things we wish to perform data mining on.

Thought should always be given to how to represent reality in the form of a model. Rather than just using what has been used in the past, you need to consider the goal of the data mining exercise. What are you trying to achieve? In *Chapter 3, Predicting Sports Winners with Decision Trees*, we created features by thinking about the goal (predicting winners) and used a little domain knowledge to come up with ideas for new features.

Not all features need to be numeric or categorical. Algorithms have been developed that work directly on text, graphs, and other data structures. Unfortunately, those algorithms are outside the scope of this book. In this book, we mainly use numeric or categorical features.

The `Adult` dataset is a great example of taking a complex reality and attempting to model it using features. In this dataset, the aim is to estimate if someone earns more than $50,000 per year. To download the dataset, navigate to `http://archive.ics.uci.edu/ml/datasets/Adult` and click on the **Data Folder** link. Download the `adult.data` and `adult.names` into a directory named `Adult` in your data folder.

This dataset takes a complex task and describes it in features. These features describe the person, their environment, their background, and their life status.

Open a new IPython Notebook for this chapter and set the data's filename and import pandas to load the file:

```
import os
import pandas as pd
data_folder = os.path.join(os.path.expanduser("~"), "Data",
  "Adult")
adult_filename = os.path.join(data_folder, "adult.data")
Using pandas as before, we load the file with read_csv:
adult = pd.read_csv(adult_filename, header=None,
    names=["Age", "Work-Class", "fnlwgt",
    "Education", "Education-Num",
    "Marital-Status", "Occupation",
    "Relationship", "Race", "Sex",
    "Capital-gain", "Capital-loss",
    "Hours-per-week", "Native-Country",
    "Earnings-Raw"])
```

Most of the code is the same as in the previous chapters.

The `adult` file itself contains two blank lines at the end of the file. By default, pandas will interpret the penultimate new line to be an empty (but valid) row. To remove this, we remove any line with invalid numbers (the use of `inplace` just makes sure the same Dataframe is affected, rather than creating a new one):

```
adult.dropna(how='all', inplace=True)
```

Having a look at the dataset, we can see a variety of features from `adult.columns`:

```
adult.columns
```

The results show each of the feature names that are stored inside an `Index` object from `pandas`:

```
Index(['Age', 'Work-Class', 'fnlwgt', 'Education',
'Education-Num', 'Marital-Status', 'Occupation', 'Relationship',
'Race', 'Sex', 'Capital-gain', 'Capital-loss', 'Hours-per-week',
'Native-Country', 'Earnings-Raw'], dtype='object')
```

Common feature patterns

While there are millions of ways to create features, there are some common patterns that are employed across different disciplines. However, choosing appropriate features is tricky and it is worth considering how a feature might correlate to the end result. As the adage says, don't judge a book by its cover—it is probably not worth considering the size of a book if you are interested in the message contained within.

Some commonly used features focus on the physical properties of the real world objects being studied, for example:

- Spatial properties such as the length, width, and height of an object
- Weight and/or density of the object
- Age of an object or its components
- The type of the object
- The quality of the object

Other features might rely on the usage or history of the object:

- The producer, publisher, or creator of the object
- The year of manufacturing
- The use of the object

Other features describe a dataset in terms of its components:

- Frequency of a given subcomponent, such as a word in a book
- Number of subcomponents and/or the number of different subcomponents
- Average size of the subcomponents, such as the average sentence length

Ordinal features allow us to perform ranking, sorting, and grouping of similar values. As we have seen in previous chapters, features can be numerical or categorical. Numerical features are often described as being **ordinal**. For example, three people, Alice, Bob and Charlie, may have heights of 1.5 m, 1.6 m and 1.7 m. We would say that Alice and Bob are more similar in height than are Alice and Charlie.

The Adult dataset that we loaded in the last section contains examples of continuous, ordinal features. For example, the `Hours-per-week` feature tracks how many hours per week people work. Certain operations make sense on a feature like this. They include computing the mean, standard deviation, minimum and maximum. There is a function in pandas for giving some basic summary stats of this type:

```
adult["Hours-per-week"].describe()
```

The result tells us a little about this feature.

```
count    32561.000000
mean        40.437456
std         12.347429
min          1.000000
25%         40.000000
50%         40.000000
75%         45.000000
max         99.000000
dtype: float64
```

Some of these operations do not make sense for other features. For example, it doesn't make sense to compute the sum of the education statuses.

There are also features that are not numerical, but still ordinal. The `Education` feature in the Adult dataset is an example of this. For example, a Bachelor's degree is a higher education status than finishing high school, which is a higher status than not completing high school. It doesn't quite make sense to compute the mean of these values, but we can create an approximation by taking the median value. The dataset gives a helpful feature `Education-Num`, which assigns a number that is basically equivalent to the number of years of education completed. This allows us to quickly compute the median:

```
adult["Education-Num"].median()
```

The result is 10, or finishing one year past high school. If we didn't have this, we could compute the median by creating an ordering over the education values.

Features can also be categorical. For instance, a ball can be a *tennis ball, cricket ball, football*, or any other type of ball. Categorical features are also referred to as nominal features. For nominal features, the values are either the same or they are different. While we could rank balls by size or weight, just the category alone isn't enough to compare things. A tennis ball is not a cricket ball, and it is also not a football. We could argue that a tennis ball is more similar to a cricket ball (say, in size), but the category alone doesn't differentiate this—they are the same, or they are not.

We can convert categorical features to numerical features using the one-hot encoding, as we saw in *Chapter 3, Predicting Sports Winners with Decision Trees*. For the aforementioned categories of balls, we can create three new binary features: `is a tennis ball`, `is a cricket ball`, and `is a football`. For a tennis ball, the vector would be [1, 0, 0]. A cricket ball has the values [0, 1, 0], while a football has the values [0, 0, 1]. These features are binary, but can be used as continuous features by many algorithms. One key reason for doing this is that it easily allows for direct numerical comparison (such as computing the distance between samples).

The Adult dataset contains several categorical features, with `Work-Class` being one example. While we could argue that some values are of higher rank than others (for instance, a person with a job is likely to have a better income than a person without), it doesn't make sense for all values. For example, a person working for the state government is not more or less likely to have a higher income than someone working in the private sector.

We can view the unique values for this feature in the dataset using the `unique()` function:

```
adult["Work-Class"].unique()
```

The result shows the unique values in this column:

```
array([' State-gov', ' Self-emp-not-inc', ' Private', ' Federal-gov',
       ' Local-gov', ' ?', ' Self-emp-inc', ' Without-pay',
       ' Never-worked', nan], dtype=object)
```

There are some missing values in the preceding dataset, but they won't affect our computations in this example.

Similarly, we can convert numerical features to categorical features through a process called **discretization**, as we saw in *Chapter 4, Recommending Movies Using Affiity Analysis*. We can call any person who is taller than 1.7 m tall, and any person shorter than 1.7 m short. This gives us a categorical feature (although still an ordinal one). We do lose some data here. For instance, two people, one 1.69 m tall and one 1.71 m, will be in two different categories and considered *drastically* different from each other. In contrast, a person 1.2 m tall will be considered "of roughly the same height" as the person 1.69 m tall! This loss of detail is a side effect of discretization, and it is an issue that we deal with when creating models.

In the Adult dataset, we can create a `LongHours` feature, which tells us if a person works more than 40 hours per week. This turns our continuous feature (`Hours-per-week`) into a categorical one:

```
adult["LongHours"] = adult["Hours-per-week"] > 40
```

Creating good features

Modeling, and the loss of information that the simplification causes, are the reasons why we do not have data mining methods that can just be applied to any dataset. A good data mining practitioner will have, or obtain, domain knowledge in the area they are applying data mining to. They will look at the problem, the available data, and come up with a model that represents what they are trying to achieve.

For instance, a *height* feature may describe one component of a person, but may not describe their academic performance well. If we were attempting to predict a person's grade, we may not bother measuring each person's height.

This is where data mining becomes more art than science. Extracting good features is difficult and is the topic of significant and ongoing research. Choosing better classification algorithms can improve the performance of a data mining application, but choosing better features is often a better option.

In all data mining applications, you should first outline what you are looking for before you start designing the methodology that will find it. This will dictate the types of features you are aiming for, the types of algorithms that you can use, and the expectations on the final result.

Feature selection

We will often have a large number of features to choose from, but we wish to select only a small subset. There are many possible reasons for this:

- **Reducing complexity**: Many data mining algorithms need more time and resources with increase in the number of features. Reducing the number of features is a great way to make an algorithm run faster or with fewer resources.
- **Reducing noise**: Adding extra features doesn't always lead to better performance. Extra features may confuse the algorithm, finding correlations and patterns that don't have meaning (this is common in smaller datasets). Choosing only the appropriate features is a good way to reduce the chance of random correlations that have no real meaning.
- **Creating readable models**: While many data mining algorithms will happily compute an answer for models with thousands of features, the results may be difficult to interpret for a human. In these cases, it may be worth using fewer features and creating a model that a human can understand.

Some classification algorithms can handle data with issues such as these. Getting the data right and getting the features to effectively describe the dataset you are modeling can still assist algorithms.

There are some basic tests we can perform, such as ensuring that the features are at least different. If a feature's values are all same, it can't give us extra information to perform our data mining.

The `VarianceThreshold` transformer in scikit-learn, for instance, will remove any feature that doesn't have at least a minimum level of variance in the values. To show how this works, we first create a simple matrix using NumPy:

```
import numpy as np
X = np.arange(30).reshape((10, 3))
```

The result is the numbers zero to 29, in three columns and 10 rows. This represents a synthetic dataset with 10 samples and three features:

```
array([[ 0,  1,  2],
       [ 3,  4,  5],
       [ 6,  7,  8],
       [ 9, 10, 11],
       [12, 13, 14],
       [15, 16, 17],
```

```
        [18, 19, 20],
        [21, 22, 23],
        [24, 25, 26],
        [27, 28, 29]])
```

Then, we set the entire second column/feature to the value 1:

```
X[:,1] = 1
```

The result has lots of variance in the first and third rows, but no variance in the second row:

```
array([[ 0,  1,  2],
       [ 3,  1,  5],
       [ 6,  1,  8],
       [ 9,  1, 11],
       [12,  1, 14],
       [15,  1, 17],
       [18,  1, 20],
       [21,  1, 23],
       [24,  1, 26],
       [27,  1, 29]])
```

We can now create a `VarianceThreshold` transformer and apply it to our dataset:

```
from sklearn.feature_selection import VarianceThreshold
vt = VarianceThreshold()
Xt = vt.fit_transform(X)
```

Now, the result `Xt` does not have the second column:

```
array([[ 0,  2],
       [ 3,  5],
       [ 6,  8],
       [ 9, 11],
       [12, 14],
       [15, 17],
       [18, 20],
       [21, 23],
       [24, 26],
       [27, 29]])
```

We can observe the variances for each column by printing the `vt.variances_` attribute:

```
print(vt.variances_)
```

The result shows that while the first and third column contains at least some information, the second column had no variance:

```
array([ 74.25,    0.  ,  74.25])
```

A simple and obvious test like this is always good to run when seeing data for the first time. Features with no variance do not add any value to a data mining application; however, they can slow down the performance of the algorithm.

Selecting the best individual features

If we have a number of features, the problem of finding the best subset is a difficult task. It relates to solving the data mining problem itself, multiple times. As we saw in *Chapter 4, Recommending Movies Using Affinity Analysis*, subset-based tasks increase exponentially as the number of features increase. This exponential growth in time needed is also true for finding the best subset of features.

A workaround to this problem is not to look for a subset that works well together, rather than just finding the best individual features. This **univariate** feature selection gives us a score based on how well a feature performs by itself. This is usually done for classification tasks, and we generally measure some type of correlation between a variable and the target class.

The `scikit-learn` package has a number of transformers for performing univariate feature selection. They include `SelectKBest`, which returns the *k* best performing features, and `SelectPercentile`, which returns the top *r%* of features. In both cases, there are a number of methods of computing the quality of a feature.

There are many different methods to compute how effectively a single feature correlates with a class value. A commonly used method is the chi-squared ($\chi 2$) test. Other methods include mutual information and entropy.

We can observe single-feature tests in action using our `Adult` dataset. First, we extract a dataset and class values from our pandas `DataFrame`. We get a selection of the features:

```
X = adult[["Age", "Education-Num", "Capital-gain", "Capital-loss",
  "Hours-per-week"]].values
```

We will also create a target class array by testing whether the `Earnings-Raw` value is above $50,000 or not. If it is, the class will be `True`. Otherwise, it will be `False`. Let's look at the code:

```
y = (adult["Earnings-Raw"] == ' >50K').values
```

Next, we create our transformer using the `chi2` function and a `SelectKBest` transformer:

```
from sklearn.feature_selection import SelectKBest
from sklearn.feature_selection import chi2
transformer = SelectKBest(score_func=chi2, k=3)
```

Running `fit_transform` will call fit and then transform with the same dataset. The result will create a new dataset, choosing only the best three features. Let's look at the code:

```
Xt_chi2 = transformer.fit_transform(X, y)
```

The resulting matrix now only contains three features. We can also get the scores for each column, allowing us to find out which features were used. Let's look at the code:

```
print(transformer.scores_)
```

The printed results give us these scores:

```
[  8.60061182e+03   2.40142178e+03   8.21924671e+07   1.37214589e+06
   6.47640900e+03]
```

The highest values are for the first, third, and fourth columns Correlates to the `Age`, `Capital-Gain`, and `Capital-Loss` features. Based on a univariate feature selection, these are the best features to choose.

If you'd like to find out more about the features in the Adult dataset, take a look at the `adult.names` file that comes with the dataset and the academic paper it references.

We could also implement other correlations, such as the Pearson's correlation coefficient. This is implemented in SciPy, a library used for scientific computing (scikit-learn uses it as a base).

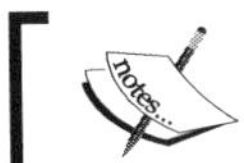

If scikit-learn is working on your computer, so is SciPy. You do not need to install anything further to get this sample working.

First, we import the `pearsonr` function from SciPy:

```
from scipy.stats import pearsonr
```

The preceding function almost fits the interface needed to be used in scikit-learn's univariate transformers. The function needs to accept two arrays (`x` and `y` in our example) as parameters and returns two arrays, the scores for each feature and the corresponding p-values. The `chi2` function we used earlier only uses the required interface, which allowed us to just pass it directly to SelectKBest.

The `pearsonr` function in SciPy accepts two arrays; however, the X array it accepts is only one dimension. We will write a wrapper function that allows us to use this for multivariate arrays like the one we have. Let's look at the code:

```
def multivariate_pearsonr(X, y):
```

We create our `scores` and `pvalues` arrays, and then iterate over each column of the dataset:

```
    scores, pvalues = [], []
    for column in range(X.shape[1]):
```

We compute the Pearson correlation for this column only and the record both the score and p-value.

```
        cur_score, cur_p = pearsonr(X[:,column], y)
        scores.append(abs(cur_score))
        pvalues.append(cur_p)
```

The Pearson value could be between `-1` and `1`. A value of `1` implies a perfect correlation between two variables, while a value of -1 implies a perfect negative correlation, that is, high values in one variable give low values in the other and vice versa. Such features are really useful to have, but would be discarded. For this reason, we have stored the absolute value in the `scores` array, rather than the original signed value.

Finally, we return the scores and `p-values` in a tuple:

```
    return (np.array(scores), np.array(pvalues))
```

Now, we can use the transformer class as before to rank the features using the Pearson correlation coefficient:

```
transformer = SelectKBest(score_func=multivariate_pearsonr, k=3)
Xt_pearson = transformer.fit_transform(X, y)
print(transformer.scores_)
```

This returns a different set of features! The features chosen this way are the first, second, and fifth columns: the `Age`, `Education`, and `Hours-per-week` worked. This shows that there is not a definitive answer to what the best features are— it depends on the metric.

We can see which feature set is better by running them through a classifier. Keep in mind that the results only indicate which subset is better for a particular classifier and/or feature combination—there is rarely a case in data mining where one method is strictly better than another in all cases! Let's look at the code:

```
from sklearn.tree import DecisionTreeClassifier
from sklearn.cross_validation import cross_val_score
clf = DecisionTreeClassifier(random_state=14)
scores_chi2 = cross_val_score(clf, Xt_chi2, y, scoring='accuracy')
scores_pearson = cross_val_score(clf, Xt_pearson, y,
  scoing='accuracy')
```

The `chi2` average here is 0.83, while the Pearson score is lower at 0.77. For this combination, `chi2` returns better results!

It is worth remembering the goal of this data mining activity: predicting wealth. Using a combination of good features and feature selection, we can achieve 83 percent accuracy using just three features of a person!

Feature creation

Sometimes, just selecting features from what we have isn't enough. We can create features in different ways from features we already have. The one-hot encoding method we saw previously is an example of this. Instead of having a category features with options *A*, *B* and *C*, we would create three new features *Is it A?*, *Is it B?*, *Is it C?*.

Creating new features may seem unnecessary and to have no clear benefit—after all, the information is already in the dataset and we just need to use it. However, some algorithms struggle when features correlate significantly, or if there are redundant features. They may also struggle if there are redundant features.

For this reason, there are various ways to create new features from the features we already have.

We are going to load a new dataset, so now is a good time to start a new IPython Notebook. Download the Advertisements dataset from `http://archive.ics.uci.edu/ml/datasets/Internet+Advertisements` and save it to your `Data` folder.

Next, we need to load the dataset with pandas. First, we set the data's filename as always:

```
import os
import numpy as np
import pandas as pd
data_folder = os.path.join(os.path.expanduser("~"), "Data")
data_filename = os.path.join(data_folder, "Ads", "ad.data")
```

There are a couple of issues with this dataset that stop us from loading it easily. First, the first few features are numerical, but pandas will load them as strings. To fix this, we need to write a converting function that will convert strings to numbers if possible. Otherwise, we will get a **NaN** (which is short for **Not a Number**), which is a special value that indicates that the value could not be interpreted as a number. It is similar to *none* or *null* in other programming languages.

Another issue with this dataset is that some values are missing. These are represented in the dataset using the string `?`. Luckily, the question mark doesn't convert to a float, so we can convert those to NaNs using the same concept. In further chapters, we will look at other ways of dealing with missing values like this.

We will create a function that will do this conversion for us:

```
def convert_number(x):
```

First, we want to convert the string to a number and see if that fails. Then, we will surround the conversion in a `try/except` block, catching a `ValueError` exception (which is what is thrown if a string cannot be converted into a number this way):

```
    try:
        return float(x)
    except ValueError:
```

Finally, if the conversion failed, we get a NaN that comes from the NumPy library we imported previously:

```
        return np.nan
```

Now, we create a dictionary for the conversion. We want to convert all of the features to floats:

```
converters = defaultdict(convert_number
```

Also, we want to set the final column (column index #1558), which is the class, to a binary feature. In the Adult dataset, we created a new feature for this. In the dataset, we will convert the feature while we load it.

```
converters[1558] = lambda x: 1 if x.strip() == "ad." else 0
```

Now we can load the dataset using `read_csv`. We use the converters parameter to pass our custom conversion into pandas:

```
ads = pd.read_csv(data_filename, header=None, converters=converters)
```

The resulting dataset is quite large, with 1,559 features and more than 2,000 rows. Here are some of the feature values the first five, printed by inserting `ads[:5]` into a new cell:

	0	1	2	3	4	5	6	7	8	9	...	1549	1550	1551	1552	1553	1554	1555	1556	1557	1558
0	125	125	1.0000	1	0	0	0	0	0	0	...	0	0	0	0	0	0	0	0	0	1
1	57	468	8.2105	1	0	0	0	0	0	0	...	0	0	0	0	0	0	0	0	0	1
2	33	230	6.9696	1	0	0	0	0	0	0	...	0	0	0	0	0	0	0	0	0	1
3	60	468	7.8000	1	0	0	0	0	0	0	...	0	0	0	0	0	0	0	0	0	1
4	60	468	7.8000	1	0	0	0	0	0	0	...	0	0	0	0	0	0	0	0	0	1

This dataset describes images on websites, with the goal of determining whether a given image is an advertisement or not.

The features in this dataset are not described well by their headings. There are two files accompanying the `ad.data` file that have more information: `ad.DOCUMENTATION` and `ad.names`. The first three features are the height, width, and ratio of the image size. The final feature is 1 if it is an advertisement and 0 if it is not.

The other features are 1 for the presence of certain words in the URL, alt text, or caption of the image. These words, such as the word *sponsor*, are used to determine if the image is likely to be an advertisement. Many of the features overlap considerably, as they are combinations of other features. Therefore, this dataset has a lot of redundant information.

With our dataset loaded in pandas, we will now extract the `x` and `y` data for our classification algorithms. The `x` matrix will be all of the columns in our Dataframe, except for the last column. In contrast, the y array will be only that last column, feature #1558. Let's look at the code:

```
X = ads.drop(1558, axis=1).values
y = ads[1558]
```

Principal Component Analysis

In some datasets, features heavily correlate with each other. For example, the speed and the fuel consumption would be heavily correlated in a go-kart with a single gear. While it can be useful to find these correlations for some applications, data mining algorithms typically do not need the redundant information.

The ads dataset has heavily correlated features, as many of the keywords are repeated across the alt text and caption.

The **Principal Component Analysis (PCA)** aims to find combinations of features that describe the dataset in less information. It aims to discover *principal components*, which are features that do not correlate with each other and explain the information—specifically the **variance**—of the dataset. What this means is that we can often capture most of the information in a dataset in fewer features.

We apply PCA just like any other transformer. It has one key parameter, which is the number of components to find. By default, it will result in as many features as you have in the original dataset. However, these principal components are ranked—the first feature explains the largest amount of the variance in the dataset, the second a little less, and so on. Therefore, finding just the first few features is often enough to explain much of the dataset. Let's look at the code:

```
from sklearn.decomposition import PCA
pca = PCA(n_components=5)
Xd = pca.fit_transform(X)
```

The resulting matrix, `Xd`, has just five features. However, let's look at the amount of variance that is explained by each of these features:

```
np.set_printoptions(precision=3, suppress=True)
pca.explained_variance_ratio_
```

The result, `array([ 0.854,  0.145,  0.001,  0.   ,  0.   ])`, shows us that the first feature accounts for 85.4 percent of the variance in the dataset, the second accounts for 14.5 percent, and so on. By the fourth feature, less than one-tenth of a percent of the variance is contained in the feature. The other 1,553 features explain even less.

The downside to transforming data with PCA is that these features are often complex combinations of the other features. For example, the first feature of the preceding code *starts* with `[-0.092, -0.995, -0.024]`, that is, multiply the first feature in the original dataset by -0.092, the second by -0.995, the third by -0.024. This *feature* has 1,558 values of this form, one for each of the original datasets (although many are zeros). Such features are indistinguishable by humans and it is hard to glean much relevant information from without a lot of experience working with them.

Using PCA can result in models that not only approximate the original dataset, but can also improve the performance in classification tasks:

```
clf = DecisionTreeClassifier(random_state=14)
scores_reduced = cross_val_score(clf, Xd, y, scoring='accuracy')
```

The resulting score is 0.9356, which is (slightly) higher than our original score using all of the original features. PCA won't always give a benefit like this, but it does more often than not.

We are using PCA here to reduce the number of features in our dataset. As a general rule, you shouldn't use it to reduce overfitting in your data mining experiments. The reason for this is that PCA doesn't take classes into account. A better solution is to use regularization. An introduction, with code, is available at `http://blog.datadive.net/selecting-good-features-part-ii-linear-models-and-regularization/`.

Another advantage is that PCA allows you to plot datasets that you otherwise couldn't easily visualize. For example, we can plot the first two features returned by PCA.

First, we tell IPython to display plots inline and import `pyplot`:

```
%matplotlib inline
from matplotlib import pyplot as plt
```

Next, we get all of the distinct classes in our dataset (there are only two: `is ad` or `not ad`):

```
classes = set(y)
```

We also assign colors to each of these classes:

```
colors = ['red', 'green']
```

We use zip to iterate over both lists at the same time:

```
for cur_class, color in zip(classes, colors):
```

We then create a mask of all of the samples that belong to the current class:

```
mask = (y == cur_class).values
```

Finally, we use the `scatter` function in `pyplot` to show where these are. We use the first two features as our `x` and `y` values in this plot.

```
plt.scatter(Xd[mask,0], Xd[mask,1], marker='o', color=color,
  label=int(cur_class))
```

Finally, outside the loop, we create a legend and show the graph, showing where the samples from each class appear:

```
plt.legend()
plt.show()
```

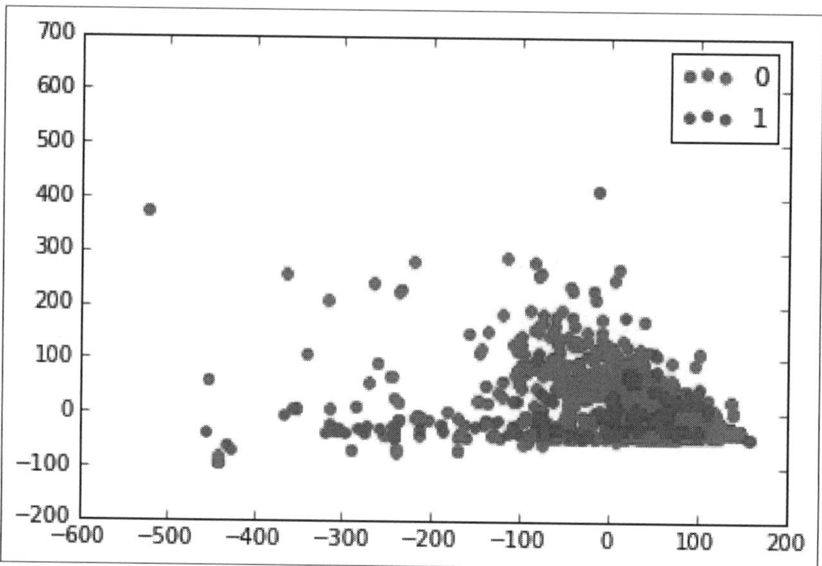

Creating your own transformer

As the complexity and type of dataset changes, you might find that you can't find an existing feature extraction transformer that fits your needs. We will see an example of this in *Chapter 7, Discovering Accounts to Follow Using Graph Mining*, where we create new features from graphs.

A transformer is akin to a converting function. It takes data of one form as input and returns data of another form as output. Transformers can be trained using some training dataset, and these trained parameters can be used to convert testing data.

The transformer API is quite simple. It takes data of a specific format as input and returns data of another format (either the same as the input or different) as output. Not much else is required of the programmer.

The transformer API

Transformers have two key functions:

- `fit()`: This takes a training set of data as input and sets internal parameters
- `transform()`: This performs the transformation itself. This can take either the training dataset, or a new dataset of the same format

Both `fit()` and `transform()` fuction should take the same data type as input, but `transform()` can return data of a different type.

We are going to create a trivial transformer to show the API in action. The transformer will take a NumPy array as input, and discretize it based on the mean. Any value higher than the mean (of the training data) will be given the value 1 and any value lower or equal to the mean will be given the value 0.

We did a similar transformation with the Adult dataset using pandas: we took the `Hours-per-week` feature and created a `LongHours` feature if the value was more than 40 hours per week. This transformer is different for two reasons. First, the code will conform to the scikit-learn API, allowing us to use it in a pipeline. Second, the code will *learn* the mean, rather than taking it as a fixed value (such as 40 in the `LongHours` example).

Implementation details

To start, open up the IPython Notebook that we used for the Adult dataset. Then, click on the **Cell menu** item and choose **Run All**. This will rerun all of the cells and ensure that the notebook is up to date.

First, we import the `TransformerMixin`, which sets the API for us. While Python doesn't have strict interfaces (as opposed to languages like Java), using a `mixin` like this allows scikit-learn to determine that the class is actually a transformer. We also need to import a function that checks the input is of a valid type. We will use that soon.

Let's look at the code:

```
from sklearn.base import TransformerMixin
from sklearn.utils import as_float_array
```

Now, create a new class that subclasses from our `mixin`:

```
class MeanDiscrete(TransformerMixin):
```

We need to define both a fit and transform function to conform to the API. In our `fit` function, we find the mean of the dataset and set an internal variable to remember that value. Let's look at the code:

```
    def fit(self, X):
```

First, we ensure that `X` is a dataset that we can work with, using the `as_float_array` function (which will also convert `X` if it can, for example, if `X` is a list of floats):

```
        X = as_float_array(X)
```

Next, we compute the mean of the array and set an internal parameter to remember this value. When `X` is a multivariate array, `self.mean` will be an array that contains the mean of each feature:

```
        self.mean = X.mean(axis=0)
```

The `fit` function also needs to return the class itself. This requirement ensures that we can perform chaining of functionality in transformers (such as calling `transformer.fit(X).transform(X)`). Let's look at the code:

```
        return self
```

Next, we define the transform function, this takes a dataset of the same type as the fit function, so we need to check we got the right input:

```
    def transform(self, X):
        X = as_float_array(X)
```

We should perform another check here too. While we need the input to be a NumPy array (or an equivalent data structure), the shape needs to be consistent too. The number of features in this array needs to be the same as the number of features the class was trained on.

```
        assert X.shape[1] == self.mean.shape[0]
```

Now, we perform the actual transformation by simply testing if the values in `X` are higher than the stored mean.

```
        return X > self.mean
```

We can then create an instance of this class and use it to transform our `X` array:

```
mean_discrete = MeanDiscrete()
X_mean = mean_discrete.fit_transform(X)
```

Unit testing

When creating your own functions and classes, it is always a good idea to do unit testing. Unit testing aims to test a single unit of your code. In this case, we want to test that our transformer does as it needs to do.

Good tests should be independently verifiable. A good way to confirm the legitimacy of your tests is by using another computer language or method to perform the calculations. In this case, I used Excel to create a dataset, and then computed the mean for each cell. Those values were then transferred here.

Unit tests should also be small and quick to run. Therefore, any data used should be of a small size. The dataset I used for creating the tests is stored in the `Xt` variable from earlier, which we will recreate in our test. The mean of these two features is 13.5 and 15.5, respectively.

To create our unit test, we import the `assert_array_equal` function from NumPy's testing, which checks whether two arrays are equal:

```
from numpy.testing import assert_array_equal
```

Next, we create our function. It is important that the test's name starts with `test_`, as this nomenclature is used for tools that automatically find and run tests. We also set up our testing data:

```
def test_meandiscrete():
    X_test = np.array([[ 0,  2],
                       [ 3,  5],
                       [ 6,  8],
                       [ 9, 11],
                       [12, 14],
                       [15, 17],
                       [18, 20],
                       [21, 23],
                       [24, 26],
                       [27, 29]])
```

We then create our transformer instance and fit it using this test data:

```
mean_discrete = MeanDiscrete()
mean_discrete.fit(X_test)
```

Next, we check whether the internal mean parameter was correctly set by comparing it with our independently verified result:

```
assert_array_equal(mean_discrete.mean, np.array([13.5, 15.5]))
```

We then run the transform to create the transformed dataset. We also create an (independently computed) array with the expected values for the output:

```
X_transformed = mean_discrete.transform(X_test)
X_expected = np.array([[ 0,  0],
                       [ 0, 0],
                       [ 0, 0],
                       [ 0, 0],
                       [ 0, 0],
                       [ 1, 1],
                       [ 1, 1],
                       [ 1, 1],
                       [ 1, 1],
                       [ 1, 1]])
```

Finally, we test that our returned result is indeed what we expected:

```
assert_array_equal(X_transformed, X_expected)
```

We can run the test by simply running the function itself:

```
test_meandiscrete()
```

If there was no error, then the test ran without an issue! You can verify this by changing some of the tests to deliberately incorrect values, and seeing that the test fails. Remember to change them back so that the test passes.

If we had multiple tests, it would be worth using a testing framework called `nose` to run our tests.

Putting it all together

Now that we have a tested transformer, it is time to put it into action. Using what we have learned so far, we create a `Pipeline`, set the first step to the `MeanDiscrete` transformer, and the second step to a Decision Tree Classifier. We then run a cross validation and print out the result. Let's look at the code:

```
from sklearn.pipeline import Pipeline
pipeline = Pipeline([('mean_discrete', MeanDiscrete()),
  ('classifier', DecisionTreeClassifier(random_state=14))])
  scores_mean_discrete = cross_val_score(pipeline, X, y,
    scoring='accuracy')
  print("Mean Discrete performance:
{0:.3f}".format(scores_mean_discrete.mean()))
```

The result is 0.803, which is not as good as before, but not bad for simple binary features.

Summary

In this chapter, we looked at features and transformers and how they can be used in the data mining pipeline. We discussed what makes a good feature and how to algorithmically choose good features from a standard set. However, creating good features is more art than science and often requires domain knowledge and experience.

We then created our own transformer using an interface that allows us to use it in scikit-learn's helper functions. We will be creating more transformers in later chapters so that we can perform effective testing using existing functions.

In the next chapter, we use feature extraction on a corpus of text documents. There are many transformers and feature types for text, each with their advantages and disadvantages.

6

Social Media Insight Using Naive Bayes

Text-based datasets contain a lot of information, whether they are books, historical documents, social media, e-mail, or any of the other ways we communicate via writing. Extracting features from text-based datasets and using them for classification is a difficult problem. There are, however, some common patterns for text mining.

We look at disambiguating terms in social media using the Naive Bayes algorithm, which is a powerful and surprisingly simple algorithm. Naive Bayes takes a few shortcuts to properly compute the probabilities for classification, hence the term *naive* in the name. It can also be extended to other types of datasets quite easily and doesn't rely on numerical features. The model in this chapter is a baseline for text mining studies, as the process can work reasonably well for a variety of datasets.

We will cover the following topics in this chapter:

- Downloading data from social network APIs
- Transformers for text
- Naive Bayes classifier
- Using JSON for saving and loading datasets
- The NLTK library for extracting features from text
- The F-measure for evaluation

Disambiguation

Text is often called an **unstructured** format. There is a lot of information there, but it is just there; no headings, no required format, loose syntax and other problems prohibit the easy extraction of information from text. The data is also highly connected, with lots of mentions and cross-references—just not in a format that allows us to easily extract it!

We can compare the information stored in a book with that stored in a large database to see the difference. In the book, there are characters, themes, places, and lots of information. However, the book needs to be read and, more importantly, interpreted to gain this information. The database sits on your server with column names and data types. All the information is there and the level of interpretation needed is quite low. Information about the data, such as its type or meaning is called **metadata**, and text lacks it. A book also contains some metadata in the form of a table of contents and index but the degree is significantly lower than that of a database.

One of the problems is the term **disambiguation**. When a person uses the word bank, is this a financial message or an environmental message (such as river bank)? This type of disambiguation is quite easy in many circumstances for humans (although there are still troubles), but much harder for computers to do.

In this chapter, we will look at disambiguating the use of the term Python on Twitter's stream. A message on Twitter is called a **tweet** and is limited to 140 characters. This means there is little room for context. There isn't much metadata available although hashtags are often used to denote the topic of the tweet.

When people talk about Python, they could be talking about the following things:

- The programming language Python
- Monty Python, the classic comedy group
- The snake Python
- A make of shoe called Python

There can be many other things called Python. The aim of our experiment is to take a tweet mentioning Python and determine whether it is talking about the programming language, based only on the content of the tweet.

Downloading data from a social network

We are going to download a corpus of data from Twitter and use it to sort out spam from useful content. Twitter provides a robust API for collecting information from its servers and this API is free for small-scale usage. It is, however, subject to some conditions that you'll need to be aware of if you start using Twitter's data in a commercial setting.

First, you'll need to sign up for a Twitter account (which is free). Go to `http://twitter.com` and register an account if you do not already have one.

Next, you'll need to ensure that you only make a certain number of requests per minute. This limit is currently 180 requests per hour. It can be tricky ensuring that you don't breach this limit, so it is highly recommended that you use a library to talk to Twitter's API.

You will need a key to access Twitter's data. Go to `http://twitter.com` and sign in to your account.

When you are logged in, go to `https://apps.twitter.com/` and click on **Create New App**.

Create a name and description for your app, along with a website address. If you don't have a website to use, insert a placeholder. Leave the **Callback URL** field blank for this app—we won't need it. Agree to the terms of use (if you do) and click on **Create your Twitter application**.

Keep the resulting website open—you'll need the **access keys** that are on this page. Next, we need a library to talk to Twitter. There are many options; the one I like is simply called `twitter`, and is the *official* Twitter Python library.

You can install `twitter` using `pip3 install twitter` if you are using `pip` to install your packages. If you are using another system, check the documentation at `https://github.com/sixohsix/twitter`.

Create a new IPython Notebook to download the data. We will create several notebooks in this chapter for various different purposes, so it might be a good idea to also create a folder to keep track of them. This first notebook, `ch6_get_twitter`, is specifically for downloading new Twitter data.

First, we import the `twitter` library and set our authorization tokens. The **consumer key, consumer secret** will be available on the **Keys and Access Tokens** tab on your Twitter app's page. To get the access tokens, you'll need to click on the **Create my access token** button, which is on the same page. Enter the keys into the appropriate places in the following code:

```
import twitter
consumer_key = "<Your Consumer Key Here>"
consumer_secret = "<Your Consumer Secret Here>"
access_token = "<Your Access Token Here>"
access_token_secret = "<Your Access Token Secret Here>"
authorization = twitter.OAuth(access_token, access_token_secret,
consumer_key, consumer_secret)
```

We are going to get our tweets from Twitter's `search` function. We will create a reader that connects to `twitter` using our authorization, and then use that reader to perform searches. In the Notebook, we set the filename where the tweets will be stored:

```
import os
output_filename = os.path.join(os.path.expanduser("~"),
  "Data", "twitter", "python_tweets.json")
```

We also need the `json` library for saving our tweets:

```
import json
```

Next, create an object that can read from Twitter. We create this object with our authorization object that we set up earlier:

```
t = twitter.Twitter(auth=authorization)
```

We then open our output file for writing. We open it for appending—this allows us to rerun the script to obtain more tweets. We then use our Twitter connection to perform a search for the word Python. We only want the statuses that are returned for our dataset. This code takes the tweet, uses the `json` library to create a string representation using the `dumps` function, and then writes it to the file. It then creates a blank line under the tweet so that we can easily distinguish where one tweet starts and ends in our file:

```
with open(output_filename, 'a') as output_file:
    search_results = t.search.tweets(q="python", count=100)['statuses']
    for tweet in search_results:
        if 'text' in tweet:
            output_file.write(json.dumps(tweet))
            output_file.write("\n\n")
```

In the preceding loop, we also perform a check to see whether there is text in the tweet or not. Not all of the objects returned by twitter will be actual tweets (some will be actions to delete tweets and others). The key difference is the inclusion of text as a key, which we test for.

Running this for a few minutes will result in 100 tweets being added to the output file.

> You can keep rerunning this script to add more tweets to your dataset, keeping in mind that you may get some duplicates in the output file if you rerun it too fast (that is, before Twitter gets new tweets to return!).

Loading and classifying the dataset

After we have collected a set of tweets (our dataset), we need labels to perform classification. We are going to label the dataset by setting up a form in an IPython Notebook to allow us to enter the labels.

The dataset we have stored is *nearly* in a **JSON** format. JSON is a format for data that doesn't impose much structure and is directly readable in JavaScript (hence the name, JavaScript Object Notation). JSON defines basic objects such as numbers, strings, lists and dictionaries, making it a good format for storing datasets if they contain data that isn't numerical. If your dataset is fully numerical, you would save space and time using a matrix-based format like in NumPy.

A key difference between our dataset and *real* JSON is that we included newlines between tweets. The reason for this was to allow us to easily append new tweets (the actual JSON format doesn't allow this easily). Our format is a JSON representation of a tweet, followed by a newline, followed by the next tweet, and so on.

To parse it, we can use the `json` library but we will have to first split the file by newlines to get the actual tweet objects themselves.

Set up a new IPython Notebook (I called mine `ch6_label_twitter`) and enter the dataset's filename. This is the same filename in which we saved the data in the previous section. We also define the filename that we will use to save the labels to. The code is as follows:

```
import os
input_filename = os.path.join(os.path.expanduser("~"), "Data",
"twitter", "python_tweets.json")
labels_filename = os.path.join(os.path.expanduser("~"), "Data",
"twitter", "python_classes.json")
```

As stated, we will use the `json` library, so import that too:

```
import json
```

We create a list that will store the tweets we received from the file:

```
tweets = []
```

We then iterate over each line in the file. We aren't interested in lines with no information (they separate the tweets for us), so check if the length of the line (minus any whitespace characters) is zero. If it is, ignore it and move to the next line. Otherwise, load the tweet using `json.loads` (which loads a JSON object from a string) and add it to our list of tweets. The code is as follows:

```
with open(input_filename) as inf:
    for line in inf:
        if len(line.strip()) == 0:
            continue
        tweets.append(json.loads(line))
```

We are now interested in classifying whether an item is relevant to us or not (in this case, *relevant* means *refers to the programming language Python*). We will use the IPython Notebook's ability to embed HTML and talk between JavaScript and Python to create a viewer of tweets to allow us to easily and quickly classify the tweets as spam or not.

The code will present a new tweet to the user (you) and ask for a label: is it relevant or not? It will then store the input and present the next tweet to be labeled.

First, we create a list for storing the labels. These labels will be stored whether or not the given tweet refers to the programming language Python, and it will allow our classifier to learn how to differentiate between meanings.

We also check if we have any labels already and load them. This helps if you need to close the notebook down midway through labeling. This code will load the labels from where you left off. It is generally a good idea to consider how to save at midpoints for tasks like this. Nothing hurts quite like losing an hour of work because your computer crashed before you saved the labels! The code is as follows:

```
labels = []
if os.path.exists(labels_filename):
    with open(labels_filename) as inf:
        labels = json.load(inf)
```

Next, we create a simple function that will return the next tweet that needs to be labeled. We can work out which is the next tweet by finding the first one that hasn't yet been labeled. The code is as follows:

```
def get_next_tweet():
    return tweet_sample[len(labels)]['text']
```

The next step in our experiment is to collect information from the user (you!) on which tweets are referring to Python (the programming language) and which are not. As of yet, there is not a good, straightforward way to get interactive feedback with pure Python in IPython Notebooks. For this reason, we will use some JavaScript and HTML to get this input from the user.

Next we create some JavaScript in the IPython Notebook to run our input. Notebooks allow us to use magic functions to embed HTML and JavaScript (among other things) directly into the Notebook itself. Start a new cell with the following line at the top:

```
%%javascript
```

The code in here will be in JavaScript, hence the curly braces that are coming up. Don't worry, we will get back to Python soon. Keep in mind here that the following code must be in the same cell as the `%%javascript` magic function.

The first function we will define in JavaScript shows how easy it is to talk to your Python code from JavaScript in IPython Notebooks. This function, if called, will add a label to the `labels` array (which is in `python` code). To do this, we load the IPython **kernel** as a JavaScript object and give it a Python command to execute. The code is as follows:

```
function set_label(label){
    var kernel = IPython.notebook.kernel;
    kernel.execute("labels.append(" + label + ")");
    load_next_tweet();
}
```

At the end of that function, we call the `load_next_tweet` function. This function loads the next tweet to be labeled. It runs on the same principle; we load the IPython kernel and give it a command to execute (calling the `get_next_tweet` function we defined earlier).

However, in this case we want to get the result. This is a little more difficult. We need to define a `callback`, which is a function that is called when the data is returned. The format for defining `callback` is outside the scope of this book. If you are interested in more advanced JavaScript/Python integration, consult the IPython documentation.

The code is as follows:

```
function load_next_tweet(){
    var code_input = "get_next_tweet()";
    var kernel = IPython.notebook.kernel;
    var callbacks = { 'iopub' : {'output' : handle_output}};
    kernel.execute(code_input, callbacks, {silent:false});
}
```

The callback function is called `handle_output`, which we will define now. This function gets called when the Python function that `kernel.execute` calls returns a value. As before, the full format of this is outside the scope of this book. However, for our purposes the result is returned as data of the type text/plain, which we extract and show in the `#tweet_text div` of the form we are going to create in the next cell. The code is as follows:

```
function handle_output(out){
    var res = out.content.data["text/plain"];
    $("div#tweet_text").html(res);
}
```

Our form will have a `div` that shows the next tweet to be labeled, which we will give the `ID #tweet_text`. We also create a textbox to enable us to capture key presses (otherwise, the Notebook will capture them and JavaScript won't do anything). This allows us to use the keyboard to set labels of *1* or *0*, which is faster than using the mouse to click buttons—given that we will need to label at least 100 tweets.

Run the previous cell to embed some JavaScript into the page, although nothing will be shown to you in the results section.

We are going to use a different magic function now, `%%html`. Unsurprisingly, this magic function allows us to directly embed HTML into our Notebook. In a new cell, start with this line:

```
%%html
```

For this cell, we will be coding in HTML and a little JavaScript. First, define a `div` element to store our current tweet to be labeled. I've also added some instructions for using this form. Then, create the `#tweet_text` div that will store the text of the next tweet to be labeled. As stated before, we need to create a textbox to be able to capture key presses. The code is as follows:

```
<div name="tweetbox">
    Instructions: Click in textbox. Enter a 1 if the tweet is
relevant, enter 0 otherwise.<br>
Tweet: <div id="tweet_text" value="text"></div><br>
<input type=text id="capture"></input><br>
</div>
```

Don't run the cell just yet!

We create the JavaScript for capturing the key presses. This has to be defined after creating the form, as the `#tweet_text` div doesn't exist until the above code runs. We use the **JQuery** library (which IPython is already using, so we don't need to include the JavaScript file) to add a function that is called when key presses are made on the `#capture` textbox we defined. However, keep in mind that this is a `%%html` cell and not a JavaScript cell, so we need to enclose this JavaScript in the `<script>` tags.

We are only interested in key presses if the user presses the **0** or the **1**, in which case the relevant label is added. We can determine which key was pressed by the ASCII value stored in `e.which`. If the user presses 0 or 1, we append the label and clear out the textbox. The code is as follows:

```
<script>
$("input#capture").keypress(function(e) {
if(e.which == 48) {
    set_label(0);
    $("input#capture").val("");
}else if (e.which == 49){
    set_label(1);
    $("input#capture").val("");
  }
});
```

All other key presses are ignored.

As a last bit of JavaScript for this chapter (I promise), we call the `load_next_tweet()` function. This will set the first tweet to be labeled and then close off the JavaScript. The code is as follows:

```
load_next_tweet();
</script>
```

After you run this cell, you will get an HTML textbox, alongside the first tweet's text. Click in the textbox and enter `1` if it is relevant to our goal (in this case, it means *is the tweet related to the programming language Python*) and a 0 if it is not. After you do this, the next tweet will load. Enter the label and the next one will load. This continues until the tweets run out.

When you finish all of this, simply save the labels to the output filename we defined earlier for the class values:

```
with open(labels_filename, 'w') as outf:
    json.dump(labels, outf)
```

You can call the preceding code even if you haven't finished. Any labeling you have done to that point will be saved. Running this Notebook again will pick up where you left off and you can keep labeling your tweets.

This might take a while to do this! If you have a lot of tweets in your dataset, you'll need to classify all of them. If you are pushed for time, you can download the same dataset I used, which contains classifications.

Creating a replicable dataset from Twitter

In data mining, there are lots of variables. These aren't just in the data mining algorithms—they also appear in the data collection, environment, and many other factors. Being able to replicate your results is important as it enables you to verify or improve upon your results.

Getting 80 percent accuracy on one dataset with algorithm `X`, and 90 percent accuracy on another dataset with algorithm `Y` doesn't mean that Y is better. We need to be able to test on the same dataset in the same conditions to be able to properly compare.

On running the preceding code, you will get a different dataset to the one I created and used. The main reasons are that Twitter will return different search results for you than me based on the time you performed the search. Even after that, your labeling of tweets might be different from what I do. While there are obvious examples where *a given tweet relates to the python programming language*, there will always be gray areas where the labeling isn't obvious. One tough gray area I ran into was tweets in non-English languages that I couldn't read. In this specific instance, there are options in Twitter's API for setting the language, but even these aren't going to be perfect.

Due to these factors, it is difficult to replicate experiments on databases that are extracted from social media, and Twitter is no exception. Twitter explicitly disallows sharing datasets directly.

One solution to this is to share tweet IDs only, which you can share freely. In this section, we will first create a tweet ID dataset that we can freely share. Then, we will see how to download the original tweets from this file to recreate the original dataset.

First, we save the replicable dataset of tweet IDs. Creating another new IPython Notebook, first set up the filenames. This is done in the same way we did labeling but there is a new filename where we can store the replicable dataset. The code is as follows:

```
import os
input_filename = os.path.join(os.path.expanduser("~"), "Data",
"twitter", "python_tweets.json")
labels_filename = os.path.join(os.path.expanduser("~"), "Data",
"twitter", "python_classes.json")
replicable_dataset = os.path.join(os.path.expanduser("~"),
  "Data", "twitter", "replicable_dataset.json")
```

We load the tweets and labels as we did in the previous notebook:

```
import json
tweets = []
with open(input_filename) as inf:
    for line in inf:
        if len(line.strip()) == 0:
            continue
        tweets.append(json.loads(line))
if os.path.exists(labels_filename):
    with open(classes_filename) as inf:
        labels = json.load(inf)
```

Now we create a dataset by looping over both the tweets and labels at the same time and saving those in a list:

```
dataset = [(tweet['id'], label) for tweet, label in zip(tweets,
  labels)]
```

Finally, we save the results in our file:

```
with open(replicable_dataset, 'w') as outf:
    json.dump(dataset, outf)
```

Now that we have the tweet IDs and labels saved, we can recreate the original dataset. If you are looking to recreate the dataset I used for this chapter, it can be found in the code bundle that comes with this book.

Loading the preceding dataset is not difficult but it can take some time. Start a new IPython Notebook and set the dataset, label, and tweet ID filenames as before. I've adjusted the filenames here to ensure that you don't overwrite your previously collected dataset, but feel free to change these if you want. The code is as follows:

```
import os
tweet_filename = os.path.join(os.path.expanduser("~"), "Data",
  "twitter", "replicable_python_tweets.json")
labels_filename = os.path.join(os.path.expanduser("~"), "Data",
  "twitter", "replicable_python_classes.json")
replicable_dataset = os.path.join(os.path.expanduser("~"),
  "Data", "twitter", "replicable_dataset.json")
```

Then load the tweet IDs from the file using JSON:

```
import json
with open(replicable_dataset) as inf:
    tweet_ids = json.load(inf)
```

Saving the labels is very easy. We just iterate through this dataset and extract the IDs. We could do this quite easily with just two lines of code (open file and save tweets). However, we can't guarantee that we will get all the tweets we are after (for example, some may have been changed to private since collecting the dataset) and therefore the labels will be incorrectly indexed against the data.

As an example, I tried to recreate the dataset just one day after collecting them and already two of the tweets were missing (they might be deleted or made private by the user). For this reason, it is important to only print out the labels that we need. To do this, we first create an empty `actual labels` list to store the labels for tweets that we actually recover from `twitter`, and then create a dictionary mapping the tweet IDs to the labels.

The code is as follows:

```
actual_labels = []
label_mapping = dict(tweet_ids)
```

Next, we are going to create a `twitter` server to collect all of these tweets. This is going to take a little longer. Import the `twitter` library that we used before, creating an authorization token and using that to create the `twitter` object:

```
import twitter
consumer_key = "<Your Consumer Key Here>"
consumer_secret = "<Your Consumer Secret Here>"
access_token = "<Your Access Token Here>"
access_token_secret = "<Your Access Token Secret Here>"
authorization = twitter.OAuth(access_token, access_token_secret,
  consumer_key, consumer_secret)
t = twitter.Twitter(auth=authorization)
```

Iterate over each of the twitter IDs by extracting the IDs into a list using the following command:

```
all_ids = [tweet_id for tweet_id, label in tweet_ids]
```

Then, we open our output file to save the tweets:

```
with open(tweets_filename, 'a') as output_file:
```

The Twitter API allows us get 100 tweets at a time. Therefore, we iterate over each batch of 100 tweets:

```
    for start_index in range(0, len(tweet_ids), 100):
```

To search by ID, we first create a string that joins all of the IDs (in this batch) together:

```
        id_string = ",".join(str(i) for i in
          all_ids[start_index:start_index+100])
```

Next, we perform a **statuses/lookup** API call, which is defined by Twitter. We pass our list of IDs (which we turned into a string) into the API call in order to have those tweets returned to us:

```
        search_results = t.statuses.lookup(_id=id_string)
```

Then for each tweet in the search results, we save it to our file in the same way we did when we were collecting the dataset originally:

```
        for tweet in search_results:
            if 'text' in tweet:
                output_file.write(json.dumps(tweet))
                output_file.write("\n\n")
```

As a final step here (and still under the preceding `if` block), we want to store the labeling of this tweet. We can do this using the `label_mapping` dictionary we created before, looking up the tweet ID. The code is as follows:

```
                actual_labels.append(label_mapping[tweet['id']])
```

Run the previous cell and the code will collect all of the tweets for you. If you created a really big dataset, this may take a while—Twitter does rate-limit requests. As a final step here, save the `actual_labels` to our `classes` file:

```
with open(labels_filename, 'w') as outf:
    json.dump(actual_labels, outf)
```

Text transformers

Now that we have our dataset, how are we going to perform data mining on it?

Text-based datasets include books, essays, websites, manuscripts, programming code, and other forms of written expression. All of the algorithms we have seen so far deal with numerical or categorical features, so how do we convert our text into a format that the algorithm can deal with?

There are a number of measurements that could be taken. For instance, average word and average sentence length are used to predict the readability of a document. However, there are lots of feature types such as word occurrence which we will now investigate.

Bag-of-words

One of the simplest but highly effective models is to simply count each word in the dataset. We create a matrix, where each row represents a document in our dataset and each column represents a word. The value of the cell is the frequency of that word in the document.

Here's an excerpt from *The Lord of the Rings, J.R.R. Tolkien*:

> *Three Rings for the Elven-kings under the sky,*
>
> *Seven for the Dwarf-lords in halls of stone,*
>
> *Nine for Mortal Men, doomed to die,*
>
> *One for the Dark Lord on his dark throne*
>
> *In the Land of Mordor where the Shadows lie.*
>
> *One Ring to rule them all, One Ring to find them,*
>
> *One Ring to bring them all and in the darkness bind them.*
>
> *In the Land of Mordor where the Shadows lie.*
>
> - *J.R.R. Tolkien's epigraph to The Lord of The Rings*

The word *the* appears nine times in this quote, while the words *in*, *for*, *to*, and *one* each appear four times. The word *ring* appears three times, as does the word *of*.

We can create a dataset from this, choosing a subset of words and counting the frequency:

Word	the	one	ring	to
Frequency	9	4	3	4

We can use the `counter` class to do a simple count for a given string. When counting words, it is normal to convert all letters to lowercase, which we do when creating the string. The code is as follows:

```
s = """Three Rings for the Elven-kings under the sky,
Seven for the Dwarf-lords in halls of stone,
Nine for Mortal Men, doomed to die,
One for the Dark Lord on his dark throne
In the Land of Mordor where the Shadows lie.
One Ring to rule them all, One Ring to find them,
One Ring to bring them all and in the darkness bind them.
In the Land of Mordor where the Shadows lie. """.lower()
words = s.split()
from collections import Counter
c = Counter(words)
```

Printing `c.most_common(5)` gives the list of the top five most frequently occurring words. Ties are not handled well as only five are given and a very large number of words all share a tie for fifth place.

The bag-of-words model has three major types. The first is to use the raw frequencies, as shown in the preceding example. This does have a drawback when documents vary in size from fewer words to many words, as the overall values will be very different. The second model is to use the normalized frequency, where each document's sum equals 1. This is a much better solution as the length of the document doesn't matter as much. The third type is to simply use binary features—a value is 1 if the word occurs *at all* and 0 if it doesn't. We will use binary representation in this chapter.

Another popular (arguably more popular) method for performing normalization is called **term frequency - inverse document frequency**, or **tf-idf**. In this weighting scheme, term counts are first normalized to frequencies and then divided by the number of documents in which it appears in the corpus. We will use tf-idf in *Chapter 10, Clustering News Articles*.

There are a number of libraries for working with text data in Python. We will use a major one, called **Natural Language ToolKit (NLTK)**. The `scikit-learn` library also has the `CountVectorizer` class that performs a similar action, and it is recommended you take a look at it (we will use it in *Chapter 9, Authorship Attribution*). However the NLTK version has more options for word tokenization. If you are doing natural language processing in python, NLTK is a great library to use.

N-grams

A step up from single bag-of-words features is that of **n-grams**. An n-gram is a subsequence of *n* consecutive tokens. In this context, a word n-gram is a set of *n* words that appear in a row.

They are counted the same way, with the n-grams forming a *word* that is put in the *bag*. The value of a cell in this dataset is the frequency that a particular n-gram appears in the given document.

The value of *n* is a parameter. For English, setting it to between 2 to 5 is a good start, although some applications call for higher values.

As an example, for *n*=3, we extract the first few n-grams in the following quote:

> *Always look on the bright side of life.*

The first n-gram (of size 3) is *Always look on*, the second is *look on the*, the third is *on the bright*. As you can see, the n-grams overlap and cover three words.

Word n-grams have advantages over using single words. This simple concept introduces some context to word use by considering its local environment, without a large overhead of understanding the language computationally. A disadvantage of using n-grams is that the matrix becomes even sparser—word n-grams are unlikely to appear twice (especially in tweets and other short documents!).

Specially for social media and other short documents, word n-grams are unlikely to appear in too many different tweets, unless it is a retweet. However, in larger documents, word n-grams are quite effective for many applications.

Another form of n-gram for text documents is that of a character n-gram. Rather than using sets of words, we simply use sets of characters (although character n-grams have lots of options for how they are computed!). This type of dataset can pick up words that are misspelled, as well as providing other benefits. We will test character n-grams in this chapter and see them again in *Chapter 9, Authorship Attribution*.

Other features

There are other features that can be extracted too. These include syntactic features, such as the usage of particular words in sentences. Part-of-speech tags are also popular for data mining applications that need to understand meaning in text. Such feature types won't be covered in this book. If you are interested in learning more, I recommend *Python 3 Text Processing with NLTK 3 Cookbook, Jacob Perkins, Packt publication*.

Naive Bayes

Naive Bayes is a probabilistic model that is unsurprisingly built upon a naive interpretation of Bayesian statistics. Despite the naive aspect, the method performs very well in a large number of contexts. It can be used for classification of many different feature types and formats, but we will focus on one in this chapter: binary features in the bag-of-words model.

Bayes' theorem

For most of us, when we were taught statistics, we started from a frequentist approach. In this approach, we assume the data comes from some distribution and we aim to determine what the parameters are for that distribution. However, those parameters are (perhaps incorrectly) assumed to be fixed. We use our model to describe the data, even testing to ensure the data fits our model.

Bayesian statistics instead model how people (non-statisticians) actually reason. We have some data and we use that data to update our model about how likely something is to occur. In Bayesian statistics, we use the data to describe the model rather than using a model and confirming it with data (as per the frequentist approach).

Bayes' theorem computes the value of *P(A | B)*, that is, knowing that *B* has occurred, what is the probability of *A*. In most cases, *B* is an observed event such as *it rained yesterday*, and *A* is a prediction *it will rain today*. For data mining, *B* is usually *we observed this sample* and *A* is *it belongs to this class*. We will see how to use Bayes' theorem for data mining in the next section.

The equation for Bayes' theorem is given as follows:

$$P(A|B) = \frac{P(B|A)\,P(A)}{P(B)}.$$

As an example, we want to determine the probability that an e-mail containing the word *drugs* is spam (as we believe that such a tweet may be a pharmaceutical spam).

A, in this context, is the probability that *this tweet is spam*. We can compute *P(A)*, called the *prior belief* directly from a training dataset by computing the percentage of tweets in our dataset that are spam. If our dataset contains 30 spam messages for every 100 e-mails, *P(A)* is *30/100* or *0.3*.

B, in this context, is *this tweet contains the word 'drugs'*. Likewise, we can compute *P(B)* by computing the percentage of tweets in our dataset containing the word *drugs*. If 10 e-mails in every 100 of our training dataset contain the word *drugs*, *P(B)* is *10/100* or 0.1. Note that we don't care if the e-mail is spam or not when computing this value.

`P(B|A)` is the probability that an e-mail contains the word *drugs* if it is spam. It is also easy to compute from our training dataset. We look through our training set for spam e-mails and compute the percentage of them that contain the word *drugs*. Of our 30 spam e-mails, if 6 contain the word *drugs*, then *P(B | A)* is calculated as 6/30 or 0.2.

From here, we use Bayes' theorem to compute *P(A | B)*, which is the probability that a tweet containing the word *drugs* is spam. Using the previous equation, we see the result is 0.6. This indicates that if an e-mail has the word *drugs* in it, there is a 60 percent chance that it is spam.

Note the empirical nature of the preceding example—we use evidence directly from our training dataset, not from some preconceived distribution. In contrast, a frequentist view of this would rely on us creating a distribution of the probability of words in tweets to compute similar equations.

Naive Bayes algorithm

Looking back at our Bayes' theorem equation, we can use it to compute the probability that a given sample belongs to a given class. This allows the equation to be used as a classification algorithm.

With *C* as a given class and *D* as a sample in our dataset, we create the elements necessary for Bayes' theorem, and subsequently Naive Bayes. Naive Bayes is a classification algorithm that utilizes Bayes' theorem to compute the probability that a new data sample belongs to a particular class.

P(C) is the probability of a class, which is computed from the training dataset itself (as we did with the spam example). We simply compute the percentage of samples in our training dataset that belong to the given class.

P(D) is the probability of a given data sample. It can be difficult to compute this, as the sample is a complex interaction between different features, but luckily it is a constant across all classes. Therefore, we don't need to compute it at all. We will see later how to get around this issue.

P(D | C) is the probability of the data point belonging to the class. This could also be difficult to compute due to the different features. However, this is where we introduce the *naive* part of the Naive Bayes algorithm. We naively assume that each feature is independent of each other. Rather than computing the full probability of *P(D | C)*, we compute the probability of each feature *D1, D2, D3, …* and so on. Then, we multiply them together:

```
P(D|C) = P(D1|C) x P(D2|C).... x P(Dn|C)
```

Each of these values is relatively easy to compute with binary features; we simply compute the percentage of times it is equal in our sample dataset.

In contrast, if we were to perform a non-naive Bayes version of this part, we would need to compute the correlations between different features for each class. Such computation is infeasible at best, and nearly impossible without vast amounts of data or adequate language analysis models.

From here, the algorithm is straightforward. We compute *P(C|D)* for each possible class, ignoring the *P(D)* term. Then we choose the class with the highest probability. As the *P(D)* term is consistent across each of the classes, ignoring it has no impact on the final prediction.

How it works

As an example, suppose we have the following (binary) feature values from a sample in our dataset: `[0, 0, 0, 1]`.

Our training dataset contains two classes with 75 percent of samples belonging to the class `0`, and 25 percent belonging to the class `1`. The likelihood of the feature values for each class are as follows:

For class 0: `[0.3, 0.4, 0.4, 0.7]`

For class 1: `[0.7, 0.3, 0.4, 0.9]`

These values are to be interpreted as: *for feature 1, it is a 1 in 30 percent of cases for class 0.*

We can now compute the probability that this sample should belong to the class `0`. *P(C=0) = 0.75* which is the probability that the class is `0`.

P(D) isn't needed for the Naive Bayes algorithm. Let's take a look at the calculation:

```
P(D|C=0) = P(D1|C=0) x P(D2|C=0) x P(D3|C=0) x P(D4|C=0)
= 0.3 x 0.6 x 0.6 x 0.7
= 0.0756
```

The second and third values are 0.6, because the value of that feature in the sample was `0`. The listed probabilities are for values of `1` for each feature. Therefore, the probability of a `0` is its inverse: *P(0) = 1 – P(1)*.

Now, we can compute the probability of the data point belonging to this class. An important point to note is that we haven't computed *P(D)*, so this isn't a real probability. However, it is good enough to compare against the same value for the probability of the class 1. Let's take a look at the calculation:

```
P(C=0|D) = P(C=0) P(D|C=0)
= 0.75 * 0.0756
= 0.0567
```

Now, we compute the same values for the class 1:

```
P(C=1) = 0.25
```

`P(D)` isn't needed for naive Bayes. Let's take a look at the calculation:

```
P(D|C=1) = P(D1|C=1) x P(D2|C=1) x P(D3|C=1) x P(D4|C=1)
= 0.7 x 0.7 x 0.6 x 0.9
= 0.2646
P(C=1|D) = P(C=1)P(D|C=1)
= 0.25 * 0.2646
= 0.06615
```

Normally, *P(C=0 | D) + P(C=1 | D)* should equal to 1. After all, those are the only two possible options! However, the probabilities are not 1 due to the fact we haven't included the computation of *P(D)* in our equations here.

The data point should be classified as belonging to the class `1`. You may have guessed this while going through the equations anyway; however, you may have been a bit surprised that the final decision was so close. After all, the probabilities in computing *P(D | C)* were much, much higher for the class `1`. This is because we introduced a prior belief that most samples generally belong to the class `0`.

If the classes had been equal sizes, the resulting probabilities would be much different. Try it yourself by changing both *P(C=0)* and *P(C=1)* to 0.5 for equal class sizes and computing the result again.

Application

We will now create a pipeline that takes a tweet and determines whether it is relevant or not, based only on the content of that tweet.

To perform the word extraction, we will be using the NLTK, a library that contains a large number of tools for performing analysis on natural language. We will use NLTK in future chapters as well.

> To get NLTK on your computer, use `pip` to install the package:
> `pip3 install nltk`
> If that doesn't work, see the NLTK installation instructions at `www.nltk.org/install.html`.

We are going to create a pipeline to extract the word features and classify the tweets using Naive Bayes. Our pipeline has the following steps:

1. Transform the original text documents into a dictionary of counts using NLTK's `word_tokenize` function.
2. Transform those dictionaries into a vector matrix using the `DictVectorizer` transformer in `scikit-learn`. This is necessary to enable the Naive Bayes classifier to read the feature values extracted in the first step.
3. Train the Naive Bayes classifier, as we have seen in previous chapters.
4. We will need to create another Notebook (last one for the chapter!) called `ch6_classify_twitter` for performing the classification.

Extracting word counts

We are going to use NLTK to extract our word counts. We still want to use it in a pipeline, but NLTK doesn't conform to our transformer interface. We will therefore need to create a basic transformer to do this to obtain both `fit` and `transform` methods, enabling us to use this in a pipeline.

First, set up the `transformer` class. We don't need to fit anything in this class, as this transformer simply extracts the words in the document. Therefore, our fit is an empty function, except that it returns `self` which is necessary for transformer objects.

Our transform is a little more complicated. We want to extract each word from each document and record `True` if it was discovered. We are only using the binary features here—`True` if in the document, `False` otherwise. If we wanted to use the frequency we would set up counting dictionaries, as we have done in several of the past chapters.

Let's take a look at the code:

```
from sklearn.base import TransformerMixin
class NLTKBOW(TransformerMixin):
    def fit(self, X, y=None):
        return self
    def transform(self, X):
        return [{word: True for word in word_tokenize(document)}
                 for document in X]
```

The result is a list of dictionaries, where the first dictionary is the list of words in the first tweet, and so on. Each dictionary has a word as key and the value `true` to indicate this word was discovered. Any word not in the dictionary will be assumed to have not occurred in the tweet. Explicitly stating that a word's occurrence is `False` will also work, but will take up needless space to store.

Converting dictionaries to a matrix

This step converts the dictionaries built as per the previous step into a matrix that can be used with a classifier. This step is made quite simple through the `DictVectorizer` transformer.

The `DictVectorizer` class simply takes a list of dictionaries and converts them into a matrix. The features in this matrix are the keys in each of the dictionaries, and the values correspond to the occurrence of those features in each sample. Dictionaries are easy to create in code, but many data algorithm implementations prefer matrices. This makes `DictVectorizer` a very useful class.

In our dataset, each dictionary has words as keys and only occurs if the word actually occurs in the tweet. Therefore, our matrix will have each word as a feature and a value of `True` in the cell if the word occurred in the tweet.

To use `DictVectorizer`, simply import it using the following command:

```
from sklearn.feature_extraction import DictVectorizer
```

Training the Naive Bayes classifier

Finally, we need to set up a classifier and we are using Naive Bayes for this chapter. As our dataset contains only binary features, we use the `BernoulliNB` classifier that is designed for binary features. As a classifier, it is very easy to use. As with `DictVectorizer`, we simply import it and add it to our pipeline:

```
from sklearn.naive_bayes import BernoulliNB
```

Putting it all together

Now comes the moment to put all of these pieces together. In our IPython Notebook, set the filenames and load the dataset and classes as we have done before. Set the filenames for both the tweets themselves (not the IDs!) and the labels that we assigned to them. The code is as follows:

```
import os
input_filename = os.path.join(os.path.expanduser("~"), "Data",
  "twitter", "python_tweets.json")
labels_filename = os.path.join(os.path.expanduser("~"), "Data",
  "twitter", "python_classes.json")
```

Load the tweets themselves. We are only interested in the content of the tweets, so we extract the `text` value and store only that. The code is as follows:

```
tweets = []
with open(input_filename) as inf:
    for line in inf:
        if len(line.strip()) == 0:
            continue
        tweets.append(json.loads(line)['text'])
```

Load the labels for each of the tweets:

```
with open(classes_filename) as inf:
    labels = json.load(inf)
```

Now, create a pipeline putting together the components from before. Our pipeline has three parts:

- The `NLTKBOW` transformer we created
- A `DictVectorizer` transformer
- A `BernoulliNB` classifier

The code is as follows:

```
from sklearn.pipeline import Pipeline
pipeline = Pipeline([('bag-of-words', NLTKBOW()),
                     ('vectorizer', DictVectorizer()),
                     ('naive-bayes', BernoulliNB())
                    ])
```

We can nearly run our pipeline now, which we will do with `cross_val_score` as we have done many times before. Before *that* though, we will introduce a better evaluation metric than the accuracy metric we used before. As we will see, the use of accuracy is not adequate for datasets when the number of samples in each class is different.

Evaluation using the F1-score

When choosing an evaluation metric, it is always important to consider cases where that evaluation metric is not useful. Accuracy is a good evaluation metric in many cases, as it is easy to understand and simple to compute. However, it can be easily faked. In other words, in many cases you can create algorithms that have a high accuracy by poor utility.

While our dataset of tweets (typically, your results may vary) contains about 50 percent programming-related and 50 percent nonprogramming, many datasets aren't as **balanced** as this.

As an example, an e-mail spam filter may expect to see more than 80 percent of incoming e-mails be spam. A spam *filter* that simply labels everything as spam is quite useless; however, it will obtain an accuracy of 80 percent!

To get around this problem, we can use other evaluation metrics. One of the most commonly employed is called an *f1-score* (also called f-score, f-measure, or one of many other variations on this term).

The f1-score is defined on a *per-class* basis and is based on two concepts: the *precision* and *recall*. The *precision* is the percentage of all the samples that were predicted as belonging to a specific class that were actually from that class. The *recall* is the percentage of samples in the dataset that are in a class and actually labeled as belonging to that class.

In the case of our application, we could compute the value for both classes (relevant and not relevant). However, we are really interested in the spam. Therefore, our precision computation becomes the question: *of all the tweets that were predicted as being relevant, what percentage were actually relevant?* Likewise, the recall becomes the question: *of all the relevant tweets in the dataset, how many were predicted as being relevant?*

After you compute both the precision and recall, the f1-score is the harmonic mean of the precision and recall:

$$F_1 = 2 \cdot \frac{\text{precision} \cdot \text{recall}}{\text{precision} + \text{recall}}$$

To use the f1-score in `scikit-learn` methods, simply set the scoring parameter to *f1*. By default, this will return the f1-score of the class with label 1. Running the code on our dataset, we simply use the following line of code:

```
scores = cross_val_score(pipeline, tweets, labels, scoring='f1')
```

We then print out the average of the scores:

```
import numpy as np
print("Score: {:.3f}".format(np.mean(scores)))
```

The result is 0.798, which means we can accurately determine if a tweet using Python relates to the programing language nearly 80 percent of the time. This is using a dataset with only 200 tweets in it. Go back and collect more data and you will find that the results increase!

More data usually means a better accuracy, but it is not guaranteed!

Getting useful features from models

One question you may ask is *what are the best features for determining if a tweet is relevant or not?* We can extract this information from of our Naive Bayes model and find out which features are the best individually, according to Naive Bayes.

First we fit a new model. While the `cross_val_score` gives us a score across different folds of cross-validated testing data, it doesn't easily give us the trained models themselves. To do this, we simply fit our pipeline with the tweets, creating a new model. The code is as follows:

```
model = pipeline.fit(tweets, labels)
```

> Note that we aren't really evaluating the model here, so we don't need to be as careful with the training/testing split. However, before you put these features into practice, you should evaluate on a separate test split. We skip over that here for the sake of clarity.

A pipeline gives you access to the individual steps through the `named_steps` attribute and the name of the step (we defined these names ourselves when we created the pipeline object itself). For instance, we can get the Naive Bayes model:

```
nb = model.named_steps['naive-bayes']
```

From this model, we can extract the probabilities for each word. These are stored as log probabilities, which is simply *log(P(A | f))*, where *f* is a given feature.

The reason these are stored as log probabilities is because the actual values are very low. For instance, the first value is -3.486, which correlates to a probability under 0.03 percent. Logarithm probabilities are used in computation involving small probabilities like this as they stop underflow errors where very small values are just rounded to zeros. Given that all of the probabilities are multiplied together, a single value of 0 will result in the whole answer always being 0! Regardless, the relationship between values is still the same; the higher the value, the more useful that feature is.

We can get the most useful features by sorting the array of logarithm probabilities. We want descending order, so we simply negate the values first. The code is as follows:

```
top_features = np.argsort(-feature_probabilities[1])[:50]
```

The preceding code will just give us the indices and not the actual feature values. This isn't very useful, so we will map the feature's indices to the actual values. The key is the `DictVectorizer` step of the pipeline, which created the matrices for us. Luckily this also records the mapping, allowing us to find the feature names that correlate to different columns. We can extract the features from that part of the pipeline:

```
dv = model.named_steps['vectorizer']
```

From here, we can print out the names of the top features by looking them up in the `feature_names_` attribute of `DictVectorizer`. Enter the following lines into a new cell and run it to print out a list of the top features:

```
for i, feature_index in enumerate(top_features):
    print(i, dv.feature_names_[feature_index],
      np.exp(feature_probabilities[1][feature_index]))
```

The first few features include `:`, `http`, # and `@`. These are likely to be noise (although the use of a colon is not very common outside programming), based on the data we collected. Collecting more data is critical to smoothing out these issues. Looking through the list though, we get a number of more obvious programming features:

```
7 for 0.188679245283
11 with 0.141509433962
28 installing 0.0660377358491
29 Top 0.0660377358491
34 Developer 0.0566037735849
35 library 0.0566037735849
36 ] 0.0566037735849
37 [ 0.0566037735849
41 version 0.0471698113208
43 error 0.0471698113208
```

There are some others too that refer to Python in a work context, and therefore might be referring to the programming language (although freelance snake handlers may also use similar terms, they are less common on Twitter):

```
22 jobs 0.0660377358491
30 looking 0.0566037735849
31 Job 0.0566037735849
34 Developer 0.0566037735849
38 Freelancer 0.0471698113208
40 projects 0.0471698113208
47 We're 0.0471698113208
```

That last one is usually in the format: *We're looking for a candidate for this job*.

Looking through these features gives us quite a few benefits. We could train people to recognize these tweets, look for commonalities (which give insight into a topic), or even get rid of features that make no sense. For example, the *word* RT appears quite high in this list; however, this is a common Twitter phrase for retweet (that is, forwarding on someone else's tweet). An expert could decide to remove this word from the list, making the classifier less prone to the noise we introduced by having a small dataset.

Summary

In this chapter, we looked at text mining—how to extract features from text, how to use those features, and ways of extending those features. In doing this, we looked at putting a tweet in context—was this tweet mentioning python referring to the programming language? We downloaded data from a web-based API, getting tweets from the popular microblogging website Twitter. This gave us a dataset that we labeled using a form we built directly in the IPython Notebook.

We also looked at reproducibility of experiments. While Twitter doesn't allow you to send copies of your data to others, it allows you to send the tweet's IDs. Using this, we created code that saved the IDs and recreated most of the original dataset. Not all tweets were returned; some had been deleted in the time since the ID list was created and the dataset was reproduced.

We used a Naive Bayes classifier to perform our text classification. This is built upon the Bayes' theorem that uses data to update the model, unlike the frequentist method that often starts with the model first. This allows the model to incorporate and update new data, and incorporate a prior belief. In addition, the naive part allows to easily compute the frequencies without dealing with complex correlations between features.

The features we extracted were word occurrences—did this word occur in this tweet? This model is called bag-of-words. While this discards information about where a word was used, it still achieves a high accuracy on many datasets.

This entire pipeline of using the bag-of-words model with Naive Bayes is quite robust. You will find that it can achieve quite good scores on most text-based tasks. It is a great baseline for you, before trying more advanced models. As another advantage, the Naive Bayes classifier doesn't have any parameters that need to be set (although there are some if you wish to do some tinkering).

In the next chapter, we will look at extracting features from another type of data, graphs, in order to make recommendations on who to follow on social media.

7

Discovering Accounts to Follow Using Graph Mining

Lots of things can be represented as graphs. This is particularly true in this day of Big Data, online social networks, and the Internet of Things. In particular, online social networks are big business, with sites such as Facebook that have over 500 million active users (50 percent of them log in each day). These sites often monetize themselves by targeted advertising. However, for users to be engaged with a website, they often need to follow interesting people or pages.

In this chapter, we will look at the concept of similarity and how we can create graphs based on it. We will also see how to split this graph up into meaningful subgraphs using connected components. This simple algorithm introduces the concept of cluster analysis—splitting a dataset into subsets based on similarity. We will investigate cluster analysis in more depth in *Chapter 10, Clustering News Articles*.

The topics covered in this chapter include:

- Creating graphs from social networks
- Loading and saving built classifiers
- The NetworkX package
- Converting graphs to matrices
- Distance and similarity
- Optimizing parameters based on scoring functions
- Loss functions and scoring functions

Loading the dataset

In this chapter, our task is to recommend users on online social networks based on shared connections. Our logic is that *if two users have the same friends, they are highly similar and worth recommending to each other.*

We are going to create a small social graph from Twitter using the API we introduced in the previous chapter. The data we are looking for is a subset of users interested in a similar topic (again, the Python programming language) and a list of all of their friends (people they follow). With this data, we will check how similar two users are, based on how many friends they have in common.

> There are many other online social networks apart from Twitter. The reason we have chosen Twitter for this experiment is that their API makes it quite easy to get this sort of information. The information is available from other sites, such as Facebook, LinkedIn, and Instagram, as well. However, getting this information is more difficult.

To start collecting data, set up a new IPython Notebook and an instance of the `twitter` connection, as we did in the previous chapter. You can reuse the app information from the previous chapter or create a new one:

```
import twitter
consumer_key = "<Your Consumer Key Here>"
consumer_secret = "<Your Consumer Secret Here>"
access_token = "<Your Access Token Here>"
access_token_secret = "<Your Access Token Secret Here>"
authorization = twitter.OAuth(access_token, access_token_secret,
  consumer_key, consumer_secret)
t = twitter.Twitter(auth=authorization, retry=True)
```

Also, create the output filename:

```
import os
data_folder = os.path.join(os.path.expanduser("~"), "Data",
  "twitter")
output_filename = os.path.join(data_folder, "python_tweets.json")
```

We will also need the `json` library to save our data:

```
import json
```

Next, we will need a list of users. We will do a search for tweets, as we did in the previous chapter, and look for those mentioning the word *python*. First, create two lists for storing the tweet's text and the corresponding users. We will need the user IDs later, so we create a dictionary mapping that now. The code is as follows:

```
original_users = []
tweets = []
user_ids = {}
```

We will now perform a search for the word *python*, as we did in the previous chapter, and iterate over the search results:

```
search_results = t.search.tweets(q="python",
  count=100)['statuses']
for tweet in search_results:
```

We are only interested in tweets, not in other messages Twitter can pass along. So, we check whether there is text in the results:

```
    if 'text' in tweet:
```

If so, we record the screen name of the user, the tweet's text, and the mapping of the screen name to the user ID. The code is as follows:

```
        original_users.append(tweet['user']['screen_name'])
        user_ids[tweet['user']['screen_name']] =
          tweet['user']['id']
        tweets.append(tweet['text'])
```

Running this code will get about 100 tweets, maybe a little fewer in some cases. Not all of them will be related to the programming language, though.

Classifying with an existing model

As we learned in the previous chapter, not all tweets that mention the word *python* are going to be relating to the programming language. To do that, we will use the classifier we used in the previous chapter to get tweets based on the programming language. Our classifier wasn't perfect, but it will result in a better specialization than just doing the search alone.

In this case, we are only interested in users who are tweeting about Python, the programming language. We will use our classifier from the last chapter to determine which tweets are related to the programming language. From there, we will select only those users who were tweeting about the programming language.

To do this, we first need to save the model. Open the IPython Notebook we made in the last chapter, the one in which we built the classifier. If you have closed it, then the IPython Notebook won't remember what you did, and you will need to run the cells again. To do this, click on the **Cell** menu in the notebook and choose **Run All**.

After all of the cells have computed, choose the final blank cell. If your notebook doesn't have a blank cell at the end, choose the last cell, select the **Insert** menu, and select the **Insert Cell Below** option.

We are going to use the `joblib` library to save our model and load it.

`joblib` is included with the `scikit-learn` package.

First, import the library and create an output filename for our model (make sure the directories exist, or else they won't be created). I've stored this model in my **Models** directory, but you could choose to store them somewhere else. The code is as follows:

```
from sklearn.externals import joblib
output_filename = os.path.join(os.path.expanduser("~"), "Models",
  "twitter", "python_context.pkl")
```

Next, we use the `dump` function in `joblib`, which works like in the `json` library. We pass the model itself (which, if you have forgotten, is simply called `model`) and the output filename:

```
joblib.dump(model, output_filename)
```

Running this code will save our model to the given filename. Next, go back to the new IPython Notebook you created in the last subsection and load this model.

You will need to set the model's filename again in this Notebook by copying the following code:

```
model_filename = os.path.join(os.path.expanduser("~"), "Models",
  "twitter", "python_context.pkl")
```

Make sure the filename is the one you used just before to save the model.
Next, we need to recreate our NLTKBOW class, as it was a custom-built class and can't be loaded directly by joblib. In later chapters, we will see some better ways around this problem. For now, simply copy the entire NLTKBOW class from the previous chapter's code, including its dependencies:

```
from sklearn.base import TransformerMixin
from nltk import word_tokenize

class NLTKBOW(TransformerMixin):
    def fit(self, X, y=None):
        return self

    def transform(self, X):
        return [{word: True for word in word_tokenize(document)}
                 for document in X]
```

Loading the model now just requires a call to the `load` function of `joblib`:

```
from sklearn.externals import joblib
context_classifier = joblib.load(model_filename)
```

Our `context_classifier` works exactly like the `model` object of the notebook we saw in *Chapter 6, Social Media Insight Using Naive Bayes*, It is an instance of a `Pipeline`, with the same three steps as before (`NLTKBOW`, `DictVectorizer`, and a `BernoulliNB` classifier).

Calling the `predict` function on this model gives us a prediction as to whether our tweets are relevant to the programming language. The code is as follows:

```
y_pred = context_classifier.predict(tweets)
```

The `ith` item in `y_pred` will be 1 if the `ith` tweet is (predicted to be) related to the programming language, or else it will be 0. From here, we can get just the tweets that are relevant and their relevant users:

```
relevant_tweets = [tweets[i] for i in range(len(tweets)) if y_pred[i]
  == 1]
relevant_users = [original_users[i] for i in range(len(tweets)) if
  y_pred[i] == 1]
```

Using my data, this comes up to 46 relevant users. A little lower than our 100 tweets/users from before, but now we have a basis for building our social network.

Getting follower information from Twitter

Next, we need to get the *friends* of each of these users. A friend is a person whom the user is following. The API for this is called `friends/ids`, and it has both good and bad points. The good news is that it returns up to 5,000 friend IDs in a single API call. The bad news is that you can only make 15 calls every 15 minutes, which means it will take you at least 1 minute per user to get all followers—more if they have more than 5,000 friends (which happens more often than you may think).

However, the code is relatively easy. We will package it as a function, as we will use this code in the next two sections. First, we will create the function signature that takes our Twitter connection and a user's ID. The function will return all of the followers for that user, so we will also create a list to store these in. We will also need the time module, so we import that as well. We will first go through the composition of the function, but then I'll give you the unbroken function in its entirety. The code is as follows:

```
import time
def get_friends(t, user_id):
    friends = []
```

While it may be surprising, many Twitter users have more than 5,000 friends. So, we will need to use Twitter's **pagination**. Twitter manages multiple *pages* of data through the use of a cursor. When you ask Twitter for information, it gives that information along with a *cursor*, which is an integer that Twitter users to track your request. If there is no more information, this cursor is 0; otherwise, you can use the supplied cursor to get the next page of results. To start with, we set the cursor to -1, indicating the start of the results:

```
    cursor = -1
```

Next, we keep looping while this cursor is not equal to 0 (as, when it is, there is no more data to collect). We then perform a request for the user's followers and add them to our list. We do this in a `try` block, as there are possible errors that can happen that we can handle. The follower's IDs are stored in the `ids` key of the `results` dictionary. After obtaining that information, we update the cursor. It will be used in the next iteration of the loop. Finally, we check if we have more than 10,000 friends. If so, we break out of the loop. The code is as follows:

```
    while cursor != 0:
        try:
            results = t.friends.ids(user_id= user_id,
              cursor=cursor, count=5000)
            friends.extend([friend for friend in results['ids']])
```

```
        cursor = results['next_cursor']
        if len(friends) >= 10000:
            break
```

It is worth inserting a warning here. We are dealing with data from the Internet, which means weird things can and do happen regularly. A problem I ran into when developing this code was that some users have many, many, many thousands of friends. As a fix for this issue, we will put a failsafe here, exiting if we reach more than 10,000 users. If you want to collect the full dataset, you can remove these lines, but beware that it may get stuck on a particular user for a very long time.

We now handle the errors that can happen. The most likely error that can occur happens if we accidentally reached our API limit (while we have a `sleep` to stop that, it can occur if you stop and run your code before this `sleep` finishes). In this case, `results is None` and our code will fail with a `TypeError`. In this case, we wait for 5 minutes and try again, hoping that we have reached our next 15-minute window. There may be another `TypeError` that occurs at this time. If one of them does, we raise it and will need to handle it separately. The code is as follows:

```
    except TypeError as e:
        if results is None:
            print("You probably reached your API limit,
              waiting for 5 minutes")
            sys.stdout.flush()
            time.sleep(5*60) # 5 minute wait
        else:
            raise e
```

The second error that can happen occurs at Twitter's end, such as asking for a user that doesn't exist or some other data-based error. In this case, don't try this user anymore and just return any followers we did get (which, in this case, is likely to be 0). The code is as follows:

```
    except twitter.TwitterHTTPError as e:
        break
```

Now, we will handle our API limit. Twitter only lets us ask for follower information 15 times every 15 minutes, so we will wait for 1 minute before continuing. We do this in a `finally` block so that it happens even if an error occurs:

```
    finally:
        time.sleep(60)
```

We complete our function by returning the friends we collected:

```
        return friends
```

The full function is given as follows:

```
    import time
    def get_friends(t, user_id):
        friends = []
        cursor = -1
        while cursor != 0:
            try:
                results = t.friends.ids(user_id= user_id,
                  cursor=cursor, count=5000)
                friends.extend([friend for friend in
                  results['ids']])
                cursor = results['next_cursor']
                if len(friends) >= 10000:
                    break
            except TypeError as e:
                if results is None:
                    print("You probably reached your API limit,
                      waiting for 5 minutes")
                    sys.stdout.flush()
                    time.sleep(5*60) # 5 minute wait
                else:
                    raise e
            except twitter.TwitterHTTPError as e:
                    break
                  finally:
                      time.sleep(60)
        return friends
```

Building the network

Now we are going to build our network. Starting with our original users, we will get the friends for each of them and store them in a dictionary (after obtaining the user's ID from our `user_id` dictionary):

```
    friends = {}
    for screen_name in relevant_users:
        user_id = user_ids[screen_name]
        friends[user_id] = get_friends(t, user_id)
```

Next, we are going to remove any user who doesn't have any friends. For these users, we can't really make a recommendation in this way. Instead, we might have to look at their content or people who follow them. We will leave that out of the scope of this chapter, though, so let's just remove these users. The code is as follows:

```
friends = {user_id:friends[user_id] for user_id in friends
           if len(friends[user_id]) > 0}
```

We now have between 30 and 50 users, depending on your initial search results. We are now going to increase that amount to 150. The following code will take quite a long time to run—given the limits on the API, we can only get the friends for a user once every minute. Simple math will tell us that 150 users will take 150 minutes, or 2.5 hours. Given the time we are going to be spending on getting this data, it pays to ensure we get only *good* users.

What makes a good user, though? Given that we will be looking to make recommendations based on shared connections, we will search for users based on shared connections. We will get the friends of our existing users, starting with those users who are better connected to our existing users. To do that, we maintain a count of all the times a user is in one of our `friends` lists. It is worth considering the goals of the application when considering your sampling strategy. For this purpose, getting lots of similar users enables the recommendations to be more regularly applicable.

To do this, we simply iterate over all the `friends` lists we have and then count each time a friend occurs.

```
from collections import defaultdict
def count_friends(friends):
    friend_count = defaultdict(int)
    for friend_list in friends.values():
        for friend in friend_list:
            friend_count[friend] += 1
    return friend_count
```

Computing our current friend count, we can then get the most connected (that is, most friends from our existing list) person from our sample. The code is as follows:

```
friend_count
reverse=True) = count_friends(friends)
from operator import itemgetter
best_friends = sorted(friend_count.items(), key=itemgetter(1),
```

From here, we set up a loop that continues until we have the friends of 150 users. We then iterate over all of our best friends (which happens in order of the number of people who have them as friends) until we find a user whose friends we haven't already got. We then get the friends of that user and update the `friends` counts. Finally, we work out who is the most connected user who we haven't already got in our list:

```
while len(friends) < 150:
    for user_id, count in best_friends:
        if user_id not in friends:
            break
        friends[user_id] = get_friends(t, user_id)
    for friend in friends[user_id]:
        friend_count[friend] += 1
    best_friends = sorted(friend_count.items(),
      key=itemgetter(1), reverse=True)
```

The codes will then loop and continue until we reach 150 users.

You may want to set these value lower, such as 40 or 50 users (or even just skip this bit of code temporarily). Then, complete the chapter's code and get a feel for how the results work. After that, reset the number of users in this loop to 150, leave the code to run for a few hours, and then come back and rerun the later code.

Given that collecting that data probably took over 2 hours, it would be a good idea to save it in case we have to turn our computer off. Using the `json` library, we can easily save our friends dictionary to a file:

```
import json
friends_filename = os.path.join(data_folder, "python_friends.json")
with open(friends_filename, 'w') as outf:
    json.dump(friends, outf)
```

If you need to load the file, use the `json.load` function:

```
with open(friends_filename) as inf:
    friends = json.load(inf)
```

Creating a graph

Now, we have a list of users and their friends and many of these users are taken from friends of other users. This gives us a graph where some users are friends of other users (although not necessarily the other way around).

A graph is a set of nodes and edges. Nodes are usually objects—in this case, they are our users. The edges in this initial graph indicate that *user A is a friend of user B*. We call this a directed graph, as the order of the nodes matters. Just because user A is a friend of user B, that doesn't imply that user B is a friend of user A. We can visualize this graph using the **NetworkX** package.

Once again, you can use `pip` to install NetworkX: `pip3 install networkx`.

First, we create a directed graph using NetworkX. By convention, when importing NetworkX, we use the abbreviation `nx` (although this isn't necessary). The code is as follows:

```
import networkx as nx
G = nx.DiGraph()
```

We will only visualize our key users, not all of the friends (as there are many thousands of these and it is hard to visualize). We get our main users and then add them to our graph as nodes. The code is as follows:

```
main_users = friends.keys()
G.add_nodes_from(main_users)
```

Next we set up the edges. We create an edge from a user to another user if the second user is a friend of the first user. To do this, we iterate through all of the friends:

```
for user_id in friends:
    for friend in friends[user_id]:
```

We ensure that the friend is one of our main users (as we currently aren't interested in the other ones), and add the edge if they are. The code is as follows:

```
        if friend in main_users:
            G.add_edge(user_id, friend)
```

We can now visualize network using NetworkX's `draw` function, which uses `matplotlib`. To get the image in our notebook, we use the `inline` function on `matplotlib` and then call the `draw` function. The code is as follows:

```
%matplotlib inline
nx.draw(G)
```

The results are a bit hard to make sense of; they show that there are some nodes with few connections but many nodes with many connections:

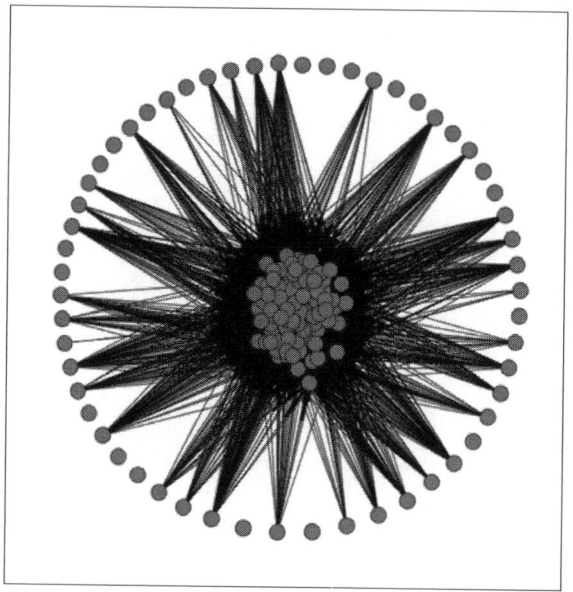

We can make the graph a bit bigger by using `pyplot` to handle the creation of the figure. To do that, we import `pyplot`, create a large figure, and then call NetworkX's `draw` function (NetworkX uses `pyplot` to draw its figures):

```
from matplotlib import pyplot as plt
plt.figure(3,figsize=(20,20))
nx.draw(G, alpha=0.1, edge_color='b')
```

The results are too big for a page here, but by making the graph bigger, an outline of how the graph appears can now be seen. In my graph, there was a major group of users all highly connected to each other, and most other users didn't have many connections at all. I've zoomed in on just the center of the network here and set the edge color to blue with a low `alpha` in the preceding code.

As you can see, it is very well connected in the center!

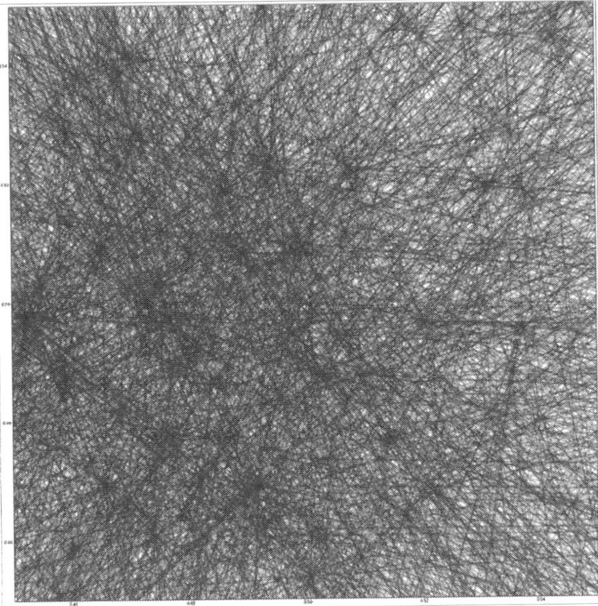

This is actually a property of our method of choosing new users—we choose those who are already well linked in our graph, so it is likely they will just make this group larger. For social networks, generally the number of connections a user has follows a power law. A small percentage of users have many connections, and others have only a few. The shape of the graph is often described as having a *long tail*. Our dataset doesn't follow this pattern, as we collected our data by getting friends of users we already had.

Creating a similarity graph

Our task in this chapter is recommendation through shared friends. As mentioned previously, our logic is that, *if two users have the same friends, they are highly similar*. We could recommend one user to the other on this basis.

We are therefore going to take our existing graph (which has edges relating to friendship) and create a new graph. The nodes are still users, but the edges are going to be weighted edges. A weighted edge is simply an edge with a `weight` property. The logic is that a higher weight indicates more similarity between the two nodes than a lower weight. This is context-dependent. If the weights represent distance, then the lower weights indicate more similarity.

For our application, the weight will be the similarity of the two users connected by that edge (based on the number of friends they share). This graph also has the property that it is not directed. This is due to our similarity computation, where the similarity of user A to user B is the same as the similarity of user B to user A.

There are many ways to compute the similarity between two lists like this. For example, we could compute the number of friends the two have in common. However, this measure is always going to be higher for people with more friends. Instead, we can normalize it by dividing by the total number of distinct friends the two have. This is called the **Jaccard Similarity**.

The Jaccard Similarity, always between 0 and 1, represents the percentage overlap of the two. As we saw in *Chapter 2, Classifying with scikit-learn Estimators*, normalization is an important part of data mining exercises and generally a good thing to do (unless you have a specific reason not to).

To compute this Jaccard similarity, we divide the intersection of the two sets of followers by the union of the two. These are `set` operations and we have `lists`, so we will need to convert the `friends` lists to sets first. The code is as follows:

```
friends = {user: set(friends[user]) for user in friends}
```

We then create a function that computes the similarity of two sets of `friends` lists. The code is as follows:

```
def compute_similarity(friends1, friends2):
return len(friends1 & friends2) / len(friends1 | friends2)
```

From here, we can create our weighted graph of the similarity between users. We will use this quite a lot in the rest of the chapter, so we will create a function to perform this action. Let's take a look at the threshold parameter:

```
def create_graph(followers, threshold=0):
    G = nx.Graph()
```

We iterate over all combinations of users, ignoring instances where we are comparing a user with themselves:

```
        for user1 in friends.keys():
            for user2 in friends.keys():
                if user1 == user2:
                    continue
```

We compute the weight of the edge between the two users:

```
                weight = compute_similarity(friends[user1],
friends[user2])
```

Next, we will only add the edge if it is above a certain threshold. This stops us from adding edges we don't care about—for example, edges with weight 0. By default, our threshold is 0, so we will be including all edges right now. However, we will use this parameter later in the chapter. The code is as follows:

```
            if weight >= threshold:
```

If the weight is above the threshold, we add the two users to the graph (they won't be added as a duplicate if they are already in the graph):

```
                G.add_node(user1)
                G.add_node(user2)
```

We then add the edge between them, setting the weight to be the computed similarity:

```
                G.add_edge(user1, user2, weight=weight)
```

Once the loops have finished, we have a completed graph and we return it from the function:

```
    return G
```

We can now create a graph by calling this function. We start with no threshold, which means all links are created. The code is as follows:

```
G = create_graph(friends)
```

The result is a very strongly connected graph—all nodes have edges, although many of those will have a weight of 0. We will see the weight of the edges by drawing the graph with line widths relative to the weight of the edge—thicker lines indicate higher weights.

Due to the number of nodes, it makes sense to make the figure larger to get a clearer sense of the connections:

```
plt.figure(figsize=(10,10))
```

We are going to draw the edges with a weight, so we need to draw the nodes first. NetworkX uses layouts to determine where to put the nodes and edges, based on certain criteria. Visualizing networks is a very difficult problem, especially as the number of nodes grows. Various techniques exist for visualizing networks, but the degree to which they work depends heavily on your dataset, personal preferences, and the aim of the visualization. I found that the `spring_layout` worked quite well, but other options such as `circular_layout` (which is a good default if nothing else works), `random_layout`, `shell_layout`, and `spectral_layout` also exist.

> Visit `http://networkx.lanl.gov/reference/drawing.html` for more details on layouts in NetworkX. Although it adds some complexity, the `draw_graphviz` option works quite well and is worth investigating for better visualizations. It is well worth considering in real-world uses.

Let's use `spring_layout` for visualization:

```
pos = nx.spring_layout(G)
```

Using our `pos` layout, we can then position the nodes:

```
nx.draw_networkx_nodes(G, pos)
```

Next, we draw the edges. To get the weights, we iterate over the edges in the graph (in a specific order) and collect the weights:

```
edgewidth = [ d['weight'] for (u,v,d) in G.edges(data=True)]
```

We then draw the edges:

```
nx.draw_networkx_edges(G, pos, width=edgewidth)
```

The result will depend on your data, but it will typically show a graph with a large set of nodes connected quite strongly and a few nodes poorly connected to the rest of the network.

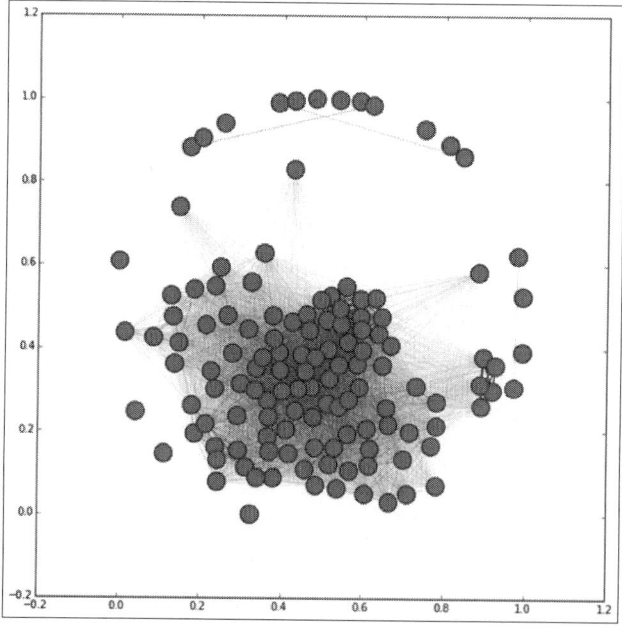

The difference in this graph compared to the previous graph is that the edges determine the similarity between the nodes based on our similarity metric and not on whether one is a friend of another (although there are similarities between the two!). We can now start extracting information from this graph in order to make our recommendations.

Finding subgraphs

From our similarity function, we could simply rank the results for each user, returning the most similar user as a recommendation—as we did with our product recommendations. Instead, we might want to find clusters of users that are all similar to each other. We could advise these users to start a group, create advertising targeting this segment, or even just use those clusters to do the recommendations themselves.

Finding these clusters of similar users is a task called cluster analysis. It is a difficult task, with complications that classification tasks do not typically have. For example, evaluating classification results is relatively easy—we compare our results to the ground truth (from our training set) and see what percentage we got right. With cluster analysis, though, there isn't typically a ground truth. Evaluation usually comes down to seeing if the clusters *make sense*, based on some preconceived notion we have of what the cluster should look like. Another complication with cluster analysis is that the model can't be trained against the expected result to learn—it has to use some approximation based on a mathematical model of a cluster, not what the user is hoping to achieve from the analysis.

Connected components

One of the simplest methods for clustering is to find the **connected components** in a graph. A connected component is a set of nodes in a graph that are connected via edges. Not all nodes need to be connected to each other to be a connected component. However, for two nodes to be in the same connected component, there needs to be a way to travel from one node to another in that connected component.

> Connected components do not consider edge weights when being computed; they only check for the presence of an edge. For that reason, the code that follows will remove any edge with a low weight.

NetworkX has a function for computing connected components that we can call on our graph. First, we create a new graph using our `create_graph` function, but this time we pass a threshold of 0.1 to get only those edges that have a weight of at least 0.1.

```
G = create_graph(friends, 0.1)
```

We then use NetworkX to find the connected components in the graph:

```
sub_graphs = nx.connected_component_subgraphs(G)
```

To get a sense of the sizes of the graph, we can iterate over the groups and print out some basic information:

```
for i, sub_graph in enumerate(sub_graphs):
    n_nodes = len(sub_graph.nodes())
    print("Subgraph {0} has {1} nodes".format(i, n_nodes))
```

The results will tell you how big each of the connected components is. My results had one big subgraph of 62 users and lots of little ones with a dozen or fewer users.

We can alter the threshold to alter the connected components. This is because a higher threshold has fewer edges connecting nodes, and therefore will have smaller connected components and more of them. We can see this by running the preceding code with a higher threshold:

```
G = create_graph(friends, 0.25)
sub_graphs = nx.connected_component_subgraphs(G)
for i, sub_graph in enumerate(sub_graphs):
    n_nodes = len(sub_graph.nodes())
    print("Subgraph {0} has {1} nodes".format(i, n_nodes))
```

The preceding code gives us much smaller nodes and more of them. My largest cluster was broken into at least three parts and none of the clusters had more than 10 users. An example cluster is shown in the following figure, and the connections within this cluster are also shown. Note that, as it is a connected component, there were no edges from nodes in this component to other nodes in the graph (at least, with the threshold set at 0.25):

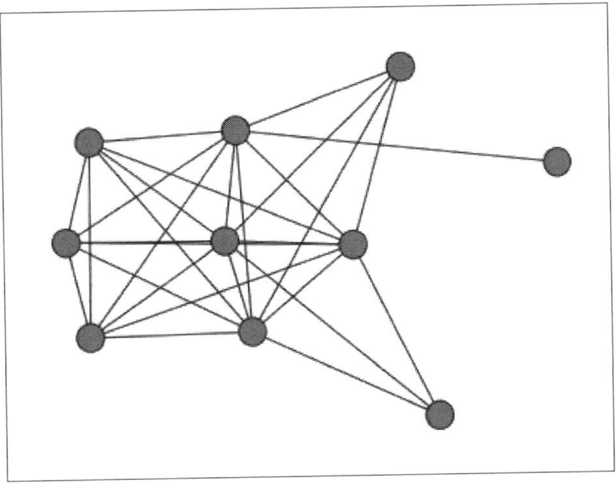

We can graph the entire set too, showing each connected component in a different color. As these connected components are not connected to each other, it actually makes little sense to plot these on a single graph. This is because the positioning of the nodes and components is arbitrary, and it can confuse the visualization. Instead, we can plot each separately on a separate subfigure.

In a new cell, obtain the connected components and also the count of the connected components:

```
sub_graphs = nx.connected_component_subgraphs(G)
n_subgraphs = nx.number_connected_components(G)
```

`sub_graphs` is a generator, not a list of the connected components. For this reason, use `nx.number_connected_components` to find out how many connected components there are; don't use `len`, as it doesn't work due to the way that NetworkX stores this information. This is why we need to recompute the connected components here.

Create a new `pyplot` figure and give enough room to show all of our connected components. For this reason, we allow the graph to increase in size with the number of connected components:

```
fig = plt.figure(figsize=(20, (n_subgraphs * 3)))
```

Next, iterate over each connected component and add a subplot for each. The parameters to add_subplot are the number of rows of subplots, the number of columns, and the index of the subplot we are interested in. My visualization uses three columns, but you can try other values instead of three (just remember to change both values):

```
for i, sub_graph in enumerate(sub_graphs):
    ax = fig.add_subplot(int(n_subgraphs / 3), 3, i)
```

By default, pyplot shows plots with axis labels, which are meaningless in this context. For that reason, we turn labels off:

```
    ax.get_xaxis().set_visible(False)
    ax.get_yaxis().set_visible(False)
```

Then we plot the nodes and edges (using the ax parameter to plot to the correct subplot). To do this, we also need to set up a layout first:

```
    pos = nx.spring_layout(G)
    nx.draw_networkx_nodes(G, pos, sub_graph.nodes(), ax=ax,
      node_size=500)
    nx.draw_networkx_edges(G, pos, sub_graph.edges(), ax=ax)
```

The results visualize each connected component, giving us a sense of the number of nodes in each and also how connected they are.

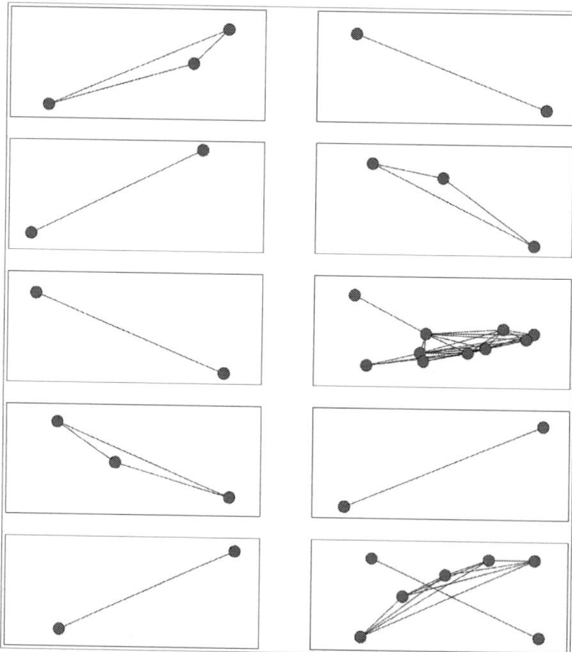

Optimizing criteria

Our algorithm for finding these connected components relies on the threshold parameter, which dictates whether edges are added to the graph or not. In turn, this directly dictates how many connected components we discover and how big they are. From here, we probably want to settle on some notion of which is the *best* threshold to use. This is a very subjective problem, and there is no definitive answer. This is a major problem with any cluster analysis task.

We can, however, determine what we think a good solution should look like and define a metric based on that idea. As a general rule, we usually want a solution where:

- Samples in the same cluster (connected components) are highly *similar* to each other
- Samples in different clusters are highly *dissimilar* to each other

The `Silhouette Coefficient` is a metric that quantifies these points. Given a single sample, we define the Silhouette Coefficient as follows:

$$s = \frac{b - a}{\max(a, b)}$$

Where a is the **intra-cluster distance** or the average distance to the other samples in the sample's cluster, and b is the inter-cluster distance or the average distance to the other samples in the *next-nearest* cluster.

To compute the overall Silhouette Coefficient, we take the mean of the Silhouettes for each sample. A clustering that provides a Silhouette Coefficient close to the maximum of 1 has clusters that have samples all similar to each other, and these clusters are very spread apart. Values near 0 indicate that the clusters all overlap and there is little distinction between clusters. Values close to the minimum of -1 indicate that samples are probably in the wrong cluster, that is, they would be better off in other clusters.

Using this metric, we want to find a solution (that is, a value for the threshold) that maximizes the Silhouette Coefficient by altering the threshold parameter. To do that, we create a function that takes the threshold as a parameter and computes the Silhouette Coefficient.

We then pass this into the `optimize` module of SciPy, which contains the `minimize` function that is used to find the minimum value of a function by altering one of the parameters. While we are interested in maximizing the Silhouette Coefficient, SciPy doesn't have a maximize function. Instead, we minimize the inverse of the Silhouette (which is basically the same thing).

The scikit-learn library has a function for computing the Silhouette Coefficient, `sklearn.metrics.silhouette_score`; however, it doesn't fix the function format that is required by the SciPy `minimize` function. The minimize function requires the variable parameter to be first (in our case, the threshold value), and any arguments to be after it. In our case, we need to pass the `friends` dictionary as an argument in order to compute the graph. The code is as follows:

```
def compute_silhouette(threshold, friends):
```

We then create the graph using the threshold parameter, and check it has at least some nodes:

```
    G = create_graph(friends, threshold=threshold)
    if len(G.nodes()) < 2:
```

The Silhouette Coefficient is not defined unless there are at least two nodes (in order for distance to be computed at all). In this case, we define the problem scope as invalid. There are a few ways to handle this, but the easiest is to return a very poor score. In our case, the minimum value that the Silhouette Coefficient can take is -1, and we will return -99 to indicate an invalid problem. Any valid solution will score higher than this. The code is as follows:

```
        return -99
```

We then extract the connected components:

```
    sub_graphs = nx.connected_component_subgraphs(G)
```

The Silhouette is also only defined if we have at least two connected components (in order to compute the inter-cluster distance), and at least one of these connected components has two members (to compute the intra-cluster distance). We test for these conditions and return our invalid problem score if it doesn't fit. The code is as follows:

```
    if not (2 <= nx.number_connected_components() < len(G.nodes())
      - 1):
        return -99
```

Next, we need to get the labels that indicate which connected component each sample was placed in. We iterate over all the connected components, noting in a dictionary which user belonged to which connected component. The code is as follows:

```
label_dict = {}
for i, sub_graph in enumerate(sub_graphs):
    for node in sub_graph.nodes():
        label_dict[node] = i
```

Then we iterate over the nodes in the graph to get the label for each node in order. We need to do this two-step process, as nodes are not clearly ordered within a graph but they do maintain their order as long as no changes are made to the graph. What this means is that, until we change the graph, we can call `.nodes()` on the graph to get the same ordering. The code is as follows:

```
labels = np.array([label_dict[node] for node in G.nodes()])
```

Next the Silhouette Coefficient function takes a *distance matrix*, not a *graph*. Addressing this is another two-step process. First, NetworkX provides a handy function `to_scipy_sparse_matrix`, which returns the graph in a matrix format that we can use:

```
X = nx.to_scipy_sparse_matrix(G).todense()
```

The Silhouette Coefficient implementation in scikit-learn, at the time of writing, doesn't support sparse matrices. For this reason, we need to call the `todense()` function. Typically, this is a bad idea—sparse matrices are usually used because the data typically shouldn't be in a dense format. In this case, it will be fine because our dataset is relatively small; however, don't try this for larger datasets.

For evaluating sparse datasets, I recommended that you look into V-Measure or Adjusted Mutual Information. These are both implemented in scikit-learn, but they have very different parameters for performing their evaluation.

However, the values are based on our weights, which are a similarity and not a distance. For a distance, higher values indicate more difference. We can convert from similarity to distance by subtracting the value from the maximum possible value, which for our weights was 1:

```
X = 1 - X
```

Now we have our distance matrix and labels, so we have all the information we need to compute the Silhouette Coefficient. We pass the metric as `precomputed`; otherwise, the matrix X will be considered a feature matrix, not a distance matrix (feature matrices are used by default nearly everywhere in scikit-learn). The code is as follows:

```
        return silhouette_score(X, labels, metric='precomputed')
```

> We have two forms of inversion happening here. The first is taking the inverse of the similarity to compute a distance function; this is needed, as the Silhouette Coefficient only accepts distances. The second is the inverting of the Silhouette Coefficient score so that we can minimize with SciPy's `optimize` module.

We have one small problem, though. This function returns the Silhouette Coefficient, which is a score where higher values are considered better. Scipy's `optimize` module only defines a `minimize` function, which works off a `loss` function where lower scores are better. We can fix this by inverting the value, which takes our `score` function and returns a `loss` function.

```
def inverted_silhouette(threshold, friends):
    return -compute_silhouette(threshold, friends)
```

This function creates a new function from an original function. When the new function is called, all of the same arguments and keywords are passed onto the original function and the return value is returned, except that this returned value is negated before it is returned.

Now we can do our actual optimization. We call the `minimize` function on the inverted `compute_silhouette` function we defined:

```
result = minimize(inverted_silhouette, 0.1, args=(friends,))
```

The parameters are as follows:

- `invert(compute_silhouette)`: This is the function we are trying to minimize (remembering that we invert it to turn it into a loss function)
- `0.1`: This is an initial guess at a threshold that will minimize the function
- `options={'maxiter':10}`: This dictates that only 10 iterations are to be performed (increasing this will probably get a better result, but will take longer to run)

- `method='nelder-mead'`: This is used to select the Nelder-Mead optimize routing (SciPy supports quite a number of different options)
- `args=(friends,)`: This passes the `friends` dictionary to the function that is being minimized

> This function will take quite a while to run. Our graph creation function isn't that fast, nor is the function that computes the Silhouette Coefficient. Decreasing the `maxiter` value will result in fewer iterations being performed, but we run the risk of finding a suboptimal solution.

Running this function, I got a threshold of 0.135 that returns 10 components. The score returned by the minimize function was -0.192. However, we must remember that we negated this value. This means our score was actually 0.192. The value is positive, which indicates that the clusters tend to be more separated than not (a good thing). We could run other models and check whether it results in a better score, which means that the clusters are better separated.

We could use this result to recommend users—if a user is in a connected component, then we can recommend other users in that component. This recommendation follows our use of the Jaccard Similarity to find good connections between users, our use of connected components to split them up into clusters, and our use of the optimization technique to find the best model in this setting.

However, a large number of users may not be connected at all, so we will use a different algorithm to find clusters for them.

Summary

In this chapter, we looked at graphs from social networks and how to do cluster analysis on them. We also looked at saving and loading models from scikit-learn by using the classification model we created in *Chapter 6, Social Media Insight Using Naive Bayes.*

We created a graph of friends from a social network, in this case Twitter. We then examined how similar two users were, based on their friends. Users with more friends in common were considered more similar, although we normalize this by considering the overall number of friends they have. This is a commonly used way to infer knowledge (such as age or general topic of discussion) based on similar users. We can use this logic for recommending users to others—if they follow user X and user Y is similar to user X, they will probably like user Y. This is, in many ways, similar to our transaction-led similarity of previous chapters.

The aim of this analysis was to recommend users, and our use of cluster analysis allowed us to find clusters of similar users. To do this, we found connected components on a weighted graph we created based on this similarity metric. We used the NetworkX package for creating graphs, using our graphs, and finding these connected components.

We then used the Silhouette Coefficient, which is a metric that evaluates how good a clustering solution is. Higher scores indicate a better clustering, according to the concepts of intra-cluster and inter-cluster distance. SciPy's `optimize` module was used to find the solution that maximises this value.

In this chapter, we compared a few opposites too. **Similarity** is a measure between two objects, where *higher* values indicate more similarity between those objects. In contrast, **distance** is a measure where *lower* values indicate more similarity. Another contrast we saw was a `loss` function, where lower scores are considered better (that is, we lost less). Its opposite is the `score` function, where *higher* scores are considered better.

In the next chapter, we will see how to extract features from another new type of data: images. We will discuss how to use neural networks to identify numbers in images and develop a program to automatically beat CAPTCHA images.

8
Beating CAPTCHAs with Neural Networks

Interpreting information contained in images has long been a difficult problem in data mining, but it is one that is really starting to be addressed. The latest research is providing algorithms to detect and understand images to the point where automated commercial surveillance systems are now being used—in real-world scenarios—by major vendors. These systems are capable of understanding and recognizing objects and people in video footage.

It is difficult to extract information from images. There is lots of raw data in an image, and the standard method for encoding images—pixels—isn't that informative by itself. Images—particularly photos—can be blurry, too close to the targets, too dark, too light, scaled, cropped, skewed, or any other of a variety of problems that cause havoc for a computer system trying to extract useful information.

In this chapter, we look at extracting text from images by using neural networks for predicting each letter. The problem we are trying to solve is to automatically understand CAPTCHA messages. CAPTCHAs are images designed to be easy for humans to solve and hard for a computer to solve, as per the acronym: Completely Automated Public Turing test to tell Computers and Humans Apart. Many websites use them for registration and commenting systems to stop automated programs flooding their site with fake accounts and spam comments.

The topics covered in this chapter include:

- Neural networks
- Creating our own dataset of CAPTCHAs and letters
- The scikit-image library for working with image data
- The PyBrain library for neural networks

- Extracting basic features from images
- Using neural networks for larger-scale classification tasks
- Improving performance using postprocessing

Artificial neural networks

Neural networks are a class of algorithm that was originally designed based on the way that human brains work. However, modern advances are generally based on mathematics rather than biological insights. A neural network is a collection of **neurons** that are connected together. Each neuron is a simple function of its inputs, which generates an output:

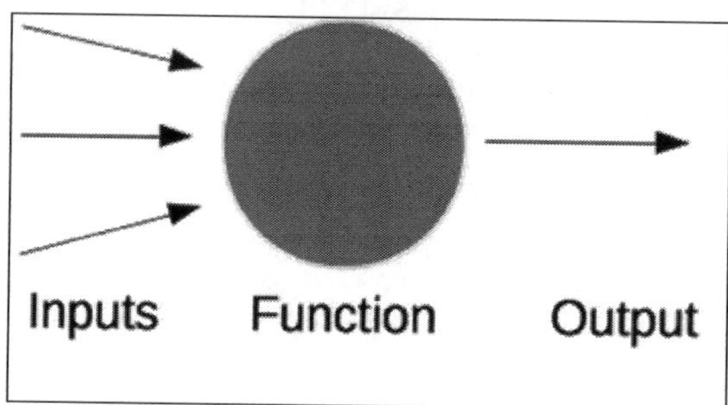

The functions that define a neuron's processing can be any standard function, such as a linear combination of the inputs, and are called the **activation function**. For the commonly used learning algorithms to work, we need the activation function to be derivable and smooth. A frequently used activation function is the logistic function, which is defined by the following equation (*k* is often simply 1, *x* is the inputs into the neuron, and *L* is normally 1, that is, the maximum value of the function):

$$f(x) = \frac{L}{1 + \mathrm{e}^{-k(x - x_0)}}$$

The value of this graph, from -6 to +6, is shown as follows:

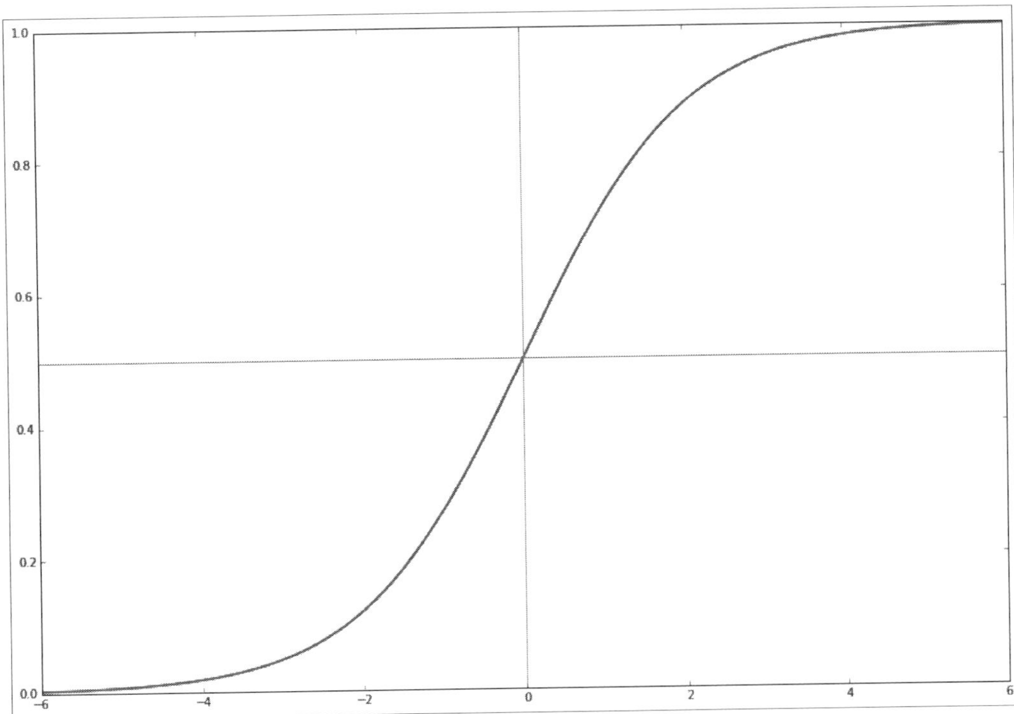

The red lines indicate that the value is 0.5 when x is zero.

Each individual neuron receives its inputs and then computes the output based on these values. Neural networks are simply networks of these neurons connected together, and they can be very powerful for data mining applications. The combinations of these neurons, how they fit together, and how they combine to learn a model are one of the most powerful concepts in machine learning.

An introduction to neural networks

For data mining applications, the arrangement of neurons is usually in layers. The first layer, the **input layer**, takes the inputs from the dataset. The outputs of each of these neurons are computed and then passed along to the neurons in the next layer. This is called a **feed-forward neural network**. We will refer to these simply as neural networks for this chapter. There are other types of neural networks too that are used for different applications. We will see another type of network in *Chapter 11, Classifying Objects in Images Using Deep Learning*.

The outputs of one layer become the inputs of the next layer, continuing until we reach the final layer: the, **output layer**. These outputs represent the predictions of the neural network as the classification. Any layer of neurons between the input layer and the output layer is referred to as a **hidden layer**, as they learn a representation of the data not intuitively interpretable by humans. Most neural networks have at least three layers, although most modern applications use networks with many more layers than that.

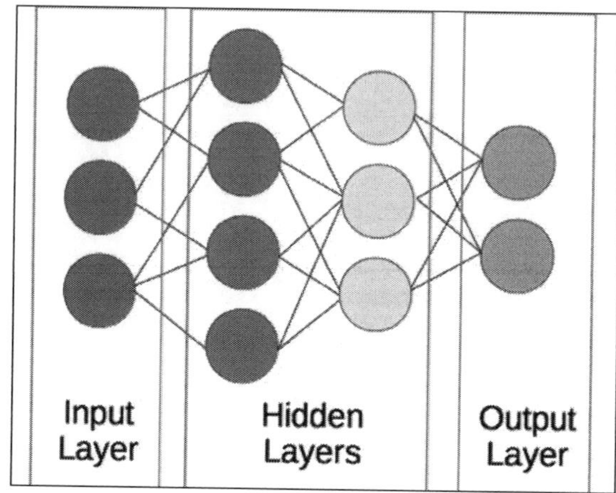

Typically, we consider fully connected layers. The outputs of each neuron in a layer go to all neurons in the next layer. While we do define a fully connected network, many of the weights will be set to zero during the training process, effectively removing these links. Fully connected neural networks are also simpler and more efficient to program than other connection patterns.

As the function of the neurons is normally the logistic function, and the neurons are fully connected to the next layer, the parameters for building and training a neural network must be other factors. The first factor for neural networks is in the building phase: the size of the neural network. This includes how many layers the neural network has and how many neurons it has in each hidden layer (the size of the input and output layers is usually dictated by the dataset).

The second parameter for neural networks is determined in the training phase: the weight of the connections between neurons. When one neuron connects to another, this connection has an associated **weight** that is multiplied by the signal (the output of the first neuron). If the connection has a weight of 0.8, the neuron is activated, and it outputs a value of 1, the resulting input to the next neuron is 0.8. If the first neuron is not activated and has a value of 0, this stays at 0.

The combination of an appropriately sized network and well-trained weights determines how accurate the neural network can be when making classifications. The word "appropriately" also doesn't necessarily mean bigger, as neural networks that are too large can take a long time to train and can more easily overfit the training data.

Weights are normally set randomly to start with, but are then updated during the training phase.

We now have a classifier that has initial parameters to set (the size of the network) and parameters to train from the dataset. The classifier can then be used to predict the target of a data sample based on the inputs, much like the classification algorithms we have used in previous chapters. But first, we need a dataset to train and test with.

Creating the dataset

In this chapter, we will take on the role of the bad guy. We want to create a program that can beat CAPTCHAs, allowing our comment spam program to advertise on someone's website. It should be noted that our CAPTCHAs will be a little easier that those used on the web today and that spamming isn't a very nice thing to do.

Our CAPTCHAs will be individual English words of four letters only, as shown in the following image:

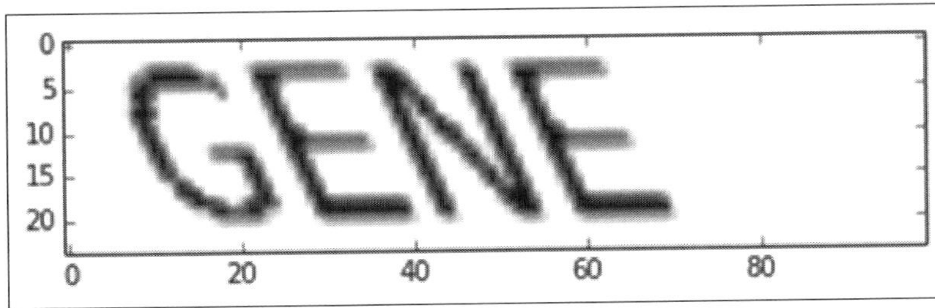

Our goal will be to create a program that can recover the word from images like this. To do this, we will use four steps:

1. Break the image into individual letters.
2. Classify each individual letter.
3. Recombine the letters to form a word.
4. Rank words with a dictionary to try to fix errors.

Our CAPTCHA-busting algorithm will make the following assumptions. First, the word will be a whole and valid four-character English word (in fact, we use the same dictionary for creating and busting CAPTCHAs). Second, the word will only contain uppercase letters. No symbols, numbers, or spaces will be used. We are going to make the problem slightly harder: we are going to perform a *shear* transform to the text, along with varying rates of shearing.

Drawing basic CAPTCHAs

Next, we develop our function for creating our CAPTCHA. Our goal here is to draw an image with a word on it, along with a shear transform. We are going to use the `PIL` library to draw our CAPTCHAs and the `scikit-image` library to perform the shear transform. The `scikit-image` library can read images in a NumPy array format that `PIL` can export to, allowing us to use both libraries.

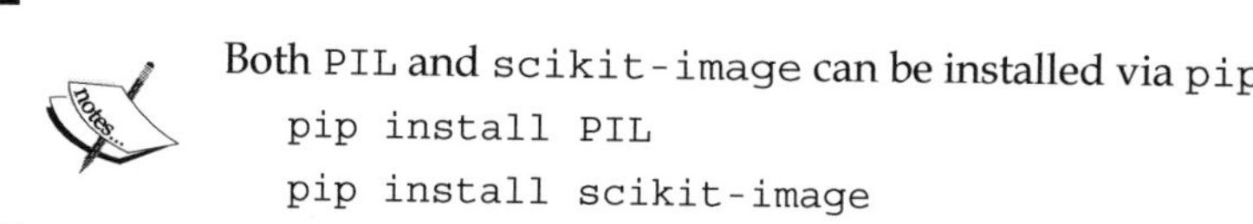

Both `PIL` and `scikit-image` can be installed via `pip`:

```
pip install PIL
pip install scikit-image
```

First, we import the necessary libraries and modules. We import NumPy and the `Image` drawing functions as follows:

```
import numpy as np
from PIL import Image, ImageDraw, ImageFont
from skimage import transform as tf
```

Then we create our base function for generating CAPTCHAs. This function takes a word and a shear value (which is normally between 0 and 0.5) to return an image in a NumPy array format. We allow the user to set the size of the resulting image, as we will use this function for single-letter training samples as well. The code is as follows:

```
def create_captcha(text, shear=0, size=(100, 24)):
```

We create a new image using L for the format, which means black-and-white pixels only, and create an instance of the `ImageDraw` class. This allows us to draw on this image using `PIL`. The code is as follows:

```
    im = Image.new("L", size, "black")
    draw = ImageDraw.Draw(im)
```

Next we set the font of the CAPTCHA we will use. You will need a font file and the filename in the following code (`Coval.otf`) should point to it (I just placed the file in the `Notebook's` directory.

```
font = ImageFont.truetype(r"Coval.otf", 22)
draw.text((2, 2), text, fill=1, font=font)
```

You can get the Coval font I used from the Open Font Library at `http://openfontlibrary.org/en/font/bretan`.

We convert the PIL image to a NumPy array, which allows us to use `scikit-image` to perform a shear on it. The `scikit-image` library tends to use NumPy arrays for most of its computation. The code is as follows:

```
image = np.array(im)
```

We then apply the shear transform and return the image:

```
affine_tf = tf.AffineTransform(shear=shear)
image = tf.warp(image, affine_tf)
return image / image.max()
```

In the last line, we normalize by dividing by the maximum value, ensuring our feature values are in the range 0 to 1. This normalization can happen in the data preprocessing stage, the classification stage, or somewhere else.

From here, we can now generate images quite easily and use `pyplot` to display them. First, we use our inline display for the `matplotlib` graphs and import `pyplot`. The code is as follows:

```
%matplotlib inline
from matplotlib import pyplot as plt
```

Then we create our first CAPTCHA and show it:

```
image = create_captcha("GENE", shear=0.5)
plt.imshow(image, cmap='Greys')
```

The result is the image shown at the start of this section: our CAPTCHA.

Splitting the image into individual letters

Our CAPTCHAs are words. Instead of building a classifier that can identify the thousands and thousands of possible words, we will break the problem down into a smaller problem: predicting letters.

The next step in our algorithm for beating these CAPTCHAs involves segmenting the word to discover each of the letters within it. To do this, we are going to create a function that finds contiguous sections of black pixels on the image and extract them as sub-images. These are (or at least should be) our letters.

First we import the `label` and `regionprops` functions, which we will use in this function:

```
from skimage.measure import label, regionprops
```

Our function will take an image, and return a list of subimages, where each sub-image is a letter from the original word in the image:

```
def segment_image(image):
```

The first thing we need to do is to detect where each letter is. To do this, we will use the label function in `scikit-image`, which finds connected sets of pixels that have the same value. This has analogies to our connected component discovery in *Chapter 7, Discovering Accounts to Follow Using Graph Mining*.

The `label` function takes an image and returns an array of the same shape as the original. However, each *connected region* has a different number in the array and pixels that are not in a connected region have the value 0. The code is as follows:

```
    labeled_image = label(image > 0)
```

We will extract each of these sub-images and place them into a list:

```
    subimages = []
```

The `scikit-image` library also contains a function for extracting information about these regions: `regionprops`. We can iterate over these regions and work on each individually:

```
    for region in regionprops(labeled_image):
```

From here, we can query the `region` object for information about the current region. For our algorithm, we need to obtain the starting and ending coordinates of the current region:

```
        start_x, start_y, end_x, end_y = region.bbox
```

We can then extract the sub-images by indexing the image (remember it is represented as a simple NumPy array, so we can easily index it) using the starting and ending positions of the sub-image, and adding the selected sub-image to our list. The code is as follows:

```
            subimages.append(image[start_x:end_x,start_y:end_y])
```

Finally (and outside the loop) we return the discovered sub-images, each (hopefully) containing the section of the image with an individual letter in it. However, if we didn't find any sub-images, we just return the original image as our only sub-image. The code is as follows:

```
        if len(subimages) == 0:
            return [image,]
        return subimages
```

We can then get the sub-images from the example CAPTCHA using this function:

```
    subimages = segment_image(image)
```

We can also view each of these sub-images:

```
    f, axes = plt.subplots(1, len(subimages), figsize=(10, 3))
    for i in range(len(subimages)):
        axes[i].imshow(subimages[i], cmap="gray")
```

The result will look something like this:

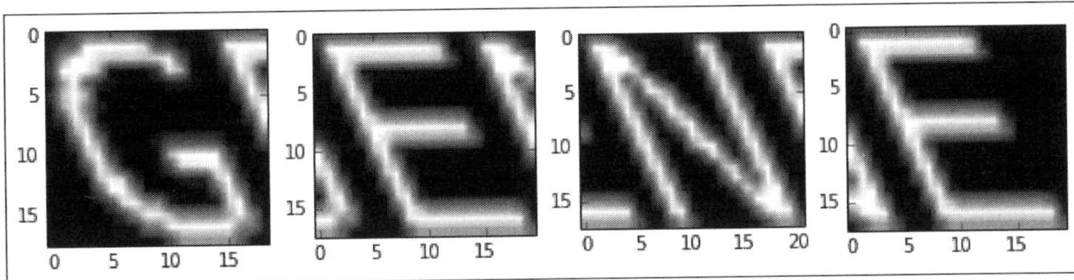

As you can see, our image segmentation does a reasonable job, but the results are still quite messy, with bits of previous letters showing.

Creating a training dataset

Using this function, we can now create a dataset of letters, each with different shear values. From this, we will train a neural network to recognize each letter from the image.

We first set up our random state and an array that holds the options for letters and shear values that we will randomly select from. There isn't much surprise here, but if you haven't used NumPy's `arange` function before, it is similar to Python's `range` function—except this one works with NumPy arrays and allows the step to be a float. The code is as follows:

```
from sklearn.utils import check_random_state
random_state = check_random_state(14)
letters = list("ABCDEFGHIJKLMNOPQRSTUVWXYZ")
shear_values = np.arange(0, 0.5, 0.05)
```

We then create a function (for generating a single sample in our training dataset) that randomly selects a letter and a shear value from the available options. The code is as follows:

```
def generate_sample(random_state=None):
    random_state = check_random_state(random_state)
    letter = random_state.choice(letters)
    shear = random_state.choice(shear_values)
```

We then return the image of the letter, along with the target value representing the letter in the image. Our classes will be 0 for A, 1 for B, 2 for C, and so on. The code is as follows:

```
    return create_captcha(letter, shear=shear, size=(20, 20)),
      letters.index(letter)
```

Outside the function block, we can now call this code to generate a new sample and then show it using `pyplot`:

```
image, target = generate_sample(random_state)
plt.imshow(image, cmap="Greys")
print("The target for this image is: {0}".format(target))
```

We can now generate all of our dataset by calling this several thousand times. We then put the data into NumPy arrays, as they are easier to work with than lists. The code is as follows:

```
dataset, targets = zip(*(generate_sample(random_state) for i in
range(3000)))
dataset = np.array(dataset, dtype='float')
targets =  np.array(targets)
```

Our targets are integer values between 0 and 26, with each representing a letter of the alphabet. Neural networks don't usually support multiple values from a single neuron, instead preferring to have multiple outputs, each with values 0 or 1. We therefore perform one hot-encoding of the targets, giving us a target array that has 26 outputs per sample, using values near 1 if that letter is likely and near 0 otherwise. The code is as follows:

```
from sklearn.preprocessing import OneHotEncoder
onehot = OneHotEncoder()
y = onehot.fit_transform(targets.reshape(targets.shape[0],1))
```

The library we are going to use doesn't support sparse arrays, so we need to turn our sparse matrix into a dense NumPy array. The code is as follows:

```
y = y.todense()
```

Adjusting our training dataset to our methodology

Our training dataset differs from our final methodology quite significantly. Our dataset here is nicely created individual letters, fitting the 20-pixel by 20-pixel image. The methodology involves extracting the letters from words, which may squash them, move them away from the center, or create other problems.

Ideally, the data you train your classifier on should mimic the environment it will be used in. In practice, we make concessions, but aim to minimize the differences as much as possible.

For this experiment, we would ideally extract letters from actual CAPTCHAs and label those. In the interests of speeding up the process a bit, we will just run our segmentation function on the training dataset and return those letters instead.

We will need the `resize` function from `scikit-image`, as our sub-images won't always be 20 pixels by 20 pixels. The code is as follows:

```
from skimage.transform import resize
```

From here, we can run our `segment_image` function on each sample and then resize them to 20 pixels by 20 pixels. The code is as follows:

```
dataset = np.array([resize(segment_image(sample)[0], (20, 20)) for
sample in dataset])
```

Finally, we will create our dataset. This `dataset` array is three-dimensional, as it is an array of two-dimensional images. Our classifier will need a two-dimensional array, so we simply flatten the last two dimensions:

```
X = dataset.reshape((dataset.shape[0], dataset.shape[1] * dataset.
shape[2]))
```

Finally, using the `train_test_split` function of scikit-learn, we create a set of data for training and one for testing. The code is as follows:

```
from sklearn.cross_validation import train_test_split
X_train, X_test, y_train, y_test = \
    train_test_split(X, y, train_size=0.9)
```

Training and classifying

We are now going to build a neural network that will take an image as input and try to predict which (single) letter is in the image.

We will use the training set of single letters we created earlier. The dataset itself is quite simple. We have a 20 by 20 pixel image, each pixel 1 (black) or 0 (white). These represent the 400 features that we will use as inputs into the neural network. The outputs will be 26 values between 0 and 1, where higher values indicate a higher likelihood that the associated letter (the first neuron is A, the second is B, and so on) is the letter represented by the input image.

We are going to use the PyBrain library for our neural network.

As with all the libraries we have seen so far, PyBrain can be installed from pip: `pip install pybrain`.

The `PyBrain` library uses its own dataset format, but luckily it isn't too difficult to create training and testing datasets using this format. The code is as follows:

```
from pybrain.datasets import SupervisedDataSet
```

First, we iterate over our training dataset and add each as a sample into a new `SupervisedDataSet` instance. The code is as follows:

```
training = SupervisedDataSet(X.shape[1], y.shape[1])
for i in range(X_train.shape[0]):
    training.addSample(X_train[i], y_train[i])
```

Then we iterate over our testing dataset and add each as a sample into a new `SupervisedDataSet` instance for testing. The code is as follows:

```
testing = SupervisedDataSet(X.shape[1], y.shape[1])
for i in range(X_test.shape[0]):
    testing.addSample(X_test[i], y_test[i])
```

Now we can build a neural network. We will create a basic three-layer network that consists of an input layer, an output layer, and a single hidden layer between them. The number of neurons in the input and output layers is fixed. 400 features in our dataset dictates that we need 400 neurons in the first layer, and 26 possible targets dictate that we need 26 output neurons.

Determining the number of neurons in the hidden layers can be quite difficult. Having too many results in a sparse network and means it is difficult to train enough neurons to properly represent the data. This usually results in overfitting the training data. If there are too few results in neurons that try to do too much of the classification each and again don't train properly, underfitting the data is the problem. I have found that creating a funnel shape, where the middle layer is between the size of the inputs and the size of the outputs, is a good starting place. For this chapter, we will use 100 neurons in the hidden layer, but playing with this value may yield better results.

We import the `buildNetwork` function and tell it to build a network based on our necessary dimensions. The first value, `X.shape[1]`, is the number of neurons in the input layer and it is set to the number of features (which is the number of columns in `X`). The second feature is our decided value of 100 neurons in the hidden layer. The third value is the number of outputs, which is based on the shape of the target array `y`. Finally, we set network to use a bias neuron to each layer (except for the output layer), effectively a neuron that always activates (but still has connections with a weight that are trained). The code is as follows:

```
from pybrain.tools.shortcuts import buildNetwork
net = buildNetwork(X.shape[1], 100, y.shape[1], bias=True)
```

From here, we can now train the network and determine good values for the weights. But how do we train a neural network?

Back propagation

The back propagation (**backprop**) algorithm is a way of assigning blame to each neuron for incorrect predictions. Starting from the output layer, we compute which neurons were incorrect in their prediction, and adjust the weights into those neurons by a small amount to attempt to fix the incorrect prediction.

These neurons made their mistake because of the neurons giving them input, but more specifically due to the weights on the connections between the neuron and its inputs. We then alter these weights by altering them by a small amount. The amount of change is based on two aspects: the partial derivative of the error function of the neuron's individual weights and the *learning rate*, which is a parameter to the algorithm (usually set at a very low value). We compute the gradient of the error of the function, multiply it by the learning rate, and subtract that from our weights. This is shown in the following example. The gradient will be positive or negative, depending on the error, and subtracting the weight will always attempt to correct the weight *towards* the correct prediction. In some cases, though, the correction will move towards something called a **local optima**, which is better than similar weights but not the best possible set of weights.

This process starts at the output layer and goes back each layer until we reach the input layer. At this point, the weights on all connections have been updated.

PyBrain contains an implementation of the backprop algorithm, which is called on the neural network through a `trainer` class. The code is as follows:

```
from pybrain.supervised.trainers import BackpropTrainer
trainer = BackpropTrainer(net, training, learningrate=0.01,
weightdecay=0.01)
```

The backprop algorithm is run iteratively using the training dataset, and each time the weights are adjusted a little. We can stop running backprop when the error reduces by a very small amount, indicating that the algorithm isn't improving the error much more and it isn't worth continuing the training. In theory, we would run the algorithm until the error doesn't change at all. This is called convergence, but in practice this takes a very long time for little gain.

Alternatively, and much more simply, we can just run the algorithm a fixed number of times, called **epochs**. The higher the number of epochs, the longer the algorithm will take and the better the results will be (with a declining improvement for each epoch). We will train for 20 epochs for this code, but trying larger values will increase the performance (if only slightly). The code is as follows:

```
trainer.trainEpochs(epochs=20)
```

After running the previous code, which may take a number of minutes depending on the hardware, we can then perform predictions of samples in our testing dataset. PyBrain contains a function for this, and it is called on the `trainer` instance:

```
predictions = trainer.testOnClassData(dataset=testing)
```

From these predictions, we can use `scikit-learn` to compute the F1 score:

```
from sklearn.metrics import f1_score
print("F-score: {0:.2f}".format(f1_score(predictions,
                                y_test.argmax(axis=1) )))
```

The score here is 0.97, which is a great result for such a relatively simple model. Recall that our features were simple pixel values only; the neural network worked out how to use them.

Now that we have a classifier with good accuracy on letter prediction, we can start putting together words for our CAPTCHAs.

Predicting words

We want to predict each letter from each of these segments, and put those predictions together to form the predicted word from a given CAPTCHA.

Our function will accept a CAPTCHA and the trained neural network, and it will return the predicted word:

```
def predict_captcha(captcha_image, neural_network):
```

We first extract the sub-images using the `segment_image` function we created earlier:

```
    subimages = segment_image(captcha_image)
```

We will be building our word from each of the letters. The sub-images are ordered according to their location, so usually this will place the letters in the correct order:

```
    predicted_word = ""
```

Next we iterate over the sub-images:

```
    for subimage in subimages:
```

Each sub-image is unlikely to be exactly 20 pixels by 20 pixels, so we will need to resize it in order to have the correct size for our neural network.

```
        subimage = resize(subimage, (20, 20))
```

We will activate our neural network by sending the sub-image data into the input layer. This propagates through our neural network and returns the given output. All this happened in our testing of the neural network earlier, but we didn't have to explicitly call it. The code is as follows:

```
        outputs = net.activate(subimage.flatten())
```

The output of the neural network is 26 numbers, each relative to the likelihood that the letter at the given index is the predicted letter. To get the actual prediction, we get the index of the maximum value of these outputs and look up our letters list from before for the actual letter. For example, if the value is highest for the fifth output, the predicted letter will be *E*. The code is as follows:

```
            prediction = np.argmax(outputs)
```

We then append the predicted letter to the predicted word we are building:

```
            predicted_word += letters[prediction]
```

After the loop completes, we have gone through each of the letters and formed our predicted word:

```
        return predicted_word
```

We can now test on a word using the following code. Try different words and see what sorts of errors you get, but keep in mind that our neural network only knows about capital letters.

```
word = "GENE"
captcha = create_captcha(word, shear=0.2)
print(predict_captcha(captcha, net))
```

We can codify this into a function, allowing us to perform predictions more easily. We also leverage our assumption that the words will be only four-characters long to make prediction a little easier. Try it without the `prediction = prediction[:4]` line and see what types of errors you get. The code is as follows:

```
def test_prediction(word, net, shear=0.2):
    captcha = create_captcha(word, shear=shear)
    prediction = predict_captcha(captcha, net)
    prediction = prediction[:4]
    return word == prediction, word, prediction
```

The returned results specify whether the prediction is correct, the original word, and the predicted word.

This code correctly predicts the word *GENE*, but makes mistakes with other words. How accurate is it? To test, we will create a dataset with a whole bunch of four-letter English words from NLTK. The code is as follows:

```
from nltk.corpus import words
```

The `words` instance here is actually a corpus object, so we need to call `words()` on it to extract the individual words from this corpus. We also filter to get only four-letter words from this list. The code is as follows:

```
valid_words = [word.upper() for word in words.words() if len(word) ==
4]
```

We can then iterate over all of the words to see how many we get correct by simply counting the correct and incorrect predictions:

```
num_correct = 0
num_incorrect = 0
for word in valid_words:
    correct, word, prediction = test_prediction(word, net,
                                                shear=0.2)
if correct:
        num_correct += 1
    else:
        num_incorrect += 1
print("Number correct is {0}".format(num_correct))
print("Number incorrect is {0}".format(num_incorrect))
```

The results we get are 2,832 correct and 2,681 incorrect for an accuracy of just over 51 percent. From our original 97 percent per-letter accuracy, this is a big decline. What happened?

The first factor to impact is our accuracy. All other things being equal, if we have four letters, and 97 percent accuracy per-letter, then we can expect about an 88 percent success rate (all other things being equal) getting four letters in a row (0.88≈0.974). A single error in a single letter's prediction results in the wrong word being predicted.

The second impact is the shear value. Our dataset chose randomly between shear values of 0 to 0.5. The previous test used a shear of 0.2. For a value of 0, I get 75 percent accuracy; for a shear of 0.5, the result is much worse at 2.5 percent. The higher the shear, the lower the performance.

The next impact is that our letters were randomly chosen for the dataset. In reality, this is not true at all. Letters, such as E, appear much more frequently than other letters, such as Q. Letters that appear reasonably commonly but are frequently mistaken for each other, will also contribute to the error.

We can table which letters are frequently mistaken for each other using a confusion matrix, which is a two dimensional array. Its rows and columns each represent an individual class.

Each cell represents the number of times that a sample is actually from one class (represented by the row) and predicted to be in the second class (represented by the column). For example, if the value of the cell (`4,2`) is 6, it means that there were six cases where a sample with the letter D was predicted as being a letter B.

```
from sklearn.metrics import confusion_matrix
cm = confusion_matrix(np.argmax(y_test, axis=1), predictions)
```

Ideally, a confusion matrix should only have values along the diagonal. The cells (`i, i`) have values, but any other cell has a value of zero. This indicates that the predicted classes are exactly the same as the actual classes. Values that aren't on the diagonal represent errors in the classification.

We can also plot this using `pyplot`, showing graphically which letters are confused with each other. The code is as follows:

```
plt.figure(figsize=(10, 10))
plt.imshow(cm)
```

We set the axis and tick marks to easily reference the letters each index corresponds to:

```
tick_marks = np.arange(len(letters))
plt.xticks(tick_marks, letters)
plt.yticks(tick_marks, letters)
plt.ylabel('Actual')
plt.xlabel('Predicted')
plt.show()
```

The result is shown in the next graph. It can be quite clearly seen that the main source of error is U being mistaken for an H nearly every single time!

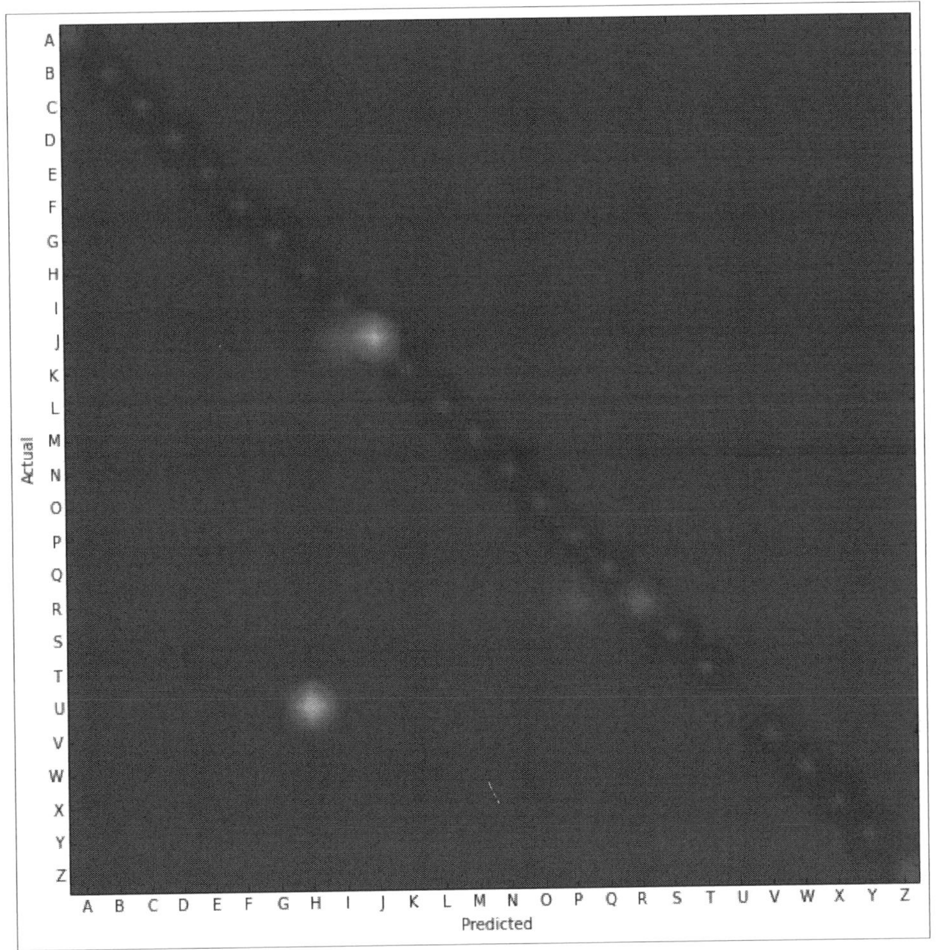

The letter U appears in 17 percent of words in our list. For each word that a U appears in, we can expect this to be wrong. U actually appears more often than H (which is in around 11 percent of words), indicating we could get a cheap (although possibly not a robust) boost in accuracy by changing any H prediction into a U.

In the next section, we will do something a bit smarter and actually use the dictionary to search for similar words.

Improving accuracy using a dictionary

Rather than just returning the given prediction, we can check whether the word actually exists in our dictionary. If it does, then that is our prediction. If it isn't in the dictionary, we can try and find a word that is similar to it and predict that instead. Note that this strategy relies on our assumption that all CAPTCHA words will be valid English words, and therefore this strategy wouldn't work for a random sequence of characters. This is one reason why some CAPTCHAs don't use words.

There is one issue here—how do we determine the closest word? There are many ways to do this. For instance, we can compare the lengths of words. Two words that have a similar length could be considered more similar. However, we commonly consider words to be similar if they have the same letters in the same positions. This is where the edit distance comes in.

Ranking mechanisms for words

The **Levenshtein edit distance** is a commonly used method for comparing two short strings to see how similar they are. It isn't very scalable, so it isn't commonly used for very long strings. The edit distance computes the number of steps it takes to go from one word to another. The steps can be one of the following three actions:

1. Insert a new letter into the word at any position.
2. Delete any letter from the word.
3. Substitute a letter for another one.

The minimum number of actions needed to transform the first word into the second is given as the distance. Higher values indicate that the words are less similar.

This distance is available in NLTK as `nltk.metrics.edit_distance`. We can call it using on two strings and it returns the edit distance:

```
from nltk.metrics import edit_distance
steps = edit_distance("STEP", "STOP")
print("The number of steps needed is: {0}".format(steps))
```

When used with different words, the edit distance is quite a good approximation to what many people would intuitively feel are similar words. The edit distance is great for testing spelling mistakes, dictation errors, and name matching (where you can mix up your Marc and Mark spelling quite easily).

However, it isn't very good. We don't really expect letters to be moved around, just individual letter comparisons to be wrong. For this reason, we will create a different distance metric, which is simply the number of letters in the same positions that are incorrect. The code is as follows:

```
def compute_distance(prediction, word):
    return len(prediction) - sum(prediction[i] == word[i] for i in
range(len(prediction)))
```

We subtract the value from the length of the prediction word (which is four) to make it a distance metric where lower values indicate more similarity between the words.

Putting it all together

We can now test our improved prediction function using similar code to before. First we define a prediction, which also takes our list of valid words:

```
from operator import itemgetter
def improved_prediction(word, net, dictionary, shear=0.2):
    captcha = create_captcha(word, shear=shear)
    prediction = predict_captcha(captcha, net)
    prediction = prediction[:4]
```

Up to this point, the code is as before. We do our prediction and limit it to the first four characters. However, we now check if the word is in the dictionary or not. If it is, we return that as our prediction. If it is not, we find the next nearest word. The code is as follows:

```
    if prediction not in dictionary:
```

We compute the distance between our predicted word and each other word in the dictionary, and sort it by distance (lowest first). The code is as follows:

```
        distances = sorted([(word, compute_distance(prediction, word))
                            for word in dictionary],
 key=itemgetter(1))
```

We then get the best matching word—that is, the one with the lowest distance—and predict that word:

```
        best_word = distances[0]
        prediction = best_word[0]
```

We then return the correctness, word, and prediction as before:

```
    return word == prediction, word, prediction
```

The changes in our testing code are highlighted in the following code:

```
num_correct = 0
num_incorrect = 0
for word in valid_words:
    correct, word, prediction = improved_prediction(word, net, valid_
words, shear=0.2)
    if correct:
        num_correct += 1
    else:
        num_incorrect += 1
print("Number correct is {0}".format(num_correct))
print("Number incorrect is {0}".format(num_incorrect))
```

The preceding code will take a while to run (computing all of the distances will take some time) but the net result is 3,037 samples correct and 2,476 samples incorrect. This is an accuracy of 55 percent for a boost of 4 percentage points. The reason this improvement is so low is that multiple words all have the same similarity, and the algorithm is choosing the *best* one randomly between this set of most similar words. For example, the first word in the list, AANI (I just chose the first word in the list, which is a dog-headed ape from Egyptian mythology), has 44 candidate words that are all the same distance from the word. This gives just a 1/44 chance of choosing the correct word from this list.

If we were to cheat and count the prediction as correct if the actual word was any one of the best candidates, we would rate 78 percent of predictions as correct (to see this code, check out the code in the bundle).

To further improve the results, we can work on our distance metric, perhaps using information from our confusion matrix to find *commonly confused letters* or some other improvement upon this. This iterative improvement is a feature of many data mining methodologies, and it mimics the scientific method—have an idea, test it out, analyze the results, and use that to improve the next idea.

Summary

In this chapter, we worked with images in order to use simple pixel values to predict the letter being portrayed in a CAPTCHA. Our CAPTCHAs were a bit simplified; we only used complete four-letter English words. In practice, the problem is much harder—as it should be! With some improvements, it would be possible to solve much harder CAPTCHAs with neural networks and a methodology similar to what we discussed. The `scikit-image` library contains lots of useful functions for extracting shapes from images, functions for improving contrast, and other image tools that will help.

We took our larger problem of predicting words, and created a smaller and simple problem of predicting letters. From here, we were able to create a feed-forward neural network to accurately predict which letter was in the image. At this stage, our results were very good with 97 percent accuracy.

Neural networks are simply connected sets of neurons, which are basic computation devices consisting of a single function. However, when you connect these together, they can solve incredibly complex problems. Neural networks are the basis for deep learning, which is one of the most effective areas of data mining at the moment.

Despite our great per-letter accuracy, the performance when predicting a word drops to just over 50 percent when trying to predict a whole word. There were several factors for this, representing the difficulty of taking a problem from an experiment to the real world.

We improved our accuracy using a dictionary, searching for the best matching word. To do this, we considered the commonly used edit distance; however, we simplified it because we were only concerned with individual mistakes on letters, not insertions or deletions. This improvement netted some benefit, but there are still many improvements you could try to further boost the accuracy.

In the next chapter, we will continue with string comparisons. We will attempt to determine which author (out of a set of authors) wrote a particular document—using only the content and no other information!

9
Authorship Attribution

Authorship analysis is, predominately, a text mining task that aims to identify certain aspects about an author, based only on the content of their writings. This could include characteristics such as age, gender, or background. In the specific **authorship attribution** task, we aim to identify who out of a set of authors wrote a particular document. This is a classic case of a classification task. In many ways, authorship analysis tasks are performed using standard data mining methodologies, such as cross fold validation, feature extraction, and classification algorithms.

In this chapter, we will use the problem of authorship attribution to piece together the parts of the data mining methodology we developed in the previous chapters. We identify the problem and discuss the background and knowledge of the problem. This lets us choose features to extract, which we will build a pipeline for achieving. We will test two different types of features: function words and character n-grams. Finally, we will perform an in-depth analysis of the results. We will work with a book dataset, and then a very messy real-world corpus of e-mails.

The topics we will cover in this chapter are as follows:

- Feature engineering and how the features differ based on application
- Revisiting the bag-of-words model with a specific goal in mind
- Feature types and the character n-grams model
- Support vector machines
- Cleaning up a messy dataset for data mining

Attributing documents to authors

Authorship analysis has a background in **stylometry**, which is the study of an author's style of writing. The concept is based on the idea that everyone learns language slightly differently, and measuring the nuances in people's writing will enable us to tell them apart using only the content of their writing.

The problem has been historically performed using manual analysis and statistics, which is a good indication that it could be automated with data mining. Modern authorship analysis studies are almost entirely data mining-based, although quite a significant amount of work is still done with more manually driven analysis using linguistic styles.

Authorship analysis has many subproblems, and the main ones are as follows:

- **Authorship profiling**: This determines the age, gender, or other traits of the author based on the writing. For example, we can detect the first language of a person speaking English by looking for specific ways in which they speak the language.
- **Authorship verification**: This checks *whether the author of this document also wrote the other document*. This problem is what you would normally think about in a legal court setting. For instance, the suspect's writing style (content-wise) would be analyzed to see if it matched the ransom note.
- **Authorship clustering**: This is an extension of authorship verification, where we use cluster analysis to group documents from a big set into clusters, and each cluster is written by the same author.

However, the most common form of authorship analysis study is that of authorship attribution, a classification task where we attempt to predict which of a set of authors wrote a given document.

Applications and use cases

Authorship analysis has a number of use cases. Many use cases are concerned with problems such as verifying authorship, proving shared authorship/provenance, or linking social media profiles with real-world users.

In a historical sense, we can use authorship analysis to verify whether certain documents were indeed written by their supposed authors. Controversial authorship claims include some of Shakespeare's plays, the Federalist papers from the USA's foundation period, and other historical texts.

Authorship studies alone cannot prove authorship, but can provide evidence for or against a given theory. For example, we can analyze Shakespeare's plays to determine his writing style, before testing whether a given sonnet actually does originate from him.

A more modern use case is that of linking social network accounts. For example, a malicious online user could set up accounts on multiple online social networks. Being able to link them allows authorities to track down the user of a given account—for example, if it is harassing other online users.

Another example used in the past is to be a backbone to provide expert testimony in court to determine whether a given person wrote a document. For instance, the suspect could be accused of writing an e-mail harassing another person. The use of authorship analysis could determine whether it is likely that person did in fact write the document. Another court-based use is to settle claims of stolen authorship. For example, two authors may claim to have written a book, and authorship analysis could provide evidence on which is the likely author.

Authorship analysis is not foolproof though. A recent study found that attributing documents to authors can be made considerably harder by simply asking people, who are otherwise untrained, to hide their writing style. This study also looked at a framing exercise where people were asked to write in the style of another person. This framing of another person proved quite reliable, with the faked document commonly attributed to the person being framed.

Despite these issues, authorship analysis is proving useful in a growing number of areas and is an interesting data mining problem to investigate.

Attributing authorship

Authorship attribution is a classification task by which we have a set of candidate authors, a set of documents from each of those authors (the training set), and a set of documents of unknown authorship (the test set). If the documents of unknown authorship definitely belong to one of the candidates, we call this a **closed problem**.

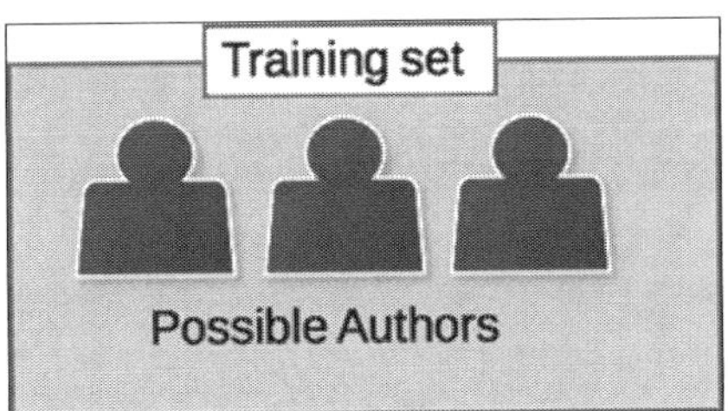

If we cannot be sure of that, we call this an open problem. This distinction isn't just specific to authorship attribution though—any data mining application where the actual class may not be in the training set is considered an open problem, with the task being to find the candidate author or to select none of them.

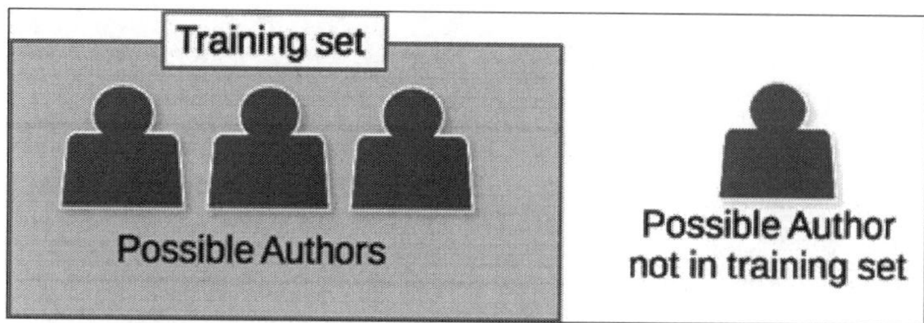

In authorship attribution, we typically have two restrictions on the tasks. First, we only use content information from the documents and not metadata about time of writing, delivery, handwriting style, and so on. There are ways to combine models from these different types of information, but that isn't generally considered authorship attribution and is more a data fusion application.

The second restriction is that we don't look at the topic of the documents; instead, we look for more salient features such as word usage, punctuation, and other text-based features. The reasoning here is that a person can write on many different topics, so worrying about the topic of their writing isn't going to model their actual authorship style. Looking at topic words can also lead to overfitting on the training data—our model may train on documents from the same author and also on the same topic. For instance, if you were to model my authorship style by looking at this book, you might conclude the words *data mining* are indicative of my style, when in fact I write on other topics as well.

From here, the pipeline for performing authorship attribution looks a lot like the one we developed in *Chapter 6, Social Media Insight Using Naive Bayes*. First, we extract features from our text. Then, we perform some feature selection on those features. Finally, we train a classification algorithm to fit a model, which we can then use to predict the class (in this case, the author) of a document.

There are some differences, mostly having to do with which features are used, that we will cover in this chapter. But first, we will define the scope of the problem.

Getting the data

The data we will use for this chapter is a set of books from Project Gutenberg at `www.gutenberg.org`, which is a repository of public domain literature works. The books I used for these experiments come from a variety of authors:

- Booth Tarkington (22 titles)
- Charles Dickens (44 titles)
- Edith Nesbit (10 titles)
- Arthur Conan Doyle (51 titles)
- Mark Twain (29 titles)
- Sir Richard Francis Burton (11 titles)
- Emile Gaboriau (10 titles)

Overall, there are 177 documents from 7 authors, giving a significant amount of text to work with. A full list of the titles, along with download links and a script to automatically fetch them, is given in the code bundle.

To download these books, we use the requests library to download the files into our data directory. First, set up the data directory and ensure the following code links to it:

```
import os
import sys
data_folder = os.path.join(os.path.expanduser("~"), "Data", "books")
```

Next, run the script from the code bundle to download each of the books from Project Gutenberg. This will place them in the appropriate subfolders of this data folder.

To run the script, download the `getdata.py` script from the `Chapter 9` folder in the code bundle. Save it to your `notebooks` folder and enter the following into a new cell:

```
!load getdata.py
```

Then, from inside your IPython Notebook, press *Shift* + *Enter* to run the cell. This will load the script into the cell. Then click the code again and press *Shift* + *Enter* to run the script itself. This will take a while, but it will print a message to let you know it is complete.

After taking a look at these files, you will see that many of them are quite messy—at least from a data analysis point of view. There is a large project Gutenberg disclaimer at the start of the files. This needs to be removed before we do our analysis.

We could alter the individual files on disk to remove this stuff. However, what happens if we were to lose our data? We would lose our changes and potentially be unable to replicate the study. For that reason, we will perform the preprocessing as we load the files—this allows us to be sure our results will be replicable (as long as the data source stays the same). The code is as follows:

```
def clean_book(document):
```

We first split the document into lines, as we can identify the start and end of the disclaimer by the starting and ending lines:

```
    lines = document.split("\n")
```

We are going to iterate through each line. We look for the line that indicates the start of the book, and the line that indicates the end of the book. We will then take the text in between as the book itself. The code is as follows:

```
    start = 0
    end = len(lines)
    for i in range(len(lines)):
        line = lines[i]
        if line.startswith("*** START OF THIS PROJECT GUTENBERG"):
            start = i + 1
        elif line.startswith("*** END OF THIS PROJECT GUTENBERG"):
            end = i - 1
```

Finally, we join those lines together with a newline character to recreate the book without the disclaimers:

```
    return "\n".join(lines[start:end])
```

From here, we can now create a function that loads all of the books, performs the preprocessing, and returns them along with a class number for each author. The code is as follows:

```
import numpy as np
```

By default, our function signature takes the parent folder containing each of the subfolders that contain the actual books. The code is as follows:

```
def load_books_data(folder=data_folder):
```

We create lists for storing the documents themselves and the author classes:

```
    documents = []
    authors = []
```

We then create a list of each of the subfolders in the parent directly, as the script creates a subfolder for each author. The code is as follows:

```
    subfolders = [subfolder for subfolder in os.listdir(folder)
                  if os.path.isdir(os.path.join(folder,
                     subfolder))]
```

Next we iterate over these subfolders, assigning each subfolder a number using `enumerate`:

```
    for author_number, subfolder in enumerate(subfolders):
```

We then create the full subfolder path and look for all documents within that subfolder:

```
        full_subfolder_path = os.path.join(folder, subfolder)
        for document_name in os.listdir(full_subfolder_path):
```

For each of those files, we open it, read the contents, preprocess those contents, and append it to our documents list. The code is as follows:

```
            with open(os.path.join(full_subfolder_path,
              document_name)) as inf:
                documents.append(clean_book(inf.read()))
```

We also append the number we assigned to this author to our authors list, which will form our classes:

```
                authors.append(author_number)
```

We then return the documents and classes (which we transform into a NumPy array for each indexing later on):

```
    return documents, np.array(authors, dtype='int')
```

We can now get our documents and classes using the following function call:

```
documents, classes = load_books_data(data_folder)
```

> This dataset fits into memory quite easily, so we can load all of the text at once. In cases where the whole dataset doesn't fit, a better solution is to extract the features from each document one-at-a-time (or in batches) and save the resulting values to a file or in-memory matrix.

Function words

One of the earliest types of features, and one that still works quite well for authorship analysis, is to use function words in a bag-of-words model. Function words are words that have little meaning on their own, but are required for creating (English) sentences. For example, the words *this* and *which* are words that are really only defined by what they do within a sentence, rather than their meaning in themselves. Contrast this with a content word such as *tiger*, which has an explicit meaning and invokes imagery of a large cat when used in a sentence.

Function words are not always clearly clarified. A good rule of thumb is to choose the most frequent words in usage (over all possible documents, not just ones from the same author). Typically, the more frequently a word is used, the better it is for authorship analysis. In contrast, the less frequently a word is used, the better it is for content-based text mining, such as in the next chapter, where we look at the topic of different documents.

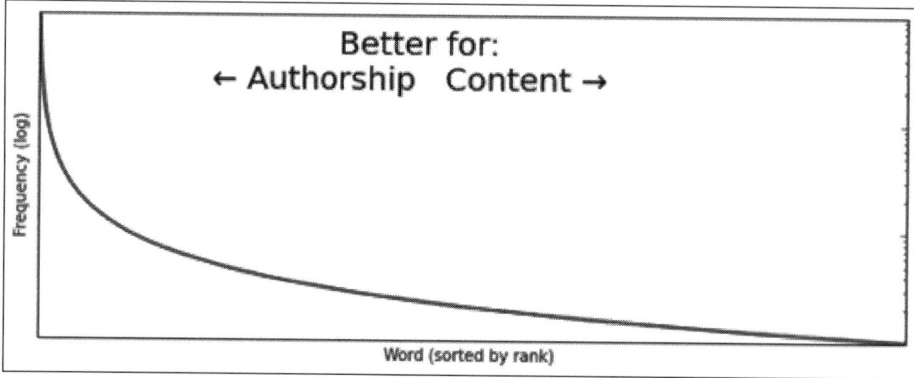

The use of function words is less defined by the content of the document and more by the decisions made by the author. This makes them good candidates for separating the authorship traits between different users. For instance, while many Americans are particular about the different in usage between *that* and *which* in a sentence, people from other countries, such as Australia, are less particular about this. This means that some Australians will lean towards almost exclusively using one word or the other, while others may use *which* much more. This difference, combined with thousands of other nuanced differences, makes a model of authorship.

Counting function words

We can count function words using the `CountVectorizer` class we used in *Chapter 6, Social Media Insight Using Naive Bayes*. This class can be passed a **vocabulary**, which is the set of words it will look for. If a vocabulary is not passed (we didn't pass one in the code of `Chapter 6`), then it will learn this vocabulary from the dataset. All the words are in the training set of documents (depending on the other parameters of course).

First, we set up our vocabulary of function words, which is just a list containing each of them. Exactly which words are function words and which are not is up for debate. I've found this list, from published research, to be quite good:

```
function_words = ["a", "able", "aboard", "about", "above", "absent",
"according" , "accordingly", "across", "after", "against",
"ahead", "albeit", "all", "along", "alongside", "although",
"am", "amid", "amidst", "among", "amongst", "amount", "an",
"and", "another", "anti", "any", "anybody", "anyone",
"anything", "are", "around", "as", "aside", "astraddle",
"astride", "at", "away", "bar", "barring", "be", "because",
"been", "before", "behind", "being", "below", "beneath",
"beside", "besides", "better", "between", "beyond", "bit",
"both", "but", "by", "can", "certain", "circa", "close",
"concerning", "consequently", "considering", "could",
"couple", "dare", "deal", "despite", "down", "due", "during",
"each", "eight", "eighth", "either", "enough", "every",
"everybody", "everyone", "everything", "except", "excepting",
"excluding", "failing", "few", "fewer", "fifth", "first",
"five", "following", "for", "four", "fourth", "from", "front",
"given", "good", "great", "had", "half", "have", "he",
"heaps", "hence", "her", "hers", "herself", "him", "himself",
"his", "however", "i", "if", "in", "including", "inside",
```

```
"instead", "into", "is", "it", "its", "itself", "keeping",
"lack", "less", "like", "little", "loads", "lots", "majority",
"many", "masses", "may", "me", "might", "mine", "minority",
"minus", "more", "most", "much", "must", "my", "myself",
"near", "need", "neither", "nevertheless", "next", "nine",
"ninth", "no", "nobody", "none", "nor", "nothing",
"notwithstanding", "number", "numbers", "of", "off", "on",
"once", "one", "onto", "opposite", "or", "other", "ought",
"our", "ours", "ourselves", "out", "outside", "over", "part",
"past", "pending", "per", "pertaining", "place", "plenty",
"plethora", "plus", "quantities", "quantity", "quarter",
"regarding", "remainder", "respecting", "rest", "round",
"save", "saving", "second", "seven", "seventh", "several",
"shall", "she", "should", "similar", "since", "six", "sixth",
"so", "some", "somebody", "someone", "something", "spite",
"such", "ten", "tenth", "than", "thanks", "that", "the",
"their", "theirs", "them", "themselves", "then", "thence",
"therefore", "these", "they", "third", "this", "those",
"though", "three", "through", "throughout", "thru", "thus",
"till", "time", "to", "tons", "top", "toward", "towards",
"two", "under", "underneath", "unless", "unlike", "until",
"unto", "up", "upon", "us", "used", "various", "versus",
"via", "view", "wanting", "was", "we", "were", "what",
"whatever", "when", "whenever", "where", "whereas",
"wherever", "whether", "which", "whichever", "while",
"whilst", "who", "whoever", "whole", "whom", "whomever",
"whose", "will", "with", "within", "without", "would", "yet",
"you", "your", "yours", "yourself", "yourselves"]
```

Now, we can set up an extractor to get the counts of these function words. We will fit this using a pipeline later:

```
from sklearn.feature_extraction.text import CountVectorizer
extractor = CountVectorizer(vocabulary=function_words)
```

Classifying with function words

Next, we import our classes. The only new thing here is the support vector machines, which we will cover in the next section (for now, just consider it a standard classification algorithm). We import the SVC class, an SVM for classification, as well as the other standard workflow tools we have seen before:

```
from sklearn.svm import SVC
from sklearn.cross_validation import cross_val_score
from sklearn.pipeline import Pipeline
from sklearn import grid_search
```

Support vector machines take a number of parameters. As I said, we will use one blindly here, before going into detail in the next section. We then use a dictionary to set which parameters we are going to search. For the `kernel` parameter, we will try `linear` and `rbf`. For `C`, we will try values of 1 and 10 (descriptions of these parameters are covered in the next section). We then create a grid search to search these parameters for the best choices:

```
parameters = {'kernel':('linear', 'rbf'), 'C':[1, 10]}
svr = SVC()
grid = grid_search.GridSearchCV(svr, parameters)
```

Gaussian kernels (such as `rbf`) only work for reasonably sized datasets, such as when the number of features is fewer than about 10,000.

Next, we set up a pipeline that takes the feature extraction step using the `CountVectorizer` (only using function words), along with our grid search using SVM. The code is as follows:

```
pipeline1 = Pipeline([('feature_extraction', extractor),
                      ('clf', grid)
                      ])
```

Next, we apply `cross_val_score` to get our cross validated score for this pipeline. The result is 0.811, which means we approximately get 80 percent of the predictions correct. For 7 authors, this is a good result!

Support vector machines

Support vector machines (SVMs) are classification algorithms based on a simple and intuitive idea. It performs classification between only two classes (although we can extend it to more classes). Suppose that our two classes can be separated by a line such that any points above the line belong to one class and any below the line belong to the other class. SVMs find this line and use it for prediction, much the same way as linear regression works. SVMs, however, find the best *line* for separating the dataset. In the following figure, we have three lines that separate the dataset: blue, black, and green. Which would you say is the best option?

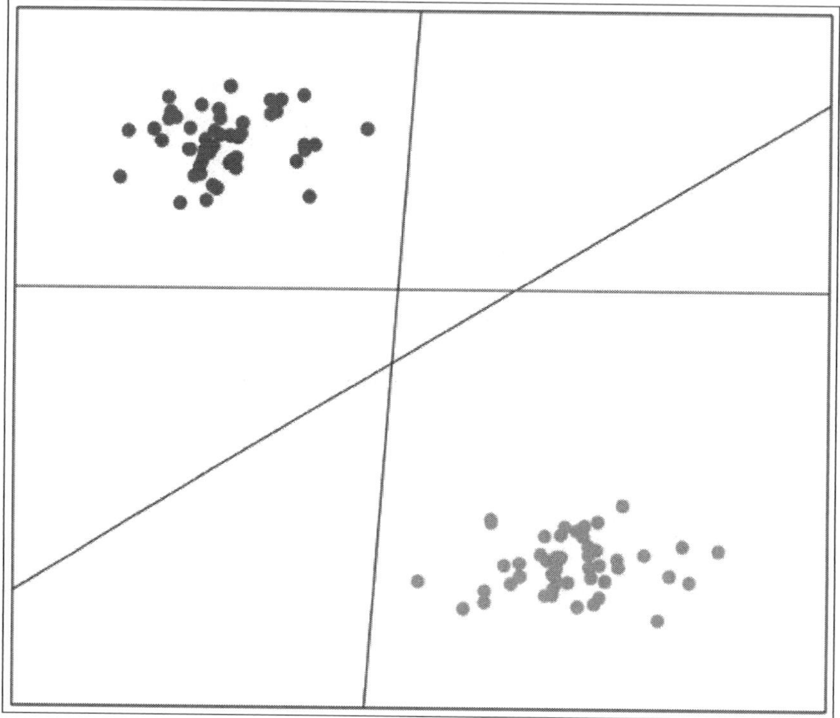

Intuitively, a person would normally choose the blue line as the *best* option, as this separates the data the most. That is, it has the maximum distance from any point in each class.

Finding this line is an optimization problem, based on finding the lines of margin with the maximum distance between them.

The derivation of these equations is outside the scope of this book, but I recommend interested readers to go through the derivations at `http://en.wikibooks.org/wiki/Support_Vector_Machines` for the details. Alternatively, you can visit `http://docs.opencv.org/doc/tutorials/ml/introduction_to_svm/introduction_to_svm.html`.

Classifying with SVMs

After training the model, we have a line of maximum margin. The classification of new samples is then simply asking the question: *does it fall above the line, or below it?* If it falls above the line, it is predicted as one class. If it is below the line, it is predicted as the other class.

For multiple classes, we create multiple SVMs—each a binary classifier. We then connect them using any one of a variety of strategies. A basic strategy is to create a **one-versus-all** classifier for each class, where we train using two classes—the given class and all other samples. We do this for each class and run each classifier on a new sample, choosing the best match from each of these. This process is performed automatically in most SVM implementations.

We saw two parameters in our previous code: `C` and the `kernel`. We will cover the `kernel` parameter in the next section, but the `C` parameter is an important parameter for fitting SVMs. The `C` parameter relates to how much the classifier should aim to predict all training samples correctly, at the risk of overfitting. Selecting a higher `C` value will find a line of separation with a smaller margin, aiming to classify all training samples correctly. Choosing a lower `C` value will result in a line of separation with a larger margin—even if that means that some training samples are incorrectly classified. In this case, a lower `C` value presents a lower chance of overfitting, at the risk of choosing a generally poorer line of separation.

One limitation with SVMs (in their basic form) is that they only separate data that is linearly separable. What happens if the data isn't? For that problem, we use kernels.

Kernels

When the data cannot be separated linearly, the trick is to embed it onto a higher dimensional space. What this means, with a lot of hand-waving about the details, is to add pseudo-features until the data is linearly separable (which will always happen if you add enough of the right kinds of features).

The trick is that we often compute the inner-produce of the samples when finding the best line to separate the dataset. Given a function that uses the dot product, we effectively manufacture new features without having to actually define those new features. This is handy because we don't know what those features were going to be anyway. We now define a `kernel` as a function that itself is the dot product of the function of two samples from the dataset, rather than based on the samples (and the made-up features) themselves.

We can now compute what that dot product is (or approximate it) and then just use that.

There are a number of kernels in common use. The `linear` kernel is the most straightforward and is simply the dot product of the two sample feature vectors, the weight feature, and a bias value. There is also a polynomial kernel, which raises the dot product to a given degree (for instance, 2). Others include the Gaussian (`rbf`) and Sigmoidal functions. In our previous code sample, we tested between the `linear` kernel and the `rbf` kernels.

The end result from all this derivation is that these kernels effectively define a distance between two samples that is used in the classification of new samples in SVMs. In theory, any distance could be used, although it may not share the same characteristics that enable easy optimization of the SVM training.

In scikit-learn's implementation of SVMs, we can define the `kernel` parameter to change which kernel function is used in computations, as we saw in the previous code sample.

Character n-grams

We saw how function words can be used as features to predict the author of a document. Another feature type is **character n-grams**. An n-gram is a sequence of `n` objects, where `n` is a value (for text, generally between 2 and 6). *Word n-grams* have been used in many studies, usually relating to the topic of the documents. However, character n-grams have proven to be of high quality for authorship attribution.

Character n-grams are found in text documents by representing the document as a sequence of characters. These n-grams are then extracted from this sequence and a model is trained. There are a number of different models for this, but a standard one is very similar to the bag-of-words model we have used earlier.

For each distinct n-gram in the training corpus, we create a feature for it. An example of an n-gram is `<e t>`, which is the letter *e*, a space, and then the letter *t* (the angle brackets are used to denote the start and end of the n-gram and aren't part of it). We then train our model using the frequency of each n-gram in the training documents and train the classifier using the created feature matrix.

> Character n-grams are defined in many ways. For instance, some applications only choose within-word characters, ignoring whitespace and punctuation. Some use this information (like our implementation in this chapter).

A common theory for why character n-grams work is that people more typically write words they can easily say and character n-grams (at least when n is between 2 and 6) are a good approximation for phonemes—the sounds we make when saying words. In this sense, using character n-grams approximates the sounds of words, which approximates your writing style. This is a common pattern when creating new features. First we have a theory on what concepts will impact the end result (authorship style) and then create features to approximate or measure those concepts.

A main feature of a character n-gram matrix is that it is sparse and increases in sparsity with higher n-values quite quickly. For an *n*-value of 2, approximately 75 percent of our feature matrix is zeros. For an *n*-value of 5, over 93 percent is zeros. This is typically less sparse than a word n-gram matrix of the same type though and shouldn't cause many issues using a classifier that is used for word-based classifications.

Extracting character n-grams

We are going to use our `CountVectorizer` class to extract character n-grams. To do that, we set the `analyzer` parameter and specify a value for *n* to extract n-grams with.

The implementation in scikit-learn uses an n-gram *range*, allowing you to extract n-grams of multiple sizes at the same time. We won't delve into different *n*-values in this experiment, so we just set the values the same. To extract n-grams of size 3, you need to specify (3, 3) as the value for the n-gram range.

We can reuse the grid search from our previous code. All we need to do is specify the new feature extractor in a new pipeline:

```
pipeline = Pipeline([('feature_extraction', CountVectorizer(analyzer='
char', ngram_range=(3, 3))),
                     ('classifier', grid)
                     ])
scores = cross_val_score(pipeline, documents, classes, scoring='f1')
print("Score: {:.3f}".format(np.mean(scores)))
```

There is a lot of implicit overlap between function words and character n-grams, as character sequences in function words are more likely to appear. However, the actual features are very different and character n-grams capture punctuation, which function words do not. For example, a character n-gram includes the full stop at the end of a sentence, while a function word-based method would only use the preceding word itself.

Using the Enron dataset

Enron was one of the largest energy companies in the world in the late 1990s, reporting revenue over $100 billion. It has over 20,000 staff and—as of the year 2000—there seemed to be no indications that something was very wrong.

In 2001, the *Enron Scandal* occurred, where it was discovered that Enron was undertaking systematic, fraudulent accounting practices. This fraud was deliberate, wide-ranging across the company, and for significant amounts of money. After this was publicly discovered, its share price dropped from more than $90 in 2000 to less than $1 in 2001. Enron shortly filed for bankruptcy in a mess that would take more than 5 years to finally be resolved.

As part of the investigation into Enron, the Federal Energy Regulatory Commission in the United States made more than 600,000 e-mails publicly available. Since then, this dataset has been used for everything from social network analysis to fraud analysis. It is also a great dataset for authorship analysis, as we are able to extract e-mails from the sent folder of individual users. This allows us to create a dataset much larger than many previous datasets.

Accessing the Enron dataset

The full set of Enron e-mails is available at `https://www.cs.cmu.edu/~./enron/`.

The full dataset is 423 MB in a compression format called `gzip`. If you don't have a Linux-based machine to decompress (unzip) this file, get an alternative program, such as 7-zip (`http://www.7-zip.org/`).

Download the full corpus and decompress it into your data folder. By default, this will decompress into a folder called `enron_mail_20110402`.

As we are looking for authorship information, we only want the e-mails we can attribute to a specific author. For that reason, we will look in each user's sent folder—that is, e-mails they have sent.

In the Notebook, setup the data folder for the Enron dataset:

```
enron_data_folder = os.path.join(os.path.expanduser("~"), "Data",
  "enron_mail_20110402", "maildir")
```

Creating a dataset loader

We can now create a function that will choose a couple of authors at random and return each of the emails in their sent folder. Specifically, we are looking for the payloads—that is, the content rather than the e-mails themselves. For that, we will need an e-mail parser. The code is as follows:

```
from email.parser import Parser
p = Parser()
```

We will be using this later to extract the payloads from the e-mail files that are in the data folder.

We will be choosing authors at random, so we will be using a random state that allows us to replicate the results if we want:

```
from sklearn.utils import check_random_state
```

With our data loading function, we are going to have a lot of options. Most of these ensure that our dataset is relatively balanced. Some authors will have thousands of e-mails in their sent mail, while others will have only a few dozen. We limit our search to only authors with at least 10 e-mails using `min_docs_author` and take a maximum of 100 e-mails from each author using the `max_docs_author` parameter. We also specify how many authors we want to get—10 by default using the `num_authors` parameter. The code is as follows:

```
def get_enron_corpus(num_authors=10, data_folder=data_folder,
                     min_docs_author=10, max_docs_author=100,
                     random_state=None):
    random_state = check_random_state(random_state)
```

Next, we list all of the folders in the data folder, which are separate e-mail addresses of Enron employees. We when randomly shuffle them, allowing us to choose a new set every time the code is run. Remember that setting the random state will allow us to replicate this result:

```
    email_addresses = sorted(os.listdir(data_folder))
    random_state.shuffle(email_addresses)
```

It may seem odd that we sort the e-mail addresses, only to shuffle them around. The `os.listdir` function doesn't always return the same results, so we sort it first to get some stability. We then shuffle using a random state, which means our shuffling can reproduce a past result if needed.

We then set up our documents and class lists. We also create an `author_num`, which will tell us which class to use for each new author. We won't use the `enumerate` trick we used earlier, as it is possible that we won't choose some authors. For example, if an author doesn't have 10 sent e-mails, we will not use it. The code is as follows:

```
    documents = []
    classes = []
    author_num = 0
```

We are also going to record which authors we used and which class number we assigned to them. This isn't for the data mining, but will be used in the visualization so we can identify the authors more easily. The dictionary will simply map e-mail usernames to class values. The code is as follows:

```
    authors = {}
```

Next, we iterate through each of the e-mail addresses and look for all subfolders with "sent" in the name, indicating a sent mail box. The code is as follows:

```
for user in email_addresses:
  users_email_folder = os.path.join(data_folder, user)
  mail_folders = [os.path.join(users_email_folder,
    subfolder) for subfolder in os.listdir(users_email_folder)
                        if "sent" in subfolder]
```

We then get each of the e-mails that are in this folder. I've surrounded this call in a try-except block, as some of the authors have subdirectories in their sent mail. We could use some more detailed code to get all of these e-mails, but for now we will just continue and ignore these users. The code is as follows:

```
try:
  authored_emails = [open(os.path.join(mail_folder,
    email_filename), encoding='cp1252').read()
  for mail_folder in mail_folders
  for email_filename in os.listdir(mail_folder)]
except IsADirectoryError:
    continue
```

Next we check we have at least 10 e-mails (or whatever `min_docs_author` is set to):

```
if len(authored_emails) < min_docs_author:
    continue
```

As a next step, if we have too many e-mails from this author, only take the first 100 (from `max_docs_author`):

```
if len(authored_emails) > max_docs_author:
    authored_emails = authored_emails[:max_docs_author]
```

Next, we parse the e-mail to extract the contents. We aren't interested in the headers—the author has little control over what goes here, so it doesn't make for good data for authorship analysis. We then add those e-mail payloads to our dataset:

```
contents = [p.parsestr(email)._payload for email in
  authored_emails]
documents.extend(contents)
```

We then append a class value for this author, for each of the e-mails we added to our dataset:

```
classes.extend([author_num] * len(authored_emails))
```

We then record the class number we used for this author and *then* increment it:

```
            authors[user] = author_num
            author_num += 1
```

We then check if we have enough authors and, if so, we break out of the loop to return the dataset. The code is as follows:

```
            if author_num >= num_authors or author_num >=
              len(email_addresses):
                break
```

We then return the datatset's documents and classes, along with our author mapping. The code is as follows:

```
        return documents, np.array(classes), authors
```

Outside this function, we can now get a dataset by making the following function call. We are going to use a random state of 14 here (as always in this book), but you can try other values or set it to *none* to get a random set each time the function is called:

```
documents, classes, authors = get_enron_corpus(data_folder=enron_data_
folder, random_state=14)
```

If you have a look at the dataset, there is still a further preprocessing set we need to undertake. Our e-mails are quite messy, but one of the worst bits (from a data analysis perspective) is that these e-mails contain writings from other authors, in the form of attached replies. Take the following e-mail, which is `documents[100]`, for instance:

I am disappointed on the timing but I understand. Thanks. Mark

-----Original Message-----

From: Greenberg, Mark

Sent: Friday, September 28, 2001 4:19 PM

To: Haedicke, Mark E.

Subject: Web Site

Mark -

FYI - I have attached below a screen shot of the proposed new look and feel for the site. We have a couple of tweaks to make, but I believe this is a much cleaner look than what we have now.

This document contains another e-mail attached to the bottom as a reply, a common e-mail pattern. The first part of the e-mail is from *Mark Haedicke*, while the second is a previous e-mail written to Mark Haedicke by *Mark Greenberg*. Only the preceding text (the first instance of **-----Original Message-----**) could be attributed to the author, and this is the only bit we are actually worried about.

Extracting this information generally is not easy. E-mail is a notoriously badly used format. Different e-mail clients add their own headers, define replies in different ways, and just do things however they want. It is really surprising that e-mail works at all in the current environment.

There are some commonly used patterns that we can look for. The `quotequail` package looks for these and can find the new part of the e-mail, discarding replies and other information.

You can install `quotequail` using pip: `pip3 install quotequail`.

We are going to write a simple function to wrap the `quotequail` functionality, allowing us to easily call it on all of our documents. First we import `quotequail` and set up the function definition:

```
import quotequail
def remove_replies(email_contents):
```

Next, we use `quotequail` to unwrap the e-mail, which returns a dictionary containing the different parts of the e-mail. The code is as follows:

```
    r = quotequail.unwrap(email_contents)
```

In some cases, `r` can be none. This happens if the e-mail couldn't be parsed. In this case, we just return the full e-mail contents. This kind of messy solution is often necessary when working with real world datasets. The code is as follows:

```
    if r is None:
        return email_contents
```

The actual part of the e-mail we are interested in is called (by `quotequail`) the `text_top`. If this exists, we return this as our interesting part of the e-mail. The code is as follows:

```
    if 'text_top' in r:
        return r['text_top']
```

If it doesn't exist, `quotequail` couldn't find it. It is possible it found other text in the e-mail. If that exists, we return only that text. The code is as follows:

```
        elif 'text' in r:
            return r['text']
```

Finally, if we couldn't get a result, we just return the e-mail contents, hoping they offer some benefit to our data analysis:

```
        return email_contents
```

We can now preprocess all of our documents by running this function on each of them:

```
documents = [remove_replies(document) for document in documents]
```

Our preceding e-mail sample is greatly clarified now and contains only the e-mail written by *Mark Greenberg*:

I am disappointed on the timing but I understand. Thanks. Mark

Putting it all together

We can use the existing parameter space and classifier from our previous experiments—all we need to do is refit it on our new data. By default, training in scikit-learn is done from scratch—subsequent calls to `fit()` will discard any previous information.

There is a class of algorithms called online learning that update the training with new samples and don't restart their training each time. We will see online learning in action later in this book, including the next chapter, *Chapter 10, Clustering News Articles*.

As before, we can compute our scores by using `cross_val_score` and print the results. The code is as follows:

```
scores = cross_val_score(pipeline, documents, classes, scoring='f1')
print("Score: {:.3f}".format(np.mean(scores)))
```

The result is 0.523, which is a reasonable result for such a messy dataset. Adding more data (such as increasing `max_docs_author` in the dataset loading) can improve these results.

Evaluation

It is generally never a good idea to base an assessment on a single number. In the case of the f-score, it is usually more robust than *tricks* that give good scores despite not being useful. An example of this is accuracy. As we said in our previous chapter, a spam classifier could predict everything as being spam and get over 80 percent accuracy, although that solution is not useful at all. For that reason, it is usually worth going more in-depth on the results.

To start with, we will look at the confusion matrix, as we did in *Chapter 8, Beating CAPTCHAs with Neural Networks*. Before we can do that, we need to predict a testing set. The previous code uses `cross_val_score`, which doesn't actually give us a trained model we can use. So, we will need to refit one. To do that, we need training and testing subsets:

```
from sklearn.cross_validation import train_test_split
training_documents, testing_documents, y_train, y_test =
train_test_split(documents, classes, random_state=14)
```

Next, we fit the pipeline to our training documents and create our predictions for the testing set:

```
pipeline.fit(training_documents, y_train)
y_pred = pipeline.predict(testing_documents)
```

At this point, you might be wondering what the best combination of parameters actually was. We can extract this quite easily from our grid search object (which is the `classifier` step of our pipeline):

```
print(pipeline.named_steps['classifier'].best_params_)
```

The results give you all of the parameters for the classifier. However, most of the parameters are the defaults that we didn't touch. The ones we did search for were `C` and `kernel`, which were set to `1` and `linear`, respectively.

Now we can create a confusion matrix:

```
from sklearn.metrics import confusion_matrix
cm = confusion_matrix(y_pred, y_test)
cm = cm / cm.astype(np.float).sum(axis=1)
```

Next we get our authors so that we can label the axis correctly. For this purpose, we use the `authors` dictionary that our Enron dataset loaded. The code is as follows:

```
sorted_authors = sorted(authors.keys(), key=lambda x:authors[x])
```

Finally, we show the confusion matrix using `matplotlib`. The only changes from the last chapter are highlighted below; just replace the letter labels with the authors from this chapter's experiments:

```
%matplotlib inline
from matplotlib import pyplot as plt
plt.figure(figsize=(10,10))
plt.imshow(cm, cmap='Blues')
tick_marks = np.arange(len(sorted_authors))
plt.xticks(tick_marks, sorted_authors)
plt.yticks(tick_marks, sorted_authors)
plt.ylabel('Actual')
plt.xlabel('Predicted')
plt.show()
```

The results are shown in the following figure:

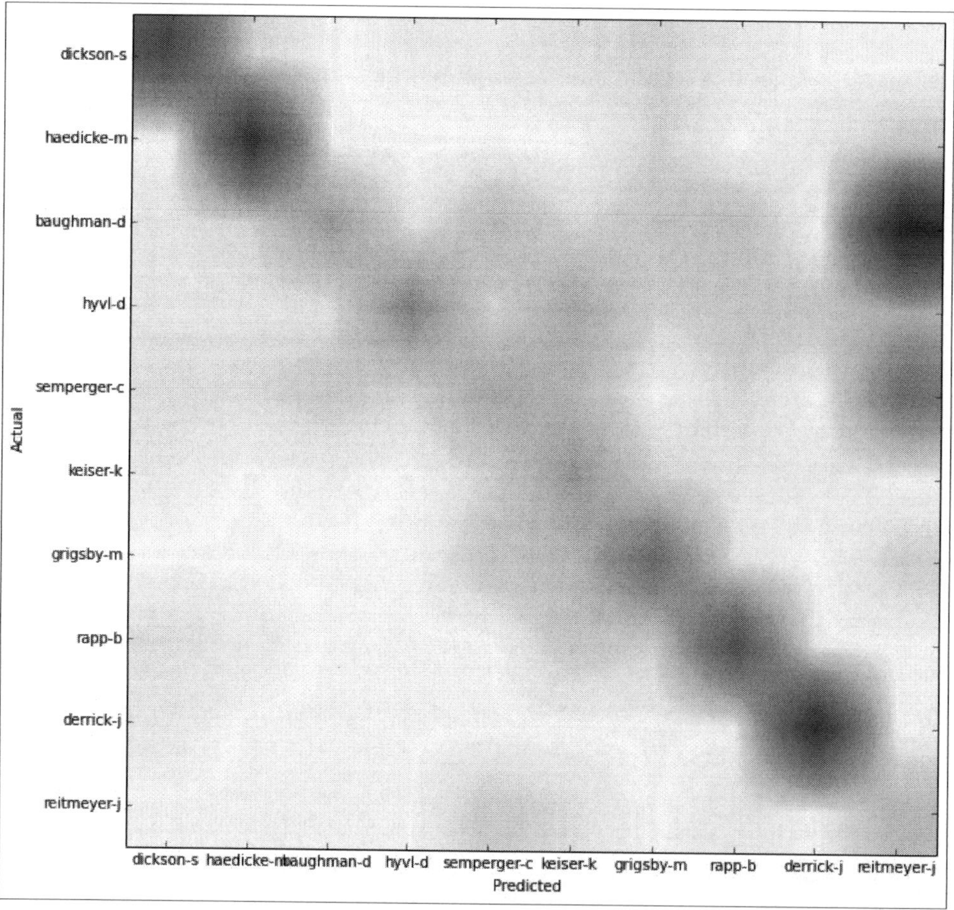

We can see that authors are predicted correctly in most cases—there is a clear diagonal line with high values. There are some large sources of error though (darker values are larger): e-mails from user `baughman-d` are typically predicted as being from `reitmeyer-j` for instance.

Summary

In this chapter, we looked at the text mining-based problem of authorship attribution. To perform this, we analyzed two types of features: function words and character n-grams. For function words, we were able to use the bag-of-words model—simply restricted to a set of words we chose beforehand. This gave us the frequencies of only those words. For character n-grams, we used a very similar workflow using the same class. However, we changed the analyzer to look at characters and not words. In addition, we used n-grams that are sequences of *n* tokens in a row—in our case characters. Word n-grams are also worth testing in some applications, as they can provide a cheap way to get the context of how a word is used.

For classification, we used SVMs that optimize a line of separation between the classes based on the idea of finding the maximum margin. Anything above the line is one class and anything below the line is another class. As with the other classification tasks we have considered, we have a set of samples (in this case, our documents).

We then used a very messy dataset, the Enron e-mails. This dataset contains lots of artefacts and other issues. This resulted in a lower accuracy than the books dataset, which was much cleaner. However, we were able to choose the correct author more than half the time, out of 10 possible authors.

In the next chapter, we consider what we can do if we don't have target classes. This is called unsupervised learning, an exploratory problem rather than a prediction problem. We also continue to deal with messy text-based datasets.

10

Clustering News Articles

In most of the previous chapters, we performed data mining knowing what we were looking for. Our use of target classes allowed us to learn how our variables model those targets during the training phase. This type of learning, where we have targets to train against, is called **supervised learning**. In this chapter, we consider what we do without those targets. This is **unsupervised learning** and is much more of an exploratory task. Rather than wanting to classify with our model, the goal in unsupervised learning is more about exploring the data to find insights.

In this chapter, we look at clustering news articles to find trends and patterns in the data. We look at how we can extract data from different websites using a link aggregation website to show a variety of news stories.

The key concepts covered in this chapter include:

- Obtaining text from arbitrary websites
- Using the reddit API to collect interesting news stories
- Cluster analysis for unsupervised data mining
- Extracting topics from documents
- Online learning for updating a model without retraining it
- Cluster ensembling to combine different models

Obtaining news articles

In this chapter, we will build a system that takes a live feed of news articles and groups them together, where the groups have similar topics. You could run the system over several weeks (or longer) to see how trends change over that time.

Our system will start with the popular link aggregation website **reddit**, which stores lists of links to other websites, as well as a comments section for discussion. Links on reddit are broken into several categories of links, called **subreddits**. There are subreddits devoted to particular TV shows, funny images, and many other things. What we are interested in is the subreddits for news. We will use the `/r/worldnews` subreddit in this chapter, but the code should work with any other subreddit.

In this chapter, our goal is to download popular stories, and then cluster them to see any major themes or concepts that occur. This will give us an insight into the popular focus, without having to manually analyze hundreds of individual stories.

Using a Web API to get data

We have used web-based APIs to extract data in several of our previous chapters. For instance, in *Chapter 7, Discovering Accounts to Follow Using Graph Mining*, we used Twitter's API to extract data. Collecting data is a critical part of the data mining pipeline, and web-based APIs are a fantastic way to collect data on a variety of topics.

There are three things you need to consider when using a web-based API for collecting data: authorization methods, rate limiting, and API endpoints.

Authorization methods allow the data provider to know who is collecting the data, in order to ensure that they are being appropriately rate-limited and that data access can be tracked. For most websites, a personal account is often enough to start collecting data, but some websites will ask you to create a formal developer account to get this access.

Rate limiting is applied to data collection, particularly free services. It is important to be aware of the rules when using APIs, as they can and do change from website to website. Twitter's API limit is 180 requests per 15 minutes (depending on the particular API call). Reddit, as we will see later, allows 30 requests per minute. Other websites impose daily limits, while others limit on a per-second basis. Even within websites, there are drastic differences for different API calls. For example, Google Maps has smaller limits and different API limits per-resource, with different allowances for the number of requests per hour.

If you find you are creating an app or running an experiment that needs more requests and faster responses, most API providers have commercial plans that allow for more calls.

API Endpoints are the actual URLs that you use to extract information. These vary from website to website. Most often, web-based APIs will follow a **RESTful** interface (short for **Representational State Transfer**). RESTful interfaces often use the same actions that HTTP does: GET, POST, and DELETE are the most common. For instance, to retrieve information on a resource, we might use the following API endpoint: `www.dataprovider.com/api/resource_type/resource_id/`.

To *get* the information, we just send a HTTP GET request to this URL. This will return information on the resource with the given type and ID. Most APIs follow this structure, although there are some differences in the implementation. Most websites with APIs will have them appropriately documented, giving you details of all the APIs that you can retrieve.

First, we set up the parameters to connect to the service. To do this, you will need a developer key for reddit. In order to get this key, log in to the `https://www.reddit.com/login` website and go to `https://www.reddit.com/prefs/apps`. From here, click on **are you a developer? create an app...** and fill out the form, setting the type as *script*. You will get your client ID and a secret, which you can add to a new IPython Notebook:

```
CLIENT_ID = "<Enter your Client ID here>"
CLIENT_SECRET = "<Enter your Client Secret here>"
```

Reddit also asks that, when you use their API, you set the user agent to a unique string that includes your username. Create a user agent string that uniquely identifies your application. I used the name of the book, `chapter 10`, and a version number of 0.1 to create my user agent, but it can be any string you like. Note that not doing this will result in your connection being heavily rate-limited:

```
USER_AGENT = "python:<your unique user agent> (by /u/<your reddit
username>)"
```

In addition, you will need to log into reddit using your username and password. If you don't have one already, sign up for a new one (it is free and you don't need to verify with personal information either).

You will need your password to complete the next step, so be careful before sharing your code to others to remove it. If you don't put your password in, set it to `none` and you will be prompted to enter it. However, due to the way IPython Notebooks work, you'll need to enter it into the command-line terminal that started the IPython server, not the notebook itself. If you can't do this, you'll need to set it in the script. The developers of the IPython Notebook are working on a plugin to fix this, but it was not yet available at the time of writing.

Now let's create the username and password:

```
USERNAME = "<your reddit username>"
PASSWORD = "<your reddit password>"
```

Next, we are going to create a function to log with this information. The reddit login API will return a token that you can use for further connections, which will be the result of this function. The code is as follows:

```
def login(username, password):
```

First, if you don't want to add your password to the script, you can set it to `None` and you will be prompted, as explained previously. The code is as follows:

```
    if password is None:
        password = getpass.getpass("Enter reddit password for user {}:
".format(username))
```

It is very important that you set the user agent to a unique value, or your connection might be severely restricted. The code is as follows:

```
    headers = {"User-Agent": USER_AGENT}
```

Next, we set up a HTTP authorization object to allow us to login at reddit's servers:

```
    client_auth = requests.auth.HTTPBasicAuth(CLIENT_ID, CLIENT_
SECRET)
```

To login, we make a POST request to the `access_token` endpoint. The data we send is our username and password, along with the grant type that is set to `password` for this example:

```
    post_data = {"grant_type": "password", "username": username,
"password": password}
```

Finally, we use the `requests` library to make the login request (this is done via a HTTP POST request) and return the result, which is a dictionary of values. One of these values is the token we will need for future requests. The code is as follows:

```
    response = requests.post("https://www.reddit.com/api/v1/access_
token", auth=client_auth, data=post_data, headers=headers)
    return response.json()
```

We can call now our function to get a token:

```
token = login(USERNAME, PASSWORD)
```

The token object is just a dictionary, but it contains the `access_token` string that we will pass with future requests. It also contains other information such as the scope of the token (which would be everything) and the time in which it expires—for example:

```
{'access_token': '<semi-random string>',  'expires_in': 3600,
'scope': '*',  'token_type': 'bearer'}
```

Reddit as a data source

Reddit (`www.reddit.com`) is a link aggregation website used by millions worldwide, although the English versions are US-centric. Any user can contribute a link to a website they found interesting, along with a title for that link. Other users can then *upvote* it, indicating that they liked the link, or *downvote* it, indicating they didn't like the link. The highest voted links are moved to the top of the page, while the lower ones are not shown. Older links are removed over time (depending on how many upvotes it has). Users who have stories upvoted earn points called *karma*, providing an incentive to submit only good stories.

Reddit also allows nonlink content, called self-posts. These contain a title and some text that the submitter enters. These are used for asking questions and starting discussions, but do not count towards a person's karma. For this chapter, we will be considering only link-based posts, and not comment-based posts.

Posts are separated into different sections of the website called *subreddits*. A subreddit is a collection of posts that are related. When a user submits a link to reddit, they choose which subreddit it goes into. Subreddits have their own administrators, and have their own rules about what is valid content for that subreddit.

By default, posts are sorted by *Hot*, which is a function of the age of a post, the number of upvotes, and the number of downvotes it has received. There is also *New*, which just gives you the most recently posted stories (and therefore contains lots of spam and bad posts), and *Top*, which is the highest voted stories for a given time period. In this chapter, we will be using *Hot*, which will give us recent, higher-quality stories (there really are a lot of poor-quality links in *New*).

Using the token we previously created, we can now obtain sets of links from a subreddit. To do that, we will use the `/r/<subredditname>` API endpoint that, by default, returns the Hot stories. We will use the `/r/worldnews` subreddit:

```
subreddit = "worldnews"
```

The URL for the previous end-point lets us create the full URL, which we can set using string formatting:

```
url = "https://oauth.reddit.com/r/{}".format(subreddit)
```

Next, we need to set the headers. This is needed for two reasons: to allow us to use the authorization token we received earlier and to set the user agent to stop our requests from being heavily restricted. The code is as follows:

```
headers = {"Authorization": "bearer {}".format(token['access_token']),
           "User-Agent": USER_AGENT}
```

Then, as before, we use the `requests` library to make the call, ensuring that we set the headers:

```
response = requests.get(url, headers=headers)
```

Calling `json()` on this will result in a Python dictionary containing the information returned by Reddit. It will contain the top 25 results from the given subreddit. We can get the title by iterating over the stories in this response. The stories themselves are stored under the dictionary's `data` key. The code is as follows:

```
for story in result['data']['children']:
    print(story['data']['title'])
```

Getting the data

Our dataset is going to consist of posts from the Hot list of the `/r/worldnews` subreddit. We saw in the previous section how to connect to reddit and how to download links. To put it all together, we will create a function that will extract the titles, links, and score for each item in a given subreddit.

We will iterate through the subreddit, getting a maximum of 100 stories at a time. We can also do pagination to get more results. We can read a large number of pages before reddit will stop us, but we will limit it to 5 pages.

As our code will be making repeated calls to an API, it is important to remember to rate-limit our calls. To do so, we will need the `sleep` function:

```
from time import sleep
```

Our function will accept a subreddit name and an authorization token. We will also accept a number of pages to read, although we will set a default of 5:

```
def get_links(subreddit, token, n_pages=5):
```

We then create a list to store the stories in:

```
stories = []
```

We saw in *Chapter 7, Discovering Accounts to Follow Using Graph Mining*, how pagination works for the Twitter API. We get a cursor with our returned results, which we send with our request. Twitter will then use this cursor to get the next page of results. The reddit API does almost exactly the same thing, except it calls the parameter `after`. We don't need it for the first page, so we initially set it to `none`. We will set it to a meaningful value after our first page of results. The code is as follows:

```
after = None
```

We then iterate for the number of pages we want to return:

```
for page_number in range(n_pages):
```

Inside the loop, we initialize our URL structure as we did before:

```
headers = {"Authorization": "bearer
{}".format(token['access_token']),
    "User-Agent": USER_AGENT}
url = "https://oauth.reddit.com/r/{}?limit=100".
    format(subreddit)
```

From the second loop onwards, we need to set the `after` parameter (otherwise, we will just get multiple copies of the same page of results). This value will be set in the previous iteration of the loop—the first loop sets the after parameter for the second loop and so on. If present, we append it to the end of our URL, telling reddit to get us the next page of data. The code is as follows:

```
if after:
    url += "&after={}".format(after)
```

Then, as before, we use the requests library to make the call and turn the result into a Python dictionary using `json()`:

```
response = requests.get(url, headers=headers)
result = response.json()
```

This result will give us the `after` parameter for the next time the loop iterates, which we can now set as follows:

```
after = result['data']['after']
```

We then sleep for 2 seconds to avoid exceeding the API limit:

```
sleep(2)
```

As the last action inside the loop, we get each of the stories from the returned result and add them to our `stories` list. We don't need all of the data—we only get the title, URL, and score. The code is as follows:

```
        stories.extend([(story['data']['title'], story['data']['url'],
story['data']['score'])
                     for story in result['data']['children']])
```

Finally (and outside the loop), we return all the stories we have found:

```
    return stories
```

Calling the `stories` function is a simple case of passing the authorization token and the subreddit name:

```
stories = get_links("worldnews", token)
```

The returned results should contain the title, URL, and 500 stories, which we will now use to extract the actual text from the resulting websites.

Extracting text from arbitrary websites

The links that we get from reddit go to arbitrary websites run by many different organizations. To make it harder, those pages were designed to be read by a human, not a computer program. This can cause a problem when trying to get the actual content/story of those results, as modern websites have a lot going on in the background. JavaScript libraries are called, style sheets are applied, advertisements are loaded using AJAX, extra content is added to sidebars, and various other things are done to make the modern webpage a complex document. These features make the modern Web what it is, but make it difficult to automatically get good information from!

Finding the stories in arbitrary websites

To start with, we will download the full webpage from each of these links and store them in our data folder, under a raw subfolder. We will process these to extract the useful information later on. This caching of results ensures that we don't have to continuously download the websites while we are working. First, we set up the data folder path:

```
import os
data_folder = os.path.join(os.path.expanduser("~"), "Data",
"websites", "raw")
```

We are going to use MD5 hashing to create unique filenames for our articles, so we will import `hashlib` to do that. A `hash` function is a function that converts some input (in our case a string containing the title) into a string that is seemingly random. The same input will always return the same output, but slightly different inputs will return drastically different outputs. It is also impossible to go from a hash value to the original value, making it a one-way function. The code is as follows:

```
import hashlib
```

We are going to simply skip any website downloads that fail. In order to make sure we don't lose too much information doing this, we maintain a simple counter of the number of errors that occur. We are going to suppress any error that occurs, which could result in a systematic problem prohibiting downloads. If this error counter is too high, we can look at what those errors were and try to fix them. For example, if the computer has no internet access, all 500 of the downloads will fail and you should probably fix that before continuing!

If there is no error in the download, zero should be the output:

```
number_errors = 0
```

Next, we iterate through each of our stories:

```
for title, url, score in stories:
```

We then create a unique output filename for our article by hashing the title. Titles in reddit don't need to be unique, which means there is a possibility of two stories having the same title and, therefore, clashing in our dataset. To get our unique filename, we simply hash the URL of the article using the MD5 algorithm. While MD5 is known to have some problems, it is unlikely that a problem (a collision) will occur in our scenario, and we don't need to worry too much even if it does and we don't need to worry too much about collisions if they do occur.

```
    output_filename = hashlib.md5(url.encode()).hexdigest()
    fullpath = os.path.join(data_folder, output_filename + ".txt")
```

Next, we download the actual page and save it to our output folder:

```
    try:
        response = requests.get(url)
        data = response.text
        with open(fullpath, 'w') as outf:
            outf.write(data)
```

If there is an error in obtaining the website, we simply skip this website and keep going. This code will work on 95 percent of websites and that is good enough for our application, as we are looking for general trends and not exactness. Note that sometimes you do care about getting 100 percent of responses, and you should adjust your code to accommodate more errors. The code to get those final 5 to 10 percent of websites will be significantly more complex. We then catch any error that could occur (it is the Internet, lots of things could go wrong), increment our error count, and continue.

```
    except Exception as e:
        number_errors += 1
        print(e)
```

If you find that too many errors occur, change the `print(e)` line to just type `raise` instead. This will cause the exception to be called, allowing you to debug the problem.

Now, we have a bunch of websites in our raw subfolder. After taking a look at these pages (open the created files in a text editor), you can see that the content is there but there are HTML, JavaScript, CSS code, as well as other content. As we are only interested in the story itself, we now need a way to extract this information from these different websites.

Putting it all together

After we get the raw data, we need to find the story in each. There are a few online sources that use data mining to achieve this. You can find them listed in *Appendix A, Next Steps....* It is rarely needed to use such complex algorithms, although you can get better accuracy using them. This is part of data mining—knowing when to use it, and when not to.

First, we get a list of each of the filenames in our raw subfolder:

```
filenames = [os.path.join(data_folder, filename)
             for filename in os.listdir(data_folder)]
```

Next, we create an output folder for the text only versions that we will extract:

```
text_output_folder = os.path.join(os.path.expanduser("~"), "Data",
                                  "websites", "textonly")
```

Next, we develop the code that will extract the text from the files. We will use the `lxml` library to parse the HTML files, as it has a good HTML parser that deals with some badly formed expressions. The code is as follows:

```
from lxml import etree
```

The actual code for extracting text is based on three steps. First, we iterate through each of the nodes in the HTML file and extract the text in it. Second, we skip any node that is JavaScript, styling, or a comment, as this is unlikely to contain information of interest to us. Third, we ensure that the content has at least 100 characters. This is a good baseline, but it could be improved upon for more accurate results.

As we said before, we aren't interested in scripts, styles, or comments. So, we create a list to ignore nodes of those types. Any node that has a type in this list will not be considered as containing the story. The code is as follows:

```
skip_node_types = ["script", "head", "style", etree.Comment]
```

We will now create a function that parses an HTML file into an `lxml etree`, and then we will create another function that parses this tree looking for text. This first function is pretty straightforward; simply open the file and create a tree using the `lxml` library's parsing function for HTML files. The code is as follows:

```
def get_text_from_file(filename):
    with open(filename) as inf:
        html_tree = lxml.html.parse(inf)
    return get_text_from_node(html_tree.getroot())
```

In the last line of that function, we call the `getroot()` function to get the root node of the tree, rather than the full `etree`. This allows us to write our text extraction function to accept any node, and therefore write a recursive function.

This function will call itself on any child nodes to extract the text from them, and then return the concatenation of any child nodes text.

If the node this function is passed doesn't have any child nodes, we just return the text from it. If it doesn't have any text, we just return an empty string. Note that we also check here for our third condition—that the text is at least 100 characters long. The code is as follows:

```
def get_text_from_node(node):
    if len(node) == 0:
        # No children, just return text from this item
        if node.text and len(node.text) > 100:
            return node.text
        else:
            return ""
```

At this point, we know that the node has child nodes, so we recursively call this function on each of those child nodes and then join the results when they return. The code is as follows:

```
    results = (get_text_from_node(child) for child in node
                   if child.tag not in skip_node_types)
    return "\n".join(r for r in results if len(r) > 1)
```

The final condition on the return result stops blank lines being returned (for example, when a node has no children and no text).

We can now run this code on all of the raw HTML pages by iterating through them, calling the text extraction function on each, and saving the results to the text-only subfolder:

```
for filename in os.listdir(data_folder):
    text = get_text_from_file(os.path.join(data_folder, filename))
    with open(os.path.join(text_output_folder, filename), 'w')
      as outf:
        outf.write(text)
```

You can evaluate the results manually by opening each of the files in the text only subfolder and checking their content. If you find too many of the results have nonstory content, try increasing the minimum 100 character limit. If you still can't get good results, or need better results for your application, try the more complex methods listed in *Appendix A, Next Steps....*

Grouping news articles

The aim of this chapter is to discover trends in news articles by clustering, or grouping, them together. To do that, we will use the k-means algorithm, a classic machine-learning algorithm originally developed in 1957.

Clustering is an unsupervised learning technique and we use clustering algorithms for exploring data. Our dataset contains approximately 500 stories, and it would be quite arduous to examine each of those stories individually. Even if we used summary statistics, that is still a lot of data. Using clustering allows us to group similar stories together, and we can explore the themes in each cluster independently.

We use clustering techniques when we don't have a clear set of target classes for our data. In that sense, clustering algorithms have little direction in their learning. They learn according to some function, regardless of the underlying meaning of the data. For this reason, it is critical to choose good features. In supervised learning, if you choose poor features, the learning algorithm can choose to not use those features. For instance, support vector machines will give little weight to features that aren't useful in classification. However, with clustering, all features are used in the final result—even if those features don't provide us with the answer we were looking for.

When performing cluster analysis on real-world data, it is always a good idea to have a sense of what sorts of features will work for your scenario. In this chapter, we will use the bag-of-words model. We are looking for topic-based groups, so we will use topic-based features to model the documents. We know those features work because of the work others have done in supervised versions of our problem. In contrast, if we were to perform an authorship-based clustering, we would use features such as those found in the *Chapter 9, Authorship Attribution* experiment.

The k-means algorithm

The k-means clustering algorithm finds centroids that best represent the data using an iterative process. The algorithm starts with a predefined set of centroids, which are normally data points taken from the training data. The *k* in k-means is the number of centroids to look for and how many clusters the algorithm will find. For instance, setting *k* to *3* will find three clusters in the dataset.

There are two phases to the k-means: assignment and updating.

In the assignment step, we set a label to every sample in the dataset linking it to the nearest centroid. For each sample nearest to centroid 1, we assign the label 1. For each sample nearest to centroid 2, we assign a label 2 and so on for each of the *k* centroids. These labels form the clusters, so we say that each data point with the label 1 is in cluster 1 (at this time only, as assignments can change as the algorithm runs).

In the updating step, we take each of the clusters and compute the centroid, which is the mean of all of the samples in that cluster.

The algorithm then iterates between the assignment step and the updating step; each time the updating step occurs, each of the centroids moves a small amount. This causes the assignments to change slightly, causing the centroids to move a small amount in the next iteration. This repeats until some stopping criterion is reached. It is common to stop after a certain number of iterations, or when the total movement of the centroids is very low. The algorithm can also complete in some scenarios, which means that the clusters are stable—the assignments do not change and neither do the centroids.

In the following figure, k-means was performed over a dataset created randomly, but with three clusters in the data. The stars represent the starting location of the centroids, which were chosen randomly by picking a random sample from the dataset. Over 5 iterations of the k-means algorithm, the centroids move to the locations represented by the triangles.

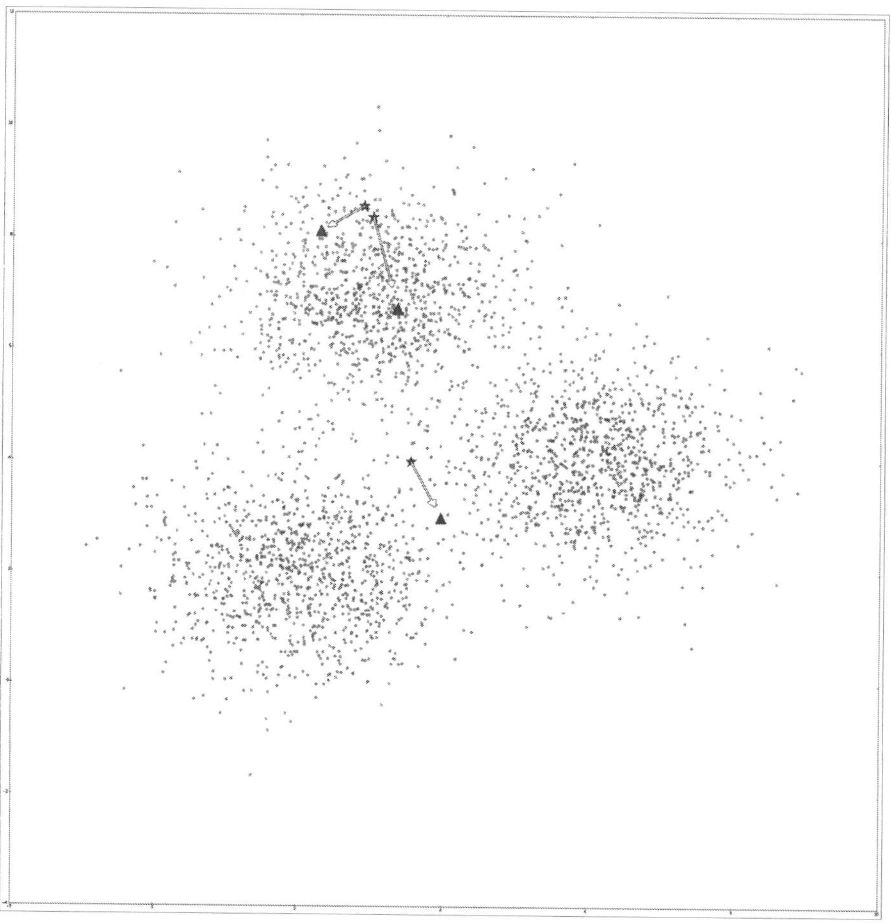

The k-means algorithm is fascinating for its mathematical properties and historical significance. It is an algorithm that (roughly) only has a single parameter, and is quite effective and frequently used, even more than 50 years after its discovery.

There is a k-means algorithm in scikit-learn, which we import from the `cluster` subpackage:

```
from sklearn.cluster import KMeans
```

We also import the `CountVectorizer` class's close cousin, `TfidfVectorizer`. This vectorizer applies a weighting to each term's counts, depending on how many documents it appears in. Terms that appear in many documents are weighted lower (by dividing the value by the log of the number of documents it appears in). For many text mining applications, using this type of weighting scheme can improve performance quite reliably. The code is as follows:

```
from sklearn.feature_extraction.text import TfidfVectorizer
```

We then set up our pipeline for our analysis. This has two steps. The first is to apply our vectorizer, and the second is to apply our k-means algorithm. The code is as follows:

```
from sklearn.pipeline import Pipeline
n_clusters = 10
pipeline = Pipeline([('feature_extraction', TfidfVectorizer(max_
df=0.4)),
                     ('clusterer', KMeans(n_clusters=n_clusters))
                     ])
```

The `max_df` parameter is set to a low value of 0.4, which says *ignore any word that occurs in more than 40 percent of documents*. This parameter is invaluable for removing function words that give little topic-based meaning on their own.

Removing any word that occurs in more than 40 percent of documents will remove function words, making this type of preprocessing quite useless for the work we saw in *Chapter 9, Authorship Attribution*.

We then fit and predict this pipeline. We have followed this process a number of times in this book so far for classification tasks, but there is a difference here—we do not give the target classes for our dataset to the fit function. This is what makes this an unsupervised learning task! The code is as follows:

```
pipeline.fit(documents)
labels = pipeline.predict(documents)
```

The `labels` variable now contains the cluster numbers for each sample. Samples with the same label are said to belong in the same cluster. It should be noted that the cluster labels themselves are meaningless: clusters 1 and 2 are no more similar than clusters 1 and 3.

We can see how many samples were placed in each cluster using the `Counter` class:

```
from collections import Counter
c = Counter(labels)
for cluster_number in range(n_clusters):
    print("Cluster {} contains {} samples".format(cluster_number,
c[cluster_number]))
```

Many of the results (keeping in mind that your dataset will be quite different to mine) consist of a large cluster with the majority of instances, several medium clusters, and some clusters with only one or two instances. This imbalance is quite normal in many clustering applications.

Evaluating the results

Clustering is mainly an exploratory analysis, and therefore it is difficult to evaluate a clustering algorithm's results effectively. A straightforward way is to evaluate the algorithm based on the criteria the algorithm tries to learn from.

> If you have a test set, you can evaluate clustering against it. For more details, visit `http://nlp.stanford.edu/IR-book/html/htmledition/evaluation-of-clustering-1.html`.

In the case of the k-means algorithm, the criterion that it uses when developing the centroids is to minimize the distance from each sample to its nearest centroid. This is called the inertia of the algorithm and can be retrieved from any `KMeans` instance that has had fit called on it:

```
pipeline.named_steps['clusterer'].inertia_
```

The result on my dataset was 343.94. Unfortunately, this value is quite meaningless by itself, but we can use it to determine how many clusters we should use. In the preceding example, we set `n_clusters` to 10, but is this the best value? The following code runs the k-means algorithm 10 times with each value of `n_clusters` from 2 to 20. For each run, it records the inertia of the result.

We only fit the X matrix once per value of n_clusters to (drastically) improve the speed of this code:

```
inertia_scores = []
n_cluster_values = list(range(2, 20))
for n_clusters in n_cluster_values:
    cur_inertia_scores = []
    X = TfidfVectorizer(max_df=0.4).fit_transform(documents)
    for i in range(10):
        km = KMeans(n_clusters=n_clusters).fit(X)
        cur_inertia_scores.append(km.inertia_)
    inertia_scores.append(cur_inertia_scores)
```

The inertia_scores variable now contains a list of inertia scores for each n_clusters value between 2 and 20. We can plot this to get a sense of how this value interacts with n_clusters:

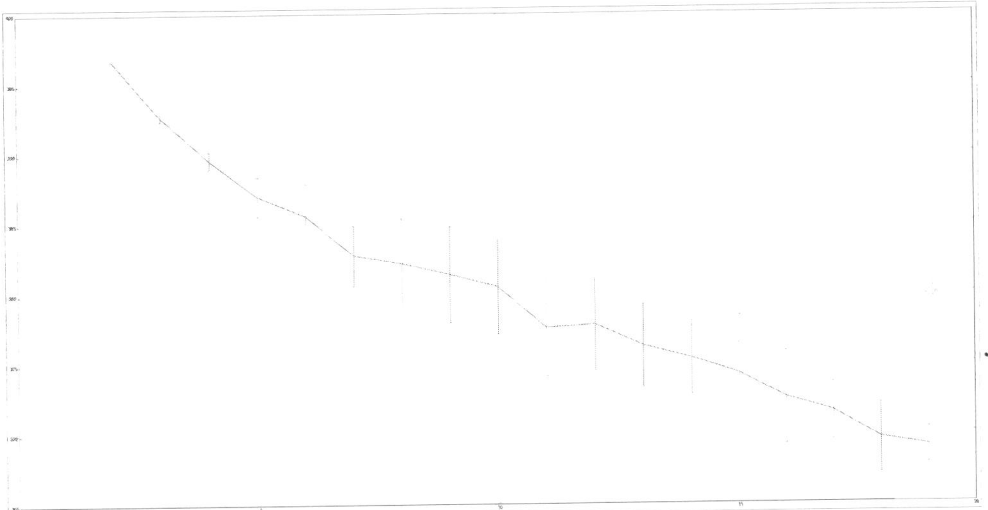

Overall, the value of the inertia should decrease with reducing improvement as the number of clusters improves, which we can broadly see from these results. The increase between values of 6 to 7 is due only to the randomness in selecting the centroids, which directly affect how good the final results are. Despite this, there is a general trend (in these results; your results may vary) that about 6 clusters is the last time a major improvement in the inertia occurred.

After this point, only slight improvements are made to the inertia, although it is hard to be specific about vague criteria such as this. Looking for this type of pattern is called the elbow rule, in that we are looking for an elbow-esque bend in the graph. Some datasets have more pronounced elbows, but this feature isn't guaranteed to even appear (some graphs may be smooth!).

Based on this analysis, we set `n_clusters` to be 6 and then rerun the algorithm:

```
n_clusters = 6
pipeline = Pipeline([('feature_extraction',
  TfidfVectorizer(max_df=0.4)),
                     ('clusterer', KMeans(n_clusters=n_clusters))
                     ])
pipeline.fit(documents)
labels = pipeline.predict(documents)
```

Extracting topic information from clusters

Now we set our sights on the clusters in an attempt to discover the topics in each. We first extract the `term` list from our feature extraction step:

```
terms = pipeline.named_steps['feature_extraction'].get_feature_names()
```

We also set up another counter for counting the size of each of our classes:

```
c = Counter(labels)
```

Iterating over each cluster, we print the size of the cluster as before. It is important to keep in mind the sizes of the clusters when evaluating the results—some of the clusters will only have one sample, and are therefore not indicative of a general trend. The code is as follows:

```
for cluster_number in range(n_clusters):
    print("Cluster {} contains {} samples".format(cluster_number,
c[cluster_number]))
```

Next (and still in the loop), we iterate over the most important terms for this cluster. To do this, we take the five largest values from the centroid, which we get by finding the features that have the highest values in the centroid itself. The code is as follows:

```
    print("  Most important terms")
    centroid = pipeline.named_steps['clusterer'].cluster_centers_
[cluster_number]
    most_important = centroid.argsort()
```

We then print out the most important five terms:

```
        for i in range(5):
```

We use the negation of `i` in this line, as our `most_important` array is sorted with lowest values first:

```
            term_index = most_important[-(i+1)]
```

We then print the rank, term, and score for this value:

```
            print("  {0}) {1} (score: {2:.4f})".format(i+1, terms[term_
    index], centroid[term_index]))
```

The results can be quite indicative of current trends. In my results (March 2015), the clusters correspond to health matters, Middle East tensions, Korean tensions, and Russian affairs. These were the main topics frequenting news around this time—although this has hardly changed for a number of years!

Using clustering algorithms as transformers

As a side note, one interesting property about the k-means algorithm (and any clustering algorithm) is that you can use it for feature reduction. There are many methods to reduce the number of features (or create new features to embed the dataset on), such as Principle Component Analysis, Latent Semantic Indexing, and many others. One issue with many of these algorithms is that they often need lots of computing power.

In the preceding example, the terms list had more than 14,000 entries in it—it is quite a large dataset. Our k-means algorithm transformed these into just six clusters. We can then create a dataset with a much lower number of features by taking the distance to each centroid as a feature. The code is as follows:

To do this, we call the transform function on a KMeans instance. Our pipeline is fit for this purpose, as it has a k-means instance at the end:

```
X = pipeline.transform(documents)
```

This calls the transform method on the final step of the pipeline, which is an instance of k-means. This results in a matrix that has six features and the number of samples is the same as the length of documents.

You can then perform your own second-level clustering on the result, or use it for classification if you have the target values. A possible workflow for this would be to perform some feature selection using the supervised data, use clustering to reduce the number of features to a more manageable number, and then use the results in a classification algorithm such as SVMs.

Clustering ensembles

In *Chapter 3, Predicting Sports Winners with Decision Trees*, we looked at a classification ensemble using the random forest algorithm, which is an ensemble of many low-quality, tree-based classifiers. Ensembling can also be performed using clustering algorithms. One of the key reasons for doing this is to smooth the results from many runs of an algorithm. As we saw before, the results from running k-means are varied, depending on the selection of the initial centroids. Variation can be reduced by running the algorithm many times and then combining the results.

Ensembling also reduces the effects of choosing parameters on the final result. Most clustering algorithms are quite sensitive to the parameter values chosen for the algorithm. Choosing slightly different parameters results in different clusters.

Evidence accumulation

As a basic ensemble, we can first cluster the data many times and record the labels from each run. We then record how many times each pair of samples was clustered together in a new matrix. This is the essence of the **Evidence Accumulation Clustering** (**EAC**) algorithm.

EAC has two major steps. The first step is to cluster the data many times using a lower-level clustering algorithm such as k-means and record the frequency that samples were in the same cluster, in each iteration. This is stored in a `coassociation` matrix. The second step is to perform a cluster analysis on the resulting `coassociation` matrix, which is performed using another type of clustering algorithm called hierarchical clustering. This has an interesting property, as it is mathematically the same as finding a tree that links all the nodes together and removing weak links.

We can create a `coassociation` matrix from an array of labels by iterating over each of the labels and recording where two samples have the same label. We use SciPy's `csr_matrix`, which is a type of sparse matrix:

```
from scipy.sparse import csr_matrix
```

Our function definition takes a set of labels:

```
def create_coassociation_matrix(labels):
```

We then record the rows and columns of each match. We do these in a list. Sparse matrices are commonly just sets of lists recording the positions of nonzero values, and `csr_matrix` is an example of this type of sparse matrix:

```
    rows = []
    cols = []
```

We then iterate over each of the individual labels:

```
    unique_labels = set(labels)
    for label in unique_labels:
```

We look for all samples that have this label:

```
        indices = np.where(labels == label)[0]
```

For each pair of samples with the preceding label, we record the position of both samples in our list. The code is as follows:

```
        for index1 in indices:
            for index2 in indices:
                rows.append(index1)
                cols.append(index2)
```

Outside all loops, we then create the data, which is simply the value 1 for every time two samples were listed together. We get the number of 1 to place by noting how many matches we had in our labels set altogether. The code is as follows:

```
    data = np.ones((len(rows),))
    return csr_matrix((data, (rows, cols)), dtype='float')
```

To get the coassociation matrix from the labels, we simply call this function:

```
C = create_coassociation_matrix(labels)
```

From here, we can add multiple instances of these matrices together. This allows us to combine the results from multiple runs of k-means. Printing out C (just enter C into a new cell and run it) will tell you how many cells have nonzero values in them. In my case, about half of the cells had values in them, as my clustering result had a large cluster (the more even the clusters, the lower the number of nonzero values).

The next step involves the hierarchical clustering of the coassociation matrix. We will do this by finding minimum spanning trees on this matrix and removing edges with a weight lower than a given threshold.

In graph theory, a spanning tree is a set of edges on a graph that connects all of the nodes together. The **Minimum Spanning Tree (MST)** is simply the spanning tree with the lowest total weight. For our application, the nodes in our graph are samples from our dataset, and the edge weights are the number of times those two samples were clustered together—that is, the value from our coassociation matrix.

In the following figure, a MST on a graph of six nodes is shown. Nodes on the graph can be used more than once in the MST. The only criterion for a spanning tree is that all nodes should be connected together.

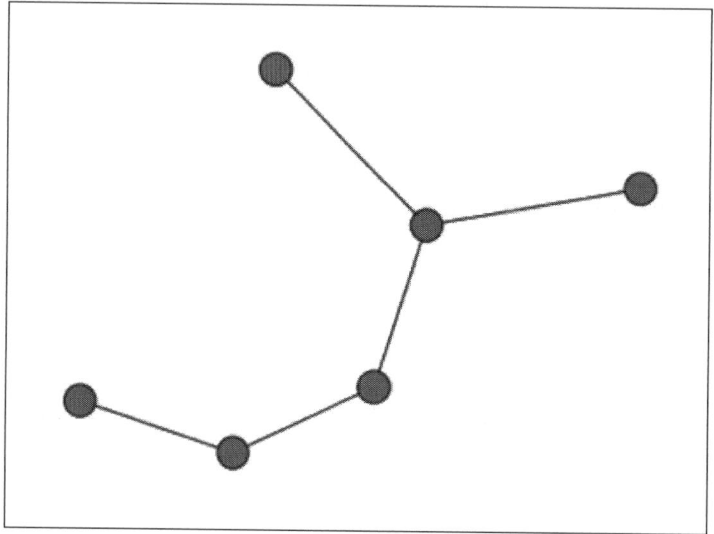

To compute the MST, we use SciPy's `minimum_spanning_tree` function, which is found in the `sparse` package:

```
from scipy.sparse.csgraph import minimum_spanning_tree
```

The `mst` function can be called directly on the sparse matrix returned by our coassociation function:

```
mst = minimum_spanning_tree(C)
```

However, in our coassociation matrix `C`, higher values are indicative of samples that are clustered together more often—a similarity value. In contrast, `minimum_spanning_tree` sees the input as a distance, with higher scores penalized. For this reason, we compute the minimum spanning tree on the negation of the coassociation matrix instead:

```
mst = minimum_spanning_tree(-C)
```

The result from the preceding function is a matrix the same size as the coassociation matrix (the number of rows and columns is the same as the number of samples in our dataset), with only the edges in the MST kept and all others removed.

We then remove any node with a weight less than a predefined threshold. To do this, we iterate over the edges in the MST matrix, removing any that are less than a specific value. We can't test this out with just a single iteration in a coassociation matrix (the values will be either 1 or 0, so there isn't much to work with). So, we will create extra labels first, create the coassociation matrix, and then add the two matrices together. The code is as follows:

```
pipeline.fit(documents)
labels2 = pipeline.predict(documents)
C2 = create_coassociation_matrix(labels2)
C_sum = (C + C2) / 2
```

We then compute the MST and remove any edge that didn't occur in both of these labels:

```
mst = minimum_spanning_tree(-C_sum)
mst.data[mst.data > -1] = 0
```

The threshold we wanted to cut off was any edge not in both clusterings—that is, with a value of 1. However, as we negated the coassociation matrix, we had to negate the threshold value too.

Lastly, we find all of the connected components, which is simply a way to find all of the samples that are still connected by edges after we removed the edges with low weights. The first returned value is the number of connected components (that is, the number of clusters) and the second is the labels for each sample. The code is as follows:

```
from scipy.sparse.csgraph import connected_components
number_of_clusters, labels = connected_components(mst)
```

In my dataset, I obtained eight clusters, with the clusters being approximately the same as before. This is hardly a surprise, given we only used two iterations of k-means; using more iterations of k-means (as we do in the next section) will result in more variance.

How it works

In the k-means algorithm, each feature is used without any regard to its weight. In essence, all features are assumed to be on the same scale. We saw the problems with not scaling features in *Chapter 2, Classifying with scikit-learn Estimators*. The result of this is that k-means is looking for circular clusters, as shown in the following screenshot:

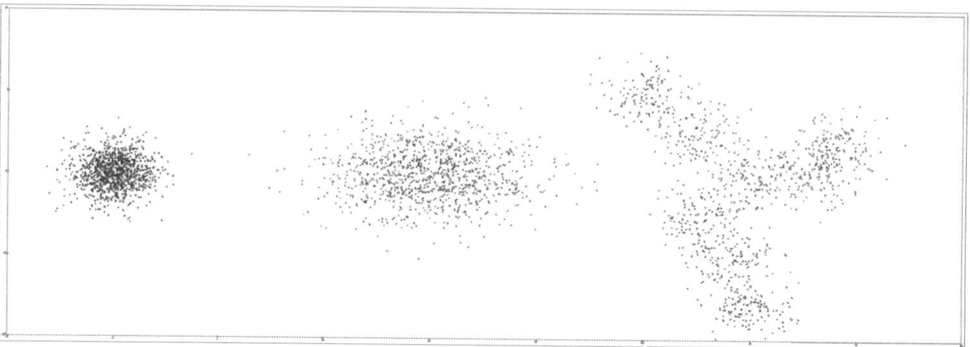

As we can see in the preceding screenshot, not all clusters have this shape. The blue cluster is circular and is of the type that k-means is very good at picking up. The red cluster is an ellipse. The k-means algorithm can pick up clusters of this shape with some feature scaling. The third cluster isn't even convex—it is an odd shape that k-means will have trouble discovering.

The EAC algorithm works by remapping the features onto a new space, in essence turning each run of the k-means algorithm into a transformer using the same principles we saw the previous section using k-means for feature reduction. In this case, though, we only use the actual label and not the distance to each centroid. This is the data that is recorded in the co-association matrix.

The result is that EAC now only cares about how close things are to each other, not how they are placed in the original feature space. There are still issues around unscaled features. Feature scaling is important and should be done anyway (we did it using `tf-idf` in this chapter, which results in feature values having the same scale).

We saw a similar type of transformation in *Chapter 9, Authorship Attribution*, through the use of kernels in SVMs. These transformations are very powerful and should be kept in mind for complex datasets.

Implementation

Putting all this altogether, we can now create a simply clustering algorithm fitting the scikit-learn interface that performs all of the steps in EAC. First, we create the basic structure of the class using scikit-learn's `ClusterMixin`:

```
from sklearn.base import BaseEstimator, ClusterMixin
class EAC(BaseEstimator, ClusterMixin):
```

Our parameters are the number of k-means clusterings to perform in the first step (to create the coassociation matrix), the threshold to cut off at, and the number of clusters to find in each k-means clustering. We set a range of `n_clusters` in order to get lots of variance in our k-means iterations. Generally, in ensemble terms, variance is a good thing; without it, the solution can be no better than the individual clusterings (that said, high variance is not an indicator that the ensemble will be better). The code is as follows:

```
    def __init__(self, n_clusterings=10, cut_threshold=0.5, n_
clusters_range=(3, 10)):
        self.n_clusterings = n_clusterings
        self.cut_threshold = cut_threshold
        self.n_clusters_range = n_clusters_range
```

Next up is the `fit` function for our `EAC` class:

```
    def fit(self, X, y=None):
```

We then perform our low-level clustering using k-means and sum the resulting coassociation matrices from each iteration. We do this in a generator to save memory, creating only the coassociation matrices when we need them. In each iteration of this generator, we create a new single k-means run with our dataset and then create the coassociation matrix for it. We use `sum` to add these together. The code is as follows:

```
        C = sum((create_coassociation_matrix(self._single_
clustering(X))
                 for i in range(self.n_clusterings)))
```

As before, we create the MST, remove any edges less than the given threshold (properly negating values as explained earlier), and find the connected components. As with any `fit` function in scikit-learn, we need to return self in order for the class to work in pipelines effectively. The code is as follows:

```
        mst = minimum_spanning_tree(-C)
        mst.data[mst.data > -self.cut_threshold] = 0
        self.n_components, self.labels_ = connected_components(mst)
        return self
```

We then write the function to cluster a single iteration. To do this, we randomly choose a number of clusters to find using NumPy's `randint` function and our `n_clusters_range` parameter, which sets the range of possible values. We then cluster and predict the dataset using k-means. The return value here will be the labels coming from k-means. The code is as follows:

```
    def _single_clustering(self, X):
        n_clusters = np.random.randint(*self.n_clusters_range)
        km = KMeans(n_clusters=n_clusters)
        return km.fit_predict(X)
```

We can now run this on our previous code by setting up a pipeline as before and using EAC where we previously used a `KMeans` instance as our final stage of the pipeline. The code is as follows:

```
pipeline = Pipeline([('feature_extraction', TfidfVectorizer(max_
df=0.4)),
                     ('clusterer', EAC())
                     ])
```

Online learning

In some cases, we don't have all of the data we need for training before we start our learning. Sometimes, we are waiting for new data to arrive, perhaps the data we have is too large to fit into memory, or we receive extra data after a prediction has been made. In cases like these, online learning is an option for training models over time.

An introduction to online learning

Online learning is the incremental updating of a model as new data arrives. Algorithms that support online learning can be trained on one or a few samples at a time, and updated as new samples arrive. In contrast, algorithms that are not online require access to all of the data at once. The standard k-means algorithm is like this, as are most of the algorithms we have seen so far in this book.

Online versions of algorithms have a means to partially update their model with only a few samples. Neural networks are a standard example of an algorithm that works in an online fashion. As a new sample is given to the neural network, the weights in the network are updated according to a learning rate, which is often a very small value such as 0.01. This means that any single instance only makes a small (but hopefully improving) change to the model.

Neural networks can also be trained in batch mode, where a group of samples are given at once and the training is done in one step. Algorithms are faster in batch mode, but use more memory.

In this same vein, we can slightly update the k-means centroids after a single or small batch of samples. To do this, we apply a learning rate to the centroid movement in the updating step of the k-means algorithm. Assuming that samples are randomly chosen from the population, the centroids should tend to move towards the positions they would have in the standard, offline, and k-means algorithm.

Online learning is related to streaming-based learning; however, there are some important differences. Online learning is capable of reviewing older samples after they have been used in the model, while a streaming-based machine learning algorithm typically only gets *one pass*—that is, one opportunity to look at each sample.

Implementation

The scikit-learn package contains the `MiniBatchKMeans` algorithm, which allows online learning. This class implements a `partial_fit` function, which takes a set of samples and updates the model. In contrast, calling `fit()` will remove any previous training and refit the model only on the new data.

`MiniBatchKMeans` follows the same clustering format as other algorithms in scikit-learn, so creating and using it is much the same as other algorithms.

Therefore, we can create a matrix `X` by extracting features from our dataset using `TfIDFVectorizer`, and then sample from this to incrementally update our model. The code is as follows:

```
vec = TfidfVectorizer(max_df=0.4)
X = vec.fit_transform(documents)
```

We then import `MiniBatchKMeans` and create an instance of it:

```
from sklearn.cluster import MiniBatchKMeans
mbkm = MiniBatchKMeans(random_state=14, n_clusters=3)
```

Next, we will randomly sample from our `X` matrix to simulate data coming in from an external source. Each time we get some data in, we update the model:

```
batch_size = 10
for iteration in range(int(X.shape[0] / batch_size)):
    start = batch_size * iteration
    end = batch_size * (iteration + 1)
    mbkm.partial_fit(X[start:end])
```

We can then get the labels for the original dataset by asking the instance to predict:

```
labels  = mbkm.predict(X)
```

At this stage, though, we can't do this in a pipeline as `TfIDFVectorizer` is not an online algorithm. To get over this, we use a `HashingVectorizer`. The `HashingVectorizer` class is a clever use of hashing algorithms to drastically reduce the memory of computing the bag-of-words model. Instead of recording the feature names, such as words found in documents, we record only hashes of those names. This allows us to *know* our *features* before we even look at the dataset, as it is the set of all possible hashes. This is a very large number, usually of the order 2^18. Using sparse matrices, we can quite easily store and compute even a matrix of this size, as a very large proportion of the matrix will have the value 0.

Currently, the `Pipeline` class doesn't allow for its use in online learning. There are some nuances in different applications that mean there isn't an obvious one-size-fits-all approach that could be implemented. Instead, we can create our own subclass of `Pipeline` that allows us to use it for online learning. We first derive our class from `Pipeline`, as we only need to implement a single function:

```
class PartialFitPipeline(Pipeline):
```

We create a class function `partial_fit`, which accepts an input matrix, and an optional set of classes (we don't need those for this experiment though):

```
    def partial_fit(self, X, y=None):
```

A pipeline, which we introduced before, is a set of transformations where the input to one step is the output of the previous step. To do this, we set the first input to our `X` matrix, and then go over each of the transformers to transform this data:

```
        Xt = X
        for name, transform in self.steps[:-1]:
```

We then transform our current dataset and continue iterating until we hit the final step (which, in our case will be the clustering algorithm):

```
            Xt = transform.transform(Xt)
```

We then call the `partial_fit` function on the final step and return the results:

```
        return self.steps[-1][1].partial_fit(Xt, y=y)
```

We can now create a pipeline to use our `MiniBatchKMeans` in online learning, alongside our `HashingVectorizer`. Other than using our new classes `PartialFitPipeline` and `HashingVectorizer`, this is the same process as used in the rest of this chapter, except we only fit on a few documents at a time. The code is as follows:

```
pipeline = PartialFitPipeline([('feature_extraction', 
HashingVectorizer()),
                              ('clusterer', MiniBatchKMeans(random_
state=14, n_clusters=3))
                              ])
batch_size = 10
for iteration in range(int(len(documents) / batch_size)):
    start = batch_size * iteration
    end = batch_size * (iteration + 1)
    pipeline.partial_fit(documents[start:end])
labels = pipeline.predict(documents)
```

There are some downsides to this approach though. For one, we can't easily find out which words are most important for each cluster. We can get around this by fitting another `CountVectorizer` and taking the hash of each word. We then look up values by hash rather than word. This is a bit cumbersome and defeats the memory gains from using `HashingVectorizer`. Further, we can't use the `max_df` parameter that we used earlier, as it requires us to know what the features mean and to count them over time.

We also can't use `tf-idf` weighting when performing training online. It would be possible to approximate this and apply such weighting, but again this is a cumbersome approach. `HashingVectorizer` is still a very useful algorithm and a great use of hashing algorithms.

Summary

In this chapter, we looked at clustering, which is an unsupervised learning approach. We use unsupervised learning to explore data, rather than for classification and prediction purposes. In the experiment here, we didn't have topics for the news items we found on reddit, so we were unable to perform classification. We used k-means clustering to group together these news stories to find common topics and trends in the data.

In pulling data from reddit, we had to extract data from arbitrary websites. This was performed by looking for large text segments, rather than a full-blown machine learning approach. There are some interesting approaches to machine learning for this task that may improve upon these results. In the Appendix of this book, I've listed, for each chapter, avenues for going beyond the scope of the chapter and improving upon the results. This includes references to other sources of information and more difficult applications of the approaches in each chapter.

We also looked at a straightforward ensemble algorithm, ECA. An ensemble is often a good way to deal with variance in the results, especially if you don't know how to choose good parameters (which is especially difficult with clustering).

Finally, we introduced online learning. This is a gateway to larger learning exercises, including Big data, which will be discussed in the final two chapters of this book. These final experiments are quite large and require management of data as well as learning a model from them.

In the next chapter, we step away from unsupervised learning and go back to classification. We will look at deep learning, which is a classification method built on complex neural networks.

11
Classifying Objects in Images Using Deep Learning

We used basic neural networks in *Chapter 8, Beating CAPTCHAs with Neural Networks*. A recent flood of research in the area has led to a number of significant advances to that base design. Today, research in neural networks is creating some of the most advanced and accurate classification algorithms in many areas.

These advances have come on the back of improvements in computational power, allowing us to train larger and more complex networks. However, the advances are much more than simply throwing more computational power at the problem. New algorithms and layer types have drastically improved performance, outside computational power.

In this chapter, we will look at determining what object is represented in an image. The pixel values will be used as input, and the neural network will then automatically find useful combinations of pixels to form higher-level features. These will then be used for the actual classification. Overall, in this chapter, we will examine the following:

- Classifying objects in images
- The different types of deep neural networks
- Theano, Lasagne, and Nolearn; libraries to build and train neural networks
- Using a GPU to improve the speed of the algorithms

Object classification

Computer vision is becoming an important part of future technology. For example, we will have access to self-driving cars in the next five years (possibly much sooner, if some rumors are to be believed). In order to achieve this, the car's computer needs to be able to see around it: obstacles, other traffic, and weather conditions.

While we can easily detect whether there is an obstacle, for example using radar, it is also important we know what that object is. If it is an animal, it may move out of the way; if it is a building, it won't move at all and we need to go around it.

Application scenario and goals

In this chapter, we will build a system that will take an image as an input and give a prediction on what the object in it is. We will take on the role of a vision system for a car, looking around at any obstacles in the way or on the side of the road. Images are of the following form:

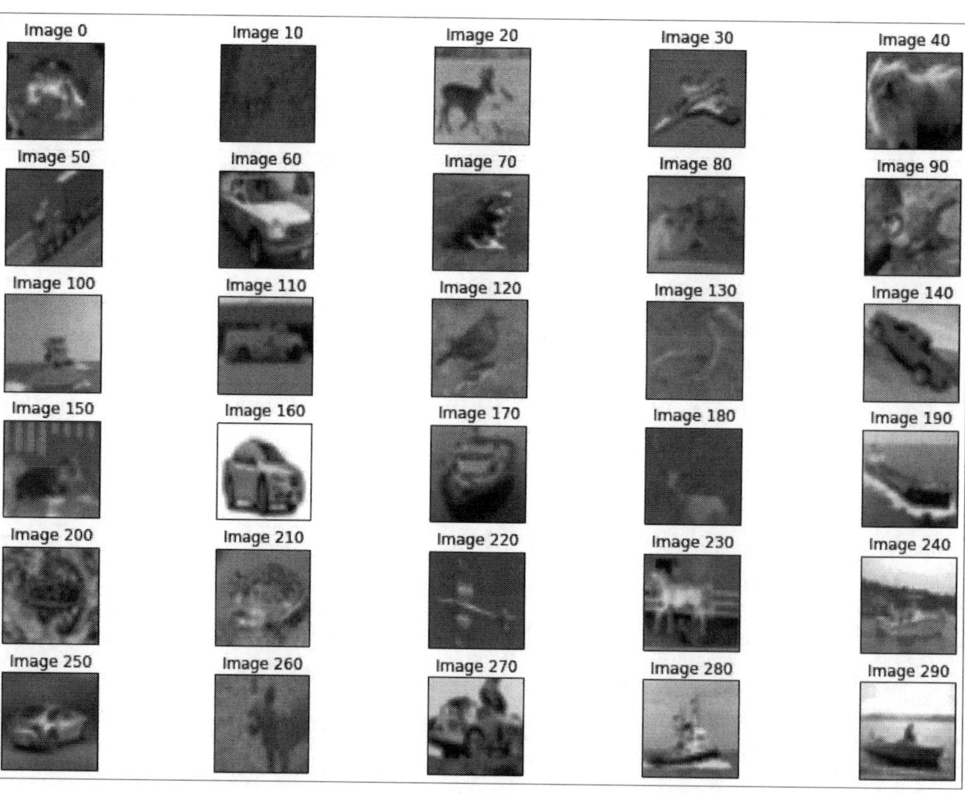

This dataset comes from a popular dataset called **CIFAR-10**. It contains 60,000 images that are 32 pixels wide and 32 pixels high, with each pixel having a red-green-blue (RGB) value. The dataset is already split into training and testing, although we will not use the testing dataset until after we complete our training.

> The CIFAR-10 dataset is available for download at: `http://www.cs.toronto.edu/~kriz/cifar.html`. Download the python version, which has already been converted to NumPy arrays.

Opening a new IPython Notebook, we can see what the data looks like. First, we set up the data filenames. We will only worry about the first batch to start with, and scale up to the full dataset size towards the end;

```
import os
data_folder = os.path.join(os.path.expanduser("~"), "Data", "cifar-10-
batches-py")
batch1_filename = os.path.join(data_folder, "data_batch_1")
```

Next, we create a function that can read the data stored in the batches. The batches have been saved using pickle, which is a python library to save objects. Usually, we can just call `pickle.load` on the file to get the object. However, there is a small issue with this data: it was saved in Python 2, but we need to open it in Python 3. In order to address this, we set the encoding to *latin* (even though we are opening it in byte mode):

```
import pickle
# Bigfix thanks to: http://stackoverflow.com/questions/11305790/
pickle-incompatability-of-numpy-arrays-between-python-2-and-3
def unpickle(filename):
    with open(filename, 'rb') as fo:
        return pickle.load(fo, encoding='latin1')
```

Using this function, we can now load the batch dataset:

```
batch1 = unpickle(batch1_filename)
```

This batch is a dictionary, containing the actual data in NumPy arrays, the corresponding labels and filenames, and finally a note to say which batch it is (this is *training batch 1 of 5*, for instance).

We can extract an image by using its index in the batch's data key:

```
image_index = 100
image = batch1['data'][image_index]
```

The image array is a NumPy array with 3,072 entries, from 0 to 255. Each value is the red, green, or blue intensity at a specific location in the image.

The images are in a different format than what matplotlib usually uses (to display images), so to show the image we first need to reshape the array and rotate the matrix. This doesn't matter so much to train our neural network (we will define our network in a way that fits with the data), but we do need to convert it for matplotlib's sake:

```
image = image.reshape((32,32, 3), order='F')
import numpy as np
image = np.rot90(image, -1)
```

Now we can show the image using matplotlib:

```
%matplotlib inline

from matplotlib import pyplot as plt
plt.imshow(image)
```

The resulting image, a boat, is displayed:

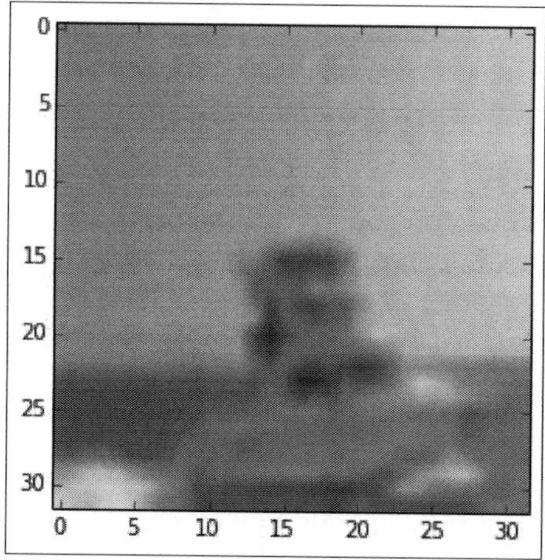

The resolution on this image is quite poor—it is only 32 pixels wide and 32 pixels high. Despite that, most people will look at the image and see a boat. Can we get a computer to do the same?

You can change the image index to show different images, getting a feel for the dataset's properties.

The aim of our project, in this chapter, is to build a classification system that can take an image like this and predict what the object in it is.

Use cases

Computer vision is used in many scenarios.

Online map websites, such as Google Maps, use computer vision for a number of reasons. One reason is to automatically blur any faces that they find, in order to give some privacy to the people being photographed as part of their Street View feature.

Face detection is also used in many industries. Modern cameras automatically detect faces, as a means to improve the quality of photos taken (the user most often wants to focus on a visible face). Face detection can also be used for identification. For example, Facebook automatically recognizes people in photos, allowing for easy tagging of friends.

As we stated before, autonomous vehicles are highly dependent on computer vision to recognize their path and avoid obstacles. Computer vision is one of the key problems that is being addressed not only in research into autonomous vehicles, not just for consumer use, but also in mining and other industries.

Other industries are using computer vision too, including warehouses examining goods automatically for defects.

The space industry is also using computer vision, helping to automate the collection of data. This is critical for effective use of spacecraft, as sending a signal from Earth to a rover on Mars can take a long time and is not possible at certain times (for instance, when the two planets are not facing each other). As we start dealing with space-based vehicles more frequently, and from a greater distance, increasing the autonomy of these spacecrafts is absolutely necessary.

The following screenshot shows the Mars rover designed and used by NASA; it made significant use of computer vision:

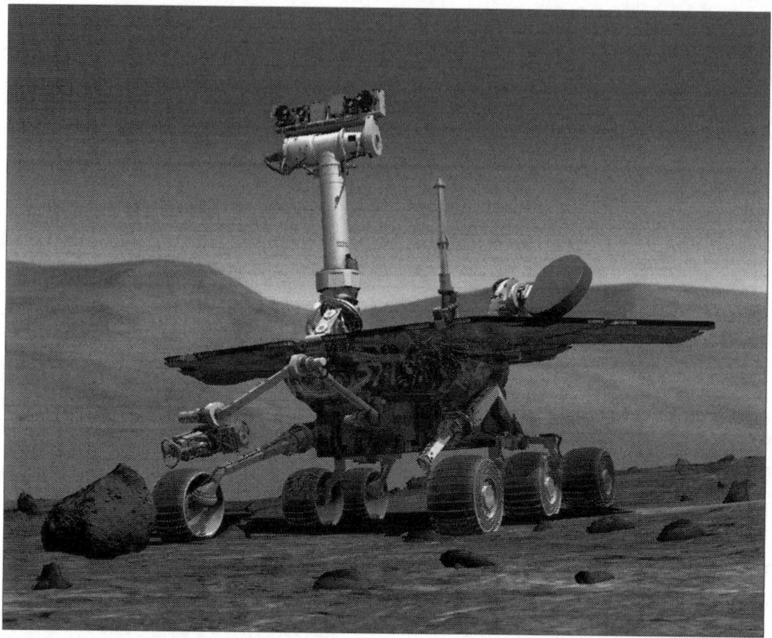

Deep neural networks

The neural networks we used in *Chapter 8, Beating CAPTCHAs with Neural Networks*, have some fantastic theoretical properties. For example, only a single hidden layer is needed to learn any mapping (although the size of the middle layer may need to be very, very big). Neural networks were a very active area of research in the 1970s and 1980s, and then these networks were no longer used, particularly compared to other classification algorithms such as support vector machines. One of the main issues was that the computational power needed to run many neural networks was more than other algorithms and more than what many people had access to.

Another issue was training the networks. While the back propagation algorithm has been known about for some time, it has issues with larger networks, requiring a very large amount of training before the weights settle.

Each of these issues has been addressed in recent times, leading to a resurgence in popularity of neural networks. Computational power is now much more easily available than 30 years ago, and advances in algorithms for training mean that we can now readily use that power.

Intuition

The aspect that differentiates deep neural networks from the more basic neural network we saw in *Chapter 8, Beating CAPTCHAs with Neural Networks,* is size. A neural network is considered deep when it has two or more hidden layers. In practice, a deep neural network is often much larger, both in the number of nodes in each layer and also the number of layers. While some of the research of the mid-2000s focused on very large numbers of layers, smarter algorithms are reducing the actual number of layers needed.

A neural network basically takes very basic features as inputs—in the case of computer vision, it is simple pixel values. Then, as that data is combined and pushed through the network, these basic features combine into more complex features. Sometimes, these features have little meaning to humans, but they represent the aspects of the sample that the computer looks for to make its classification.

Implementation

Implementing these deep neural networks can be quite challenging due to their size. A bad implementation will take significantly longer to run than a good one, and may not even run at all due to memory usage.

A basic implementation of a neural network might start by creating a node class and collecting a set of these into a layer class. Each node is then connected to a node in the next layer using an instance of an Edge class. This type of implementation, a class-based one, is good to show how networks work, but is too inefficient for larger networks.

Neural networks are, at their core, simply mathematical expressions on matrices. The weights of the connections between one network and the next can be represented as a matrix of values, where the rows represent nodes in the first layer and the columns represent the nodes in the second layer (the transpose of this matrix is used sometimes too). The value is the weight of the edge between one layer and the next. A network can then be defined as a set of these weight matrices. In addition to the nodes, we add a bias term to each layer, which is basically a node that is always on and connected to each neuron in the next layer.

This insight allows us to use mathematical operations to build, train, and use neural networks, as opposed to creating a class-based implementation. These mathematical operations are great, as many great libraries of highly optimized code have been written that we can use to perform these computations as efficiently as we can.

The `PyBrain` library that we used in *Chapter 8, Beating CAPTCHAs with Neural Networks*, does contain a simple convolutional layer for a neural network. However, it doesn't offer us some of the features that we need for this application. For larger and more customized networks, though, we need a library that gives us a bit more power. For this reason, we will be using the `Lasagne` and `nolearn` libraries. This library works on the `Theano` library, which is a useful tool for mathematical expressions.

In this chapter, we will start by implementing a basic neural network with `Lasagne` to introduce the concepts. We will then use `nolearn` to replicate our experiment in *Chapter 8, Beating CAPTCHAs with Neural Networks,* on predicting which letter is in an image. Finally, we will use a much more complex convolution neural network to perform image classification on the CIFAR dataset, which will also include running this on GPUs rather than CPUs to improve the performance.

An introduction to Theano

Theano is a library that allows you to build mathematical expressions and run them. While this may immediately not seem that different to what we normally do to write a program, in Theano, we define the function we want to perform, not the way in which it is computed. This allows Theano to optimize the evaluation of the expression and also to perform lazy computation—expressions are only actually computed when they are needed, not when they are defined.

Many programmers don't use this type of programming day-to-day, but most of them interact with a related system that does. Relational databases, specifically SQL-based ones, use this concept called the declarative paradigm. While a programmer might define a *SELECT* query on a database with a *WHERE* clause, the database interprets that and creates an optimized query based on a number of factors, such as whether the *WHERE* clause is on a primary key, the format the data is stored in, and other factors. The programmer defines what they want and the system determines how to do it.

You can install Theano using pip: `pip3 install Theano`.

Using Theano, we can define many types of functions working on scalars, arrays, and matrices, as well as other mathematical expressions. For instance, we can create a function that computes the length of the hypotenuse of a right-angled triangle:

```
import theano
from theano import tensor as T
```

First, we define the two inputs, a and b. These are simple numerical values, so we define them as scalars:

```
a = T.dscalar()
b = T.dscalar()
```

Then, we define the output, `c`. This is an expression based on the values of `a` and `b`:

```
c = T.sqrt(a ** 2 + b ** 2)
```

Note that `c` isn't a function or a value here—it is simply an expression, given `a` and `b`. Note also that `a` and `b` don't have actual values—this is an algebraic expression, not an absolute one. In order to compute on this, we define a function:

```
f = theano.function([a,b], c)
```

This basically tells Theano to create a function that takes values for `a` and `b` as inputs, and returns `c` as an output, computed on the values given. For example, `f(3, 4)` returns `5`.

While this simple example may not seem much more powerful than what we can already do with Python, we can now use our function or our mathematical expression `c` in other parts of code and the remaining mappings. In addition, while we defined `c` before the function was defined, no actual computation was done until we called the function.

An introduction to Lasagne

Theano isn't a library to build neural networks. In a similar way, NumPy isn't a library to perform machine learning; it just does the heavy lifting and is generally used from another library. Lasagne is such a library, designed specifically around building neural networks, using Theano to perform the computation.

Lasagne implements a number of modern types of neural network layers, and the building blocks for building them.

These include the following:

- **Network-in-network layers**: These are small neural networks that are easier to interpret than traditional neural network layers.
- **Dropout layers**: These randomly drop units during training, preventing overfitting, which is a major problem in neural networks.
- **Noise layers**: These introduce noise into the neurons; again, addressing the overfitting problem.

In this chapter, we will use `convolution layers` (layers that are organized to mimic the way in which human vision works). They use small collections of connected neurons that analyze only a segment of the input values (in this case, an image). This allows the network to deal with standard alterations such as dealing with translations of images. In the case of vision-based experiments, an example of an alteration dealt with by convolution layers is translating the image.

In contrast, a traditional neural network is often heavily connected—all neurons from one layer connect to all neurons in the next layer.

Convolutional networks are implemented in the `lasagne.layers.Conv1DLayer` and `lasagne.layers.Conv2DLayer` classes.

At the time of writing, Lasagne hasn't had a formal release and is not on `pip`. You can install it from `github`. In a new folder, download the source code repository using the following:

```
git clone https://github.com/Lasagne/Lasagne.git
```

From within the created Lasagne folder, you can then install the library using the following:

```
sudo python3 setup.py install
```

See `http://lasagne.readthedocs.org/en/latest/user/installation.html` for installation instructions.

Neural networks use convolutional layers (generally, just *Convolutional Neural Networks*) and also the `pooling` layers, which take the maximum output for a certain region. This reduces noise caused by small variations in the image, and reduces (or down-samples) the amount of information. This has the added benefit of reducing the amount of work needed to be done in later layers.

Lasagne also implements these pooling layers—for example in the `lasagne.layers.MaxPool2DLayer` class. Together with the convolution layers, we have all the tools needed to build a convolution neural network.

Building a neural network in Lasagne is easier than building it using just Theano. To show the principles, we will implement a basic network to lean on the Iris dataset, which we saw in *Chapter 1, Getting Started with Data Mining*. The Iris dataset is great for testing new algorithms, even complex ones such as deep neural networks.

First, open a new IPython Notebook. We will come back to the Notebook we loaded the CIFAR dataset with, later in the chapter.

First, we load the dataset:

```
from sklearn.datasets import load_iris
iris = load_iris()
X = iris.data.astype(np.float32)
y_true = iris.target.astype(np.int32)
```

Due to the way Lasagne works, we need to be a bit more explicit about the data types. This is why we converted the classes to `int32` (they are stored as `int64` in the original dataset).

We then split into training and testing datasets:

```
from sklearn.cross_validation import train_test_split
X_train, X_test, y_train, y_test = train_test_split(X, y_true, random_
state=14)
```

Next, we build our network by creating the different layers. Our dataset contains four input variables and three output classes. This gives us the size of the first and last layer, but not the layers in between. Playing around with this figure will give different results, and it is worth trailing different values to see what happens.

We start by creating an input layer, which has the same number of nodes as the dataset. We can specify a batch size (where the value is 10), which allows Lasagne to do some optimizations in training:

```
import lasagne
input_layer = lasagne.layers.InputLayer(shape=(10, X.shape[1]))
```

Next, we create our hidden layer. This layer takes its input from our input layer (specified as the first argument), which has 12 nodes, and uses the sigmoid nonlinearity, which we saw in *Chapter 8, Beating CAPTCHAs with Neural Networks*;

```
hidden_layer = lasagne.layers.DenseLayer(input_layer, num_units=12,
nonlinearity=lasagne.nonlinearities.sigmoid)
```

Next, we have our output layer that takes its input from the hidden layer, which has three nodes (which is the same as the number of classes), and uses the **softmax** nonlinearity. Softmax is more typically used in the final layer of neural networks:

```
output_layer = lasagne.layers.DenseLayer(hidden_layer, num_units=3,
                                    nonlinearity=lasagne.
nonlinearities.softmax)
```

In Lasagne's usage, this output layer is our `network`. When we enter a sample into it, it looks at this output layer and obtains the layer that is inputted into it (the first argument). This continues recursively until we reach an input layer, which applies the samples to itself, as it doesn't have an input layer to it. The activations of the neurons in the input layer are then fed into its calling layer (in our case, the `hidden_layer`), and that is then propagated up all the way to the output layer.

In order to train our network, we now need to define some training functions, which are Theano-based functions. In order to do this, we need to define a Theano expression and a function for the training. We start by creating variables for the input samples, the output given by the network, and the actual output:

```
import theano.tensor as T
net_input = T.matrix('net_input')
net_output = output_layer.get_output(net_input)
true_output = T.ivector('true_output')
```

We can now define our loss function, which tells the training function how to improve the network—it attempts to train the network to minimize the loss according to this function. The loss we will use is the categorical cross entropy, a metric on categorical data such as ours. This is a function of the output given by the network and the actual output we expected:

```
loss = T.mean(T.nnet.categorical_crossentropy(net_output,
  true_output))
```

Next, we define the function that will change the weights in our network. In order to do this, we obtain all of the parameters from the network and create a function (using a helper function given by Lasagne) that adjusts the weights to minimize our loss;

```
all_params = lasagne.layers.get_all_params(output_layer)
updates = lasagne.updates.sgd(loss, all_params, learning_rate=0.1)
```

Finally, we create Theano-based functions that perform this training and also obtain the output of the network for testing purposes:

```
import theano
train = theano.function([net_input, true_output], loss,
updates=updates)
get_output = theano.function([net_input], net_output)
```

We can then call our train function, on our training data, to perform one iteration of training the network. This involves taking each sample, computing the predicted class of it, comparing those predictions to the expected classes, and updating the weights to minimize the loss function. We then perform this 1,000 times, incrementally training our network over those iterations:

```
for n in range(1000):
    train(X_train, y_train)
```

Next, we can evaluate by computing the F-score on the outputs. First, we obtain those outputs:

```
y_output = get_output(X_test)
```

Note that `get_output` is a Theano function we obtained from our neural network, which is why we didn't need to add our network as a parameter to this line of code.

This result, `y_output`, is the activation of each of the neurons in the final output layer. The actual prediction itself is created by finding which neuron has the highest activation:

```
import numpy as np
y_pred = np.argmax(y_output, axis=1)
```

Now, `y_pred` is an array of class predictions, like we are used to in classification tasks. We can now compute the F-score using these predictions:

```
from sklearn.metrics import f1_score
print(f1_score(y_test, y_pred))
```

The result is impressively perfect—1.0! This means all the classifications were correct in the test data: a great result (although this is a simpler dataset).

As we can see, while it is possible to develop and train a network using just Lasagne, it can be a little awkward. To address this, we will be using nolearn, which is a package that further wraps this process in code that is conveniently convertible with the scikit-learn API.

Implementing neural networks with nolearn

The `nolearn` package provides wrappers for Lasagne. We lose some of the fine-tuning that can go with building a neural network by hand in Lasagne, but the code is much more readable and much easier to manage.

The `nolearn` package implements the normal sorts of complex neural networks you are likely to want to build. If you want more control than nolearn gives you, you can revert to using Lasagne, but at the cost of having to manage a bit more of the training and building process.

To get started with nolearn, we are going to reimplement the example we used in *Chapter 8, Beating CAPTCHAs with Neural Networks*, to predict which letter was represented in an image. We will recreate the dense neural network we used in *Chapter 8, Beating CAPTCHAs with Neural Networks*. To start with, we need to enter our dataset building code again in our notebook. For a description of what this code does, refer to *Chapter 8, Beating CAPTCHAs with Neural Networks*:

```
import numpy as np
from PIL import Image, ImageDraw, ImageFont
from skimage.transform import resize
from skimage import transform as tf
from skimage.measure import label, regionprops
from sklearn.utils import check_random_state
from sklearn.preprocessing import OneHotEncoder
from sklearn.cross_validation import train_test_split

def create_captcha(text, shear=0, size=(100, 24)):
    im = Image.new("L", size, "black")
    draw = ImageDraw.Draw(im)
    font = ImageFont.truetype(r"Coval.otf", 22)
    draw.text((2, 2), text, fill=1, font=font)
    image = np.array(im)
    affine_tf = tf.AffineTransform(shear=shear)
    image = tf.warp(image, affine_tf)
    return image / image.max()

def segment_image(image):
    labeled_image = label(image > 0)
    subimages = []
    for region in regionprops(labeled_image):
        start_x, start_y, end_x, end_y = region.bbox
        subimages.append(image[start_x:end_x,start_y:end_y])
    if len(subimages) == 0:
```

```
        return [image,]
    return subimages

random_state = check_random_state(14)
letters = list("ABCDEFGHIJKLMNOPQRSTUVWXYZ")
shear_values = np.arange(0, 0.5, 0.05)

def generate_sample(random_state=None):
    random_state = check_random_state(random_state)
    letter = random_state.choice(letters)
    shear = random_state.choice(shear_values)
    return create_captcha(letter, shear=shear, size=(20, 20)),
letters.index(letter)
dataset, targets = zip(*(generate_sample(random_state) for i in
range(3000)))
dataset = np.array(dataset, dtype='float')
targets =  np.array(targets)

onehot = OneHotEncoder()
y = onehot.fit_transform(targets.reshape(targets.shape[0],1))
y = y.todense().astype(np.float32)

dataset = np.array([resize(segment_image(sample)[0], (20, 20)) for
sample in dataset])
X = dataset.reshape((dataset.shape[0], dataset.shape[1] * dataset.
shape[2]))
X = X / X.max()
X = X.astype(np.float32)

X_train, X_test, y_train, y_test = \
    train_test_split(X, y, train_size=0.9, random_state=14)
```

A neural network is a collection of layers. Implementing one in nolearn is a case of organizing what those layers will look like, much as it was with PyBrain. The neural network we used in *Chapter 8, Beating CAPTCHAs with Neural Networks*, used fully connected dense layers. These are implemented in nolearn, meaning we can replicate our basic network structure here. First, we create the layers consisting of an input layer, our dense hidden layer, and our dense output layer:

```
from lasagne import layers
layers=[
        ('input', layers.InputLayer),
        ('hidden', layers.DenseLayer),
        ('output', layers.DenseLayer),
        ]
```

We then import some requirements, which we will explain as we use them:

```
from lasagne import updates
from nolearn.lasagne import NeuralNet
from lasagne.nonlinearities import sigmoid, softmax
```

Next we define the neural network, which is represented as a scikit-learn-compatible estimator:

```
net1 = NeuralNet(layers=layers,
```

Note that we haven't closed off the parenthesis—this is deliberate. At this point, we enter the parameters for the neural network, starting with the size of each layer:

```
    input_shape=X.shape,
    hidden_num_units=100,
    output_num_units=26,
```

The parameters here match the layers. In other words, the `input_shape` parameter first finds the layer in our layers that has given the name input, working much the same way as setting parameters in pipelines.

Next, we define the nonlinearities. Again, we will use `sigmoid` for the hidden layer and `softmax` for the output layer:

```
    hidden_nonlinearity=sigmoid,
    output_nonlinearity=softmax,
```

Next, we will use bias nodes, which are nodes that are always turned on in the hidden layer. Bias nodes are important to train a network, as they allow for the activations of neurons to train more specifically to their problems. As an oversimplified example, if our prediction is always off by 4, we can add a bias of -4 to remove this bias. Our bias nodes allow for this, and the training of the weights dictates the amount of bias that is used.

The biases are given as a set of weights, meaning that it needs to be the same size as the layer the bias is attaching to:

```
    hidden_b=np.zeros((100,), dtype=np.float32),
```

Next, we define how the network will train. The nolearn package doesn't have the exact same training mechanism as we used in *Chapter 8, Beating CAPTCHAs with Neural Networks*, as it doesn't have a way to decay weights. However, it does have momentum, which we will use, along with a high learning rate and low momentum value:

```
        update=updates.momentum,
        update_learning_rate=0.9,
        update_momentum=0.1,
```

Next, we define the problem as a regression problem. This may seem odd, as we are performing a classification task. However, the outputs are real-valued, and optimizing them as a regression problem appears to do much better in training than trying to optimize on classification:

```
        regression=True,
```

Finally, we set the maximum number of epochs for training at 1,000, which is a good fit between good training and not taking a long time to train (for this dataset; other datasets may require more or less training):

```
        max_epochs=1000,
```

We can now close off the parenthesis for the neural network constructor;

```
    )
```

Next, we train the network on our training dataset:

```
net1.fit(X_train, y_train)
```

Now we can evaluate the trained network. To do this, we get the output of our network and, as with the Iris example, we need to perform an `argmax` to get the actual classification by choosing the highest activation:

```
y_pred = net1.predict(X_test)
y_pred = y_pred.argmax(axis=1)
assert len(y_pred) == len(X_test)
if len(y_test.shape) > 1:
    y_test = y_test.argmax(axis=1)
print(f1_score(y_test, y_pred))
```

The results are equally impressive—another perfect score on my machine. However, your results may vary as the `nolearn` package has some randomness that can't be directly controlled at this stage.

GPU optimization

Neural networks can grow quite large in size. This has some implications for memory use; however, efficient structures such as sparse matrices mean that we don't generally run into problems fitting a neural network in memory.

The main issue when neural networks grow large is that they take a very long time to compute. In addition, some datasets and neural networks will need to run many epochs of training to get a good fit for the dataset. The neural network we will train in this chapter takes more than 8 minutes per epoch on my reasonably powerful computer, and we expect to run dozens, potentially hundreds, of epochs. Some larger networks can take hours to train a single epoch. To get the best performance, you may be considering thousands of training cycles.

The math obviously doesn't give a nice result here.

One positive is that neural networks are, at their core, full of floating point operations. There are also a large number of operations that can be performed in parallel, as neural network training is composed of mainly matrix operations. These factors mean that computing on GPUs is an attractive option to speed up this training.

When to use GPUs for computation

GPUs were originally designed to render graphics for display. These graphics are represented using matrices and mathematical equations on those matrices, which are then converted into the pixels that we see on our screen. This process involves lots of computation in parallel. While modern CPUs may have a number of cores (your computer may have 2, 4, or even 16—or more!), GPUs have thousands of small cores designed specifically for graphics.

A CPU is therefore better for sequential tasks, as the cores tend to be individually faster and tasks such as accessing the computer's memory are more efficient. It is also, honestly, easier to just let the CPU do the heavy lifting. Almost every machine learning library defaults to using the CPU, and there is extra work involved before you can use the GPU for computing. The benefits though, can be quite significant.

GPUs are therefore better suited for tasks in which there are lots of small operations on numbers that can be performed at the same time. Many machine learning tasks are like this, lending themselves to efficiency improvements through the use of a GPU.

Getting your code to run on a GPU can be a frustrating experience. It depends greatly on what type of GPU you have, how it is configured, your operating system, and whether you are prepared to make some low-level changes to your computer.

There are three main avenues to take:

- The first is to look at your computer, search for tools and drivers for your GPU and operating system, explore some of the many tutorials out there, and find one that fits your scenario. Whether this works depends on what your system is like. That said, this scenario is much easier than it was a few years ago, with better tools and drivers available to perform GPU-enabled computation.
- The second avenue is to choose a system, find good documentation on setting it up, and buy a system to match. This will work better, but can be fairly expensive—in most modern computers, the GPU is one of the most expensive parts. This is especially true if you want to get great performance out of the system—you'll need a really good GPU, which can be very expensive.
- The third avenue is to use a virtual machine, which is already configured for such a purpose. For example, Markus Beissinger has created such a system that runs on Amazon's Web Services. The system will cost you money to run, but the price is much less than that of a new computer. Depending on your location, the exact system you get and how much you use it, you are probably looking at less than $1 an hour, and often much, much less. If you use spot instances in Amazon's Web Services, you can run them for just a few cents per hour (although, you will need to develop your code to run on spot instances separately).

If you aren't able to afford the running costs of a virtual machine, I recommend that you look into the first avenue, with your current system. You may also be able to pick up a good secondhand GPU from family or a friend who constantly updates their computer (gamer friends are great for this!).

Running our code on a GPU

We are going to take the third avenue in this chapter and create a virtual machine based on *Markus Beissinger's* base system. This will run on an Amazon's EC2 service. There are many other Web services to use, and the procedure will be slightly different for each. In this section, I'll outline the procedure for Amazon.

If you want to use your own computer and have it configured to run GPU-enabled computation, feel free to skip this section.

You can get more information on how this was set up, which may also provide information on setting it up on another computer, at `http://markus.com/install-theano-on-aws/`.

To start with, go to the AWS console at:

`https://console.aws.amazon.com/console/home?region=us-east-1`

Log in with your Amazon account. If you don't have one, you will be prompted to create one, which you will need to do in order to continue.

Next, go to the EC2 service console at: `https://console.aws.amazon.com/ec2/v2/home?region=us-east-1`.

Click on **Launch Instance** and choose **N. California** as your location in the drop-down menu at the top-right.

Click on **Community AMIs** and search for `ami-b141a2f5`, which is the machine created by Markus Beissinger. Then, click on **Select**. On the next screen, choose **g2.2xlarge** as the machine type and click on **Review and Launch**. On the next screen, click on **Launch**.

At this point, you will be charged, so please remember to shut down your machines when you are done with them. You can go to the EC2 service, select the machine, and stop it. You won't be charged for machines that are not running.

You'll be prompted with some information on how to connect to your instance. If you haven't used AWS before, you will probably need to create a new key pair to securely connect to your instance. In this case, give your key pair a name, download the `pem` file, and store it in a safe place—if lost, you will not be able to connect to your instance again!

Click on **Connect** for information on using the `pem` file to connect to your instance. The most likely scenario is that you will use `ssh` with the following command:

```
ssh -i <certificante_name>.pem ubuntu@<server_ip_address>
```

Setting up the environment

When you have connected to the instance, you can install the updated `Lasagne` and `nolearn` packages.

First, clone the `git` repository for `Lasagne`, as was outlined earlier in this chapter:

```
git clone https://github.com/Lasagne/Lasagne.git
```

In order to build this library on this machine, we will need `setuptools` for Python 3, which we can install via `apt-get`, which is Ubuntu's method of installing applications and libraries; we also need the development library for NumPy. Run the following in the command line of the virtual machine:

```
sudo apt-get install python3-pip python3-numpy-dev
```

Next, we install Lasagne. First, we change to the source code directory and then run `setup.py` to build and install it:

```
cd Lasagne
sudo python3 setup.py install
```

We have installed `Lasagne` and will install `nolearn` as system-wide packages for simplicity. For those wanting a more portable solution, I recommend using `virtualenv` to install these packages. It will allow you to use different python and library versions on the same computer, and make moving the code to a new computer much easier. For more information, see `http://docs.python-guide.org/en/latest/dev/virtualenvs/`.

After Lasagne is built, we can now install nolearn. Change to the home directory and follow the same procedure, except for the nolearn package:

```
cd ~/
git clone https://github.com/dnouri/nolearn.git
cd nolearn
sudo python3 setup.py install
```

Our system is nearly set up. We need to install scikit-learn and scikit-image, as well as matplotlib. We can do all of this using `pip3`. As a dependency on these, we need the `scipy` and `matplotlib` packages as well, which aren't currently installed on this machine. I recommend using scipy and matplotlib from `apt-get` rather than `pip3`, as it can be painful in some cases to install it using `pip3`:

```
sudo apt-get install python3-scipy python3-matplotlib
sudo pip3 install scikit-learn scikit-image
```

Next, we need to get our code onto the machine. There are many ways to get this file onto your computer, but one of the easiest is to just copy-and-paste the contents.

To start with, open the IPython Notebook we used before (on your computer, not on the Amazon Virtual Machine). On the Notebook itself is a menu. Click on **File** and then **Download as**. Select **Python** and save it to your computer. This procedure downloads the code in the IPython Notebook as a python script that you can run from the command line.

Open this file (on some systems, you may need to right-click and open with a text editor). Select all of the contents and copy them to your clipboard.

On the Amazon Virtual Machine, move to the home directory and open `nano` with a new filename:

```
cd ~/
nano chapter11script.py
```

The `nano` program will open, which is a command-line text editor.

With this program open, paste the contents of your clipboard into this file. On some systems, you may need to use a file option of the ssh program, rather than pressing *Ctrl* + *V* to paste.

In `nano`, press *Ctrl* + *O* to save the file on the disk and then *Ctrl* + *X* to exit the program.

You'll also need the font file. The easiest way to do this is to download it again from the original location. To do this, enter the following:

```
wget http://openfontlibrary.org/assets/downloads/bretan/680bc56bbeeca9535
3ede363a3744fdf/bretan.zip
sudo apt-get install unzip
unzip -p bretan.zip Coval.otf > Coval.otf
```

This will unzip only one `Coval.otf` file (there are lots of files in this zip folder that we don't need).

While still in the virtual machine, you can run the program with the following command:

```
python3 chapter11script.py
```

The program will run through as it would in the IPython Notebook and the results will print to the command line.

The results should be the same as before, but the actual training and testing of the neural network will be much faster. Note that it won't be that much faster in the other aspects of the program—we didn't write the CAPTCHA dataset creation to use a GPU, so we will not obtain a speedup there.

[You may wish to shut down the Amazon virtual machine to save some money; we will be using it at the end of this chapter to run our main experiment, but will be developing the code on your main computer first.]

Application

Back on your main computer now, open the first IPython Notebook we created in this chapter—the one that we loaded the CIFAR dataset with. In this major experiment, we will take the CIFAR dataset, create a deep convolution neural network, and then run it on our GPU-based virtual machine.

Getting the data

To start with, we will take our CIFAR images and create a dataset with them. Unlike previously, we are going to preserve the pixel structure—that is,. in rows and columns. First, load all the batches into a list:

```
import numpy as np
batches = []
for i in range(1, 6):
    batch_filename = os.path.join(data_folder, "data_batch_{}".
format(i))
    batches.append(unpickle(batch1_filename))
    break
```

The last line, the break, is to test the code—this will drastically reduce the number of training examples, allowing you to quickly see if your code is working. I'll prompt you later to remove this line, after you have tested that the code works.

Next, create a dataset by stacking these batches on top of each other. We use NumPy's `vstack`, which can be visualized as adding rows to the end of the array:

```
X = np.vstack([batch['data'] for batch in batches])
```

We then normalize the dataset to the range 0 to 1 and then force the type to be a 32-bit float (this is the only datatype the GPU-enabled virtual machine can run with):

```
X = np.array(X) / X.max()
X = X.astype(np.float32)
```

We then do the same with the classes, except we perform a `hstack`, which is similar to adding columns to the end of the array. We then use the `OneHotEncoder` to turn this into a one-hot array:

```
from sklearn.preprocessing import OneHotEncoder
y = np.hstack(batch['labels'] for batch in batches).flatten()
y = OneHotEncoder().fit_transform(y.reshape(y.shape[0],1)).todense()
y = y.astype(np.float32)
```

Next, we split the dataset into training and testing sets:

```
X_train, X_test, y_train, y_test = train_test_split(X, y, test_
size=0.2)
```

Next, we reshape the arrays to preserve the original data structure. The original data was 32 by 32 pixel images, with 3 values per pixel (for the red, green, and blue values);

```
X_train = X_train.reshape(-1, 3, 32, 32)
X_test = X_test.reshape(-1, 3, 32, 32)
```

We now have a familiar training and testing dataset, along with the target classes for each. We can now build the classifier.

Creating the neural network

We will be using the `nolearn` package to build the neural network, and therefore will follow a pattern that is similar to our replication experiment in *Chapter 8, Beating CAPTCHAs with Neural Networks* replication.

First we create the layers of our neural network:

```
from lasagne import layers
layers=[
        ('input', layers.InputLayer),
        ('conv1', layers.Conv2DLayer),
        ('pool1', layers.MaxPool2DLayer),
        ('conv2', layers.Conv2DLayer),
        ('pool2', layers.MaxPool2DLayer),
        ('conv3', layers.Conv2DLayer),
        ('pool3', layers.MaxPool2DLayer),
        ('hidden4', layers.DenseLayer),
        ('hidden5', layers.DenseLayer),
        ('output', layers.DenseLayer),
        ]
```

We use dense layers for the last three layers, but before that we use convolution layers combined with pooling layers. We have three sets of these. In addition, we start (as we must) with an input layer. This gives us a total of 10 layers. As before, the size of the first and last layers is easy to work out from the dataset, although our input size will have the same shape as the dataset rather than just the same number of nodes/inputs.

Start building our neural network (remember to not close the parentheses):

```
from nolearn.lasagne import NeuralNet
nnet = NeuralNet(layers=layers,
```

Add the input shape. The shape here resembles the shape of the dataset (three values per pixel and a 32 by 32 pixel image). The first value, None, is the default batch size used by nolearn—it will train on this number of samples at once, decreasing the running time of the algorithm. Setting it to None removes this hard-coded value, giving us more flexibility in running our algorithm:

```
                input_shape=(None, 3, 32, 32),
```

To change the batch size, you will need to create a `BatchIterator` instance. Those who are interested in this parameter can view the source of the file at `https://github.com/dnouri/nolearn/blob/master/nolearn/lasagne.py`, track the `batch_iterator_train` and `batch_iterator_test` parameters, and see how they are set in the `NeuralNet` class in this file.

Next we set the size of the convolution layers. There are no strict rules here, but I found the following values to be good starting points;

```
conv1_num_filters=32,
conv1_filter_size=(3, 3),
conv2_num_filters=64,
conv2_filter_size=(2, 2),
conv3_num_filters=128,
conv3_filter_size=(2, 2),
```

The `filter_size` parameter dictates the size of the window of the image that the convolution layer looks at. In addition, we set the size of the pooling layers:

```
pool1_ds=(2,2),
pool2_ds=(2,2),
pool3_ds=(2,2),
```

We then set the size of the two hidden dense layers (the third-last and second-last layers) and also the size of the output layer, which is just the number of classes in our dataset;

```
hidden4_num_units=500,
hidden5_num_units=500,
output_num_units=10,
```

We also set a nonlinearity for the final layer, again using `softmax`;

```
output_nonlinearity=softmax,
```

We also set the learning rate and momentum. As a rule of thumb, as the number of samples increase, the learning rate should decrease:

```
update_learning_rate=0.01,
update_momentum=0.9,
```

We set regression to be `True`, as we did before, and set the number of training epochs to be low as this network will take a long time to run. After a successful run, increasing the number of epochs will result in a much better model, but you may need to wait for a day or two (or more!) for it to train:

```
regression=True,
max_epochs=3,
```

Finally, we set the verbosity as equal to 1, which will give us a printout of the results of each epoch. This allows us to know the progress of the model and also that it is still running. Another feature is that it tells us the time it takes for each epoch to run. This is pretty consistent, so you can compute the time left in training by multiplying this value by the number of remaining epochs, giving a good estimate on how long you need to wait for the training to complete:

```
                        verbose=1)
```

Putting it all together

Now that we have our network, we can train it with our training dataset:

```
nnet.fit(X_train, y_train)
```

This will take quite a while to run, even with the reduced dataset size and the reduced number of epochs. Once the code completes, you can test it as we did before:

```
from sklearn.metrics import f1_score
y_pred = nnet.predict(X_test)
print(f1_score(y_test.argmax(axis=1), y_pred.argmax(axis=1)))
```

The results will be terrible—as they should be! We haven't trained the network very much—only for a few iterations and only on one fifth of the data.

First, go back and remove the break line we put in when creating the dataset (it is in the batches loop). This will allow the code to train on all of the samples, not just some of them.

Next, change the number of epochs to 100 in the neural network definition.

Now, we upload the script to our virtual machine. As with before, click on **File | Download** as, `Python`, and save the script somewhere on your computer. Launch and connect to the virtual machine and upload the script as you did earlier (I called my script `chapter11cifar.py`—if you named yours differently, just update the following code).

The next thing we need is for the dataset to be on the virtual machine. The easiest way to do this is to go to the virtual machine and type:

```
wget http://www.cs.toronto.edu/~kriz/cifar-10-python.tar.gz
```

This will download the dataset. Once that has downloaded, you can extract the data to the `Data` folder by first creating that folder and then unzipping the data there:

```
mkdir Data
tar -zxf cifar-10-python.tar.gz -C Data
```

Finally, we can run our example with the following:

```
python3 chapter11cifar.py
```

The first thing you'll notice is a drastic speedup. On my home computer, each epoch took over 100 seconds to run. On the GPU-enabled virtual machine, each epoch takes just 16 seconds! If we tried running 100 epochs on my computer, it would take nearly three hours, compared to just 26 minutes on the virtual machine.

This drastic speedup makes trailing different models much faster. Often with trialing machine learning algorithms, the computational complexity of a single algorithm doesn't matter too much. An algorithm might take a few seconds, minutes, or hours to run. If you are only running one model, it is unlikely that this training time will matter too much—especially as prediction with most machine learning algorithms is quite quick, and that is where a machine learning model is mostly used.

However, when you have many parameters to run, you will suddenly need to train thousands of models with slightly different parameters—suddenly, these speed increases matter much more.

After 100 epochs of training, taking a whole 26 minutes, you will get a printout of the final result:

```
0.8497
```

Not too bad! We can increase the number of epochs of training to improve this further or we might try changing the parameters instead; perhaps, more hidden nodes, more convolution layers, or an additional dense layer. There are other types of layers in Lasagne that could be tried too; although generally, convolution layers are better for vision.

Summary

In this chapter, we looked at using deep neural networks, specifically convolution networks, in order to perform computer vision. We did this through the Lasagne and nolearn packages, which work off Theano. The networks were relatively easy to build with nolearn's helper functions.

The convolution networks were designed for computer vision, so it shouldn't be a surprise that the result was quite accurate. The final result shows that computer vision is indeed an effective application using today's algorithms and computational power.

We also used a GPU-enabled virtual machine to drastically speed up the process, by a factor of almost 10 for my machine. If you need extra power to run some of these algorithms, virtual machines by cloud providers can be an effective way to do this (usually for less than a dollar per hour)—just remember to turn them off when you are done!

This chapter's focus was on a very complex algorithm. Convolution networks take a long time to train and have many parameters to train. Ultimately, the size of the data was small in comparison; although it was a large dataset, we can load it all in memory without even using sparse matrices. In the next chapter, we go for a much simpler algorithm, but a much, much larger dataset that can't fit in memory. This is the basis of Big Data and it underpins applications of data mining in many large industries such as mining and social networks.

12

Working with Big Data

The amount of data is increasing at exponential rates. Today's systems are generating and recording information on customer behavior, distributed systems, network analysis, sensors and many, many more sources. While the current big trend of mobile data is pushing the current growth, the next big thing—the **Internet of Things (IoT)**—is going to further increase the rate of growth.

What this means for data mining is a new way of thinking. The complex algorithms with high run times need to be improved or discarded, while simpler algorithms that can deal with more samples are becoming more popular to use. As an example, while support vector machines are great classifiers, some variants are difficult to use on very large datasets. In contrast, simpler algorithms such as logistic regression can manage more easily in these scenarios.

In this chapter, we will investigate the following:

- Big data challenges and applications
- The MapReduce paradigm
- Hadoop MapReduce
- mrjob, a python library to run MapReduce programs on Amazon's infrastructure

Big data

What makes big data different? Most big-data proponents talk about the four Vs of big data:

1. **Volume**: The amount of data that we generate and store is growing at an increasing rate, and predictions of the future generally only suggest further increases. Today's multi-gigabyte sized hard drives will turn into exabyte hard drives in a few years, and network throughput traffic will be increasing as well. The signal to noise ratio can be quite difficult, with important data being lost in the mountain of non-important data.
2. **Velocity**: While related to volume, the velocity of data is increasing too. Modern cars have hundreds of sensors that stream data into their computers, and the information from these sensors needs to be analyzed at a subsecond level to operate the car. It isn't just a case of finding answers in the volume of data; those answers often need to come quickly.
3. **Variety**: Nice datasets with clearly defined columns are only a small part of the dataset that we have these days. Consider a social media post, which may have text, photos, user mentions, likes, comments, videos, geographic information, and other fields. Simply ignoring parts of this data that don't fit your model will lead to a loss of information, but integrating that information itself can be very difficult.
4. **Veracity**: With the increase in the amount of data, it can be hard to determine whether the data is being correctly collected—whether it is outdated, noisy, contains outliers, or generally whether it is useful at all. Being able to trust the data is hard when a human can't reliably verify the data itself. External datasets are being increasingly merged into internal ones too, giving rise to more troubles relating to the veracity of the data.

These main four Vs (others have proposed additional Vs) outline why big data is different to just lots-of-data. At these scales, the engineering problem of working with the data is often more difficult—let alone the analysis. While there are lots of snake oil salesmen that overstate the ability to use big data, it is hard to deny the engineering challenges and the potential of big-data analytics.

The algorithms we have used are to date load the dataset into memory and then to work on the in-memory version. This gives a large benefit in terms of speed of computation, as it is much faster to compute on in-memory data than having to load a sample before we use it. In addition, in-memory data allows us to iterate over the data many times, improving our model.

In big data, we can't load our data into memory, In many ways, this is a good definition for whether a problem is big data or not—if the data can fit in the memory on your computer, you aren't dealing with a big data problem.

Application scenario and goals

There are many use cases for big data, in the public and private sectors.

The most common experience people have using a big-data-based system is in Internet search, such as Google. To run these systems, a search needs to be carried out over billions of websites in a fraction of a second. Doing a basic text-based search would be inadequate to deal with such a problem. Simply storing the text of all those websites is a large problem. In order to deal with queries, new data structures and data mining methods need to be created and implemented specifically for this application.

Big data is also used in many other scientific experiments such as the Large Hadron Collider, part of which is pictured below, that stretches over 17 kilometers and contains 150 million sensors monitoring hundreds of millions of particle collisions per second. The data from this experiment is massive, with 25 petabytes created daily, after a filtering process (if filtering was not used, there would be 150 million petabytes per year). Analysis on data this big has led to amazing insights about our universe, but has been a significant engineering and analytics challenge.

Governments are increasingly using big data too, to track populations, businesses, and other aspects about their country. Tracking millions of people and billions of interactions (such as business transactions or health spending) has led to a need for big data analytics in many government organizations.

Traffic management is a particular focus of many governments around the world, who are tracking traffic using millions of sensors to determine which roads are most congested and predicting the impact of new roads on traffic levels.

Large retail organizations are using big data to improve the customer experience and reduce costs. This involves predicting customer demand in order to have the correct level of inventory, upselling customers with products they may like to purchase, and tracking transactions to look for trends, patterns, and potential frauds.

Other large businesses are also leveraging big data to automate aspects of their business and improve their offering. This includes leveraging analytics to predict future trends in their sector and track external competitors. Large businesses also use analytics to manage their own employees—tracking employees to look for signs that an employee may leave the company, in order to intervene before they do.

The information security sector is also leveraging big data in order to look for malware infections in large networks, by monitoring network traffic. This can include looking for odd traffic patterns, evidence of malware spreading, and other oddities. **Advanced Persistent Threats** (**APTs**) is another problem, where a motivated attacker will hide their code within a large network to steal information or cause damage over a long period of time. Finding APTs is often a case of forensically examining many computers, a task which simply takes too long for a human to effectively perform themselves. Analytics helps automate and analyze these forensic images to find infections.

Big data is being used in an increasing number of sectors and applications, and this trend is likely to only continue.

MapReduce

There are a number of concepts to perform data mining and general computation on big data. One of the most popular is the MapReduce model, which can be used for general computation on arbitrarily large datasets.

MapReduce originates from Google, where it was developed with distributed computing in mind. It also introduces fault tolerance and scalability improvements. The "original" research for MapReduce was published in 2004, and since then there have been thousands of projects, implementations, and applications using it.

While the concept is similar to many previous concepts, MapReduce has become a staple in big data analytics.

Intuition

MapReduce has two main steps: the Map step and the Reduce step. These are built on the functional programming concepts of mapping a function to a list and reducing the result. To explain the concept, we will develop code that will iterate over a list of lists and produce the sum of all numbers in those lists.

There are also shuffle and combine steps in the MapReduce paradigm, which we will see later.

To start with, the Map step takes a function and applies it to each element in a list. The returned result is a list of the same size, with the results of the function applied to each element.

To open a new IPython Notebook, start by creating a list of lists with numbers in each sublist:

```
a = [[1,2,1], [3,2], [4,9,1,0,2]]
```

Next, we can perform a map, using the sum function. This step will apply the sum function to each element of a:

```
sums = map(sum, a)
```

While sums is a generator (the actual value isn't computed until we ask for it), the above step is approximately equal to the following code:

```
sums = []
for sublist in a:
    results = sum(sublist)
    sums.append(results)
```

The reduce step is a little more complicated. It involves applying a function to each element of the returned result, to some starting value. We start with an initial value, and then apply a given function to that initial value and the first value. We then apply the given function to the result and the next value, and so on.

We start by creating a function that takes two numbers and adds them together.

```
def add(a, b):
  return a + b
```

We then perform the reduce. The signature of reduce is reduce(function, sequence, and initial), where the function is applied at each step to the sequence. In the first step, the initial value is used as the first value, rather than the first element of the list:

```
from functools import reduce
print(reduce(add, sums, 0))
```

The result, *25*, is the sum of each of the values in the sums list and is consequently the sum of each of the elements in the original array.

The preceding code is equal to the following:

```
initial = 0
current_result = initial
for element in sums:
    current_result = add(current_result, element)
```

In this trivial example, our code can be greatly simplified, but the real gains come from distributing the computation. For instance, if we have a million sublists and each of those sublists contained a million elements, we can distribute this computation over many computers.

In order to do this, we distribute the map step. For each of the elements in our list, we send it, along with a description of our function, to a computer. This computer then returns the result to our main computer (the master).

The master then sends the result to a computer for the reduce step. In our example of a million sublists, we would send a million jobs to different computers (the same computer may be reused after it completes our first job). The returned result would be just a single list of a million numbers, which we then compute the sum of.

The result is that no computer ever needed to store more than a million numbers, despite our original data having a trillion numbers in it.

A word count example

The implementation of MapReduce is a little more complex than just using a map and reduce step. Both steps are invoked using keys, which allows for the separation of data and tracking of values.

The map function takes a key and value pair and returns a list of *key+value* pairs. The keys for the input and output don't necessarily relate to each other. For example, for a MapReduce program that performs a word count, the input key might be a sample document's ID value, while the output key would be a given word. The input value would be the text of the document and the output value would be the frequency of each word:

```
from collections import defaultdict
def map_word_count(document_id, document):
```

We first count the frequency of each word. In this simplified example, we split the document on whitespace to obtain the words, although there are better options:

```
    counts = defaultdict(int)
    for word in document.split():
        counts[word] += 1
```

We then yield each of the word, count pairs. The word here is the key, with the count being the value in MapReduce terms:

```
    for word in counts:
        yield (word, counts[word])
```

By using the word as the key, we can then perform a **shuffle** step, which groups all of the values for each key:

```
def shuffle_words(results):
```

First, we aggregate the resulting counts for each word into a list of counts:

```
    records = defaultdict(list)
```

We then iterate over all the results that were returned by the map function;

```
    for results in results_generators:
        for word, count in results:
            records[word].append(count)
```

Next, we yield each of the words along with all the counts that were obtained in our dataset:

```
    for word in records:
        yield (word, records[word])
```

The final step is the reduce step, which takes a key value pair (the value in this case is always a list) and produces a key value pair as a result. In our example, the key is the word, the input list is the list of counts produced in the shuffle step, and the output value is the sum of the counts:

```
def reduce_counts(word, list_of_counts):
    return (word, sum(list_of_counts))
```

To see this in action, we can use the 20 newsgroups dataset, which is provided in scikit-learn:

```
from sklearn.datasets import fetch_20newsgroups
dataset = fetch_20newsgroups(subset='train')
documents = dataset.data
```

We then apply our map step. We use enumerate here to automatically generate document IDs for us. While they aren't important in this application, these keys are important in other applications;

```
map_results = map(map_word_count, enumerate(documents))
```

The actual result here is just a generator, no actual counts have been produced. That said, it is a generator that emits (word, count) pairs.

Next, we perform the shuffle step to sort these word counts:

```
shuffle_results = shuffle_words(map_results)
```

This, in essence is a MapReduce job; however, it is only running on a single thread, meaning we aren't getting any benefit from the MapReduce data format. In the next section, we will start using Hadoop, an open source provider of MapReduce, to start to get the benefits from this type of paradigm.

Hadoop MapReduce

Hadoop is a set of open source tools from Apache that includes an implementation of MapReduce. In many cases, it is the de facto implementation used by many. The project is managed by the Apache group (who are responsible for the famous web server).

The Hadoop ecosystem is quite complex, with a large number of tools. The main component we will use is Hadoop MapReduce. Other tools for working with big data that are included in Hadoop are as follows:

- **Hadoop Distributed File System (HDFS)**: This is a file system that can store files over many computers, with the goal of being robust against hardware failure while providing high bandwidth.
- **YARN**: This is a method for scheduling applications and managing clusters of computers.
- **Pig**: This is a higher level programming language for MapReduce. Hadoop MapReduce is implemented in Java, and Pig sits on top of the Java implementation, allowing you to write programs in other languages—including Python.
- **Hive**: This is for managing data warehouses and performing queries.
- **HBase**: This is an implementation of Google's BigTable, a distributed database.

These tools all solve different issues that come up when doing big data experiments, including data analytics.

There are also non-Hadoop-based implementations of MapReduce, as well as other projects with similar goals. In addition, many cloud providers have MapReduce-based systems.

Application

In this application, we will look at predicting the gender of a writer based on their use of different words. We will use a Naive Bayes method for this, trained in MapReduce. The final model doesn't need MapReduce, although we can use the Map step to do so—that is, run the prediction model on each document in a list. This is a common Map operation for data mining in MapReduce, with the reduce step simply organizing the list of predictions so they can be tracked back to the original document.

We will be using Amazon's infrastructure to run our application, allowing us to leverage their computing resources.

Getting the data

The data we are going to use is a set of blog posts that are labeled for age, gender, industry (that is, work) and, funnily enough, star sign. This data was collected from `http://blogger.com` in August 2004 and has over 140 million words in more than 600,000 posts. Each blog is probably written by just one person, with some work put into verifying this (although, we can never be really sure). Posts are also matched with the date of posting, making this a very rich dataset.

To get the data, go to `http://u.cs.biu.ac.il/~koppel/BlogCorpus.htm` and click on **Download Corpus**. From there, unzip the file to a directory on your computer.

The dataset is organized with a single blog to a file, with the filename giving the classes. For instance, one of the filenames is as follows:

```
1005545.male.25.Engineering.Sagittarius.xml
```

The filename is separated by periods, and the fields are as follows:

- **Blogger ID**: This a simple ID value to organize the identities.
- **Gender**: This is either male or female, and all the blogs are identified as one of these two options (no other options are included in this dataset).
- **Age**: The exact ages are given, but some gaps are deliberately present. Ages present are in the (inclusive) ranges of 13-17, 23-27, and 33-48. The reason for the gaps is to allow for splitting the blogs into age ranges with gaps, as it would be quite difficult to separate an 18 year old's writing from a 19 year old, and it is possible that the age itself is a little outdated.
- **Industry**: In one of 40 different industries including science, engineering, arts, and real estate. Also, included is indUnk, for unknown industry.
- **Star Sign**: This is one of the 12 astrological star signs.

All values are self-reported, meaning there may be errors or inconsistencies with labeling, but are assumed to be mostly reliable—people had the option of not setting values if they wanted to preserve their privacy in those ways.

A single file is in a `psuedo-XML` format, containing a `<Blog>` tag and then a sequence of `<post>` tags. Each of the `<post>` tag is proceeded by a `<date>` tag as well. While we can parse this as XML, it is much simpler to parse it on a line-by-line basis as the files are not exactly well-formed XML, with some errors (mostly encoding problems). To read the posts in the file, we can use a loop to iterate over the lines.

We set a test filename so we can see this in action:

```
import os
filename = os.path.join(os.path.expanduser("~"), "Data", "blogs",
"1005545.male.25.Engineering.Sagittarius.xml")
```

First, we create a list that will let us store each of the posts:

```
all_posts = []
```

Then, we open the file to read:

```
with open(filename) as inf:
```

We then set a flag indicating whether we are currently in a post. We will set this to `True` when we find a `<post>` tag indicating the start of a post and set it to `False` when we find the closing `</post>` tag;

```
    post_start = False
```

We then create a list that stores the current post's lines:

```
    post = []
```

We then iterate over each line of the file and remove white space:

```
    for line in inf:
        line = line.strip()
```

As stated before, if we find the opening `<post>` tag, we indicate that we are in a new post. Likewise, with the close `</post>` tag:

```
        if line == "<post>":
            post_start = True
        elif line == "</post>":
            post_start = False
```

When we do find the closing `</post>` tag, we also then record the full post that we have found so far. We also then start a new "current" post. This code is on the same indentation level as the previous line:

```
            all_posts.append("\n".join(post))
            post = []
```

Finally, when the line isn't a start of end tag, but we are in a post, we add the text of the current line to our current post:

```
        elif post_start:
            post.append(line)
```

If we aren't in a current post, we simply ignore the line.

We can then grab the text of each post:

```
print(all_posts[0])
```

We can also find out how many posts this author created:

```
print(len(all_posts))
```

Naive Bayes prediction

We are now going to implement the Naive Bayes algorithm (technically, a reduced version of it, without many of the features that more complex implementations have) that is able to process our dataset.

The mrjob package

The mrjob package allows us to create MapReduce jobs that can easily be transported to Amazon's infrastructure. While mrjob sounds like a sedulous addition to the Mr. Men series of children's books, it actually stands for *Map Reduce Job*. It is a great package; however, as of the time of writing, Python 3 support is still not mature yet, which is true for the Amazon EMR service that we will discuss later on.

> You can install mrjob for Python 2 versions using the following:
>
> **`sudo pip2 install mrjob`**
>
> Note that `pip` is used for version 2, not for version 3.

In essence, mrjob provides the standard functionality that most MapReduce jobs need. Its most amazing feature is that you can write the same code, test on your local machine without Hadoop, and then push to Amazon's EMR service or another Hadoop server.

This makes testing the code significantly easier, although it can't magically make a big problem small—note that any local testing uses a subset of the dataset, rather than the whole, big dataset.

Extracting the blog posts

We are first going to create a MapReduce program that will extract each of the posts from each blog file and store them as separate entries. As we are interested in the gender of the author of the posts, we will extract that too and store it with the post.

We can't do this in an IPython Notebook, so instead open a Python IDE for development. If you don't have a Python IDE (such as PyCharm), you can use a text editor. I recommend looking for an IDE that has syntax highlighting.

If you still can't find a good IDE, you can write the code in an IPython Notebook and then click on **File** | **Download As** | **Python**. Save this file to a directory and run it as we outlined in *Chapter 11, Classifying Objects in Images using Deep Learning*.

To do this, we will need the `os` and `re` libraries as we will be obtaining environment variables and we will also use a regular expression for word separation:

```
import os
import re
```

We then import the `MRJob` class, which we will inherit from our MapReduce job:

```
from mrjob.job import MRJob
```

We then create a new class that subclasses MRJob:

```
class ExtractPosts(MRJob):
```

We will use a similar loop, as before, to extract blog posts from the file. The mapping function we will define next will work off each line, meaning we have to track different posts outside of the mapping function. For this reason, we make `post_start` and `post` class variables, rather than variables inside the function:

```
    post_start = False
    post = []
```

We then define our mapper function—this takes a line from a file as input and yields blog posts. The lines are guaranteed to be ordered from the same per-job file. This allows us to use the above class variables to record current post data:

```
    def mapper(self, key, line):
```

Before we start collecting blog posts, we need to get the gender of the author of the blog. While we don't normally use the filename as part of MapReduce jobs, there is a strong need for it (as in this case) so the functionality is available. The current file is stored as an environment variable, which we can obtain using the following line of code:

```
filename = os.environ["map_input_file"]
```

We then split the filename to get the gender (which is the second token);

```
gender = filename.split(".")[1]
```

We remove whitespace from the start and end of the line (there is a lot of whitespace in these documents) and then do our post-based tracking as before;

```
line = line.strip()
if line == "<post>":
    self.post_start = True
elif line == "</post>":
    self.post_start = False
```

Rather than storing the posts in a list, as we did earlier, we yield them. This allows mrjob to track the output. We yield both the gender and the post so that we can keep a record of which gender each record matches. The rest of this function is defined in the same way as our loop above:

```
    yield gender, repr("\n".join(self.post))
    self.post = []
elif self.post_start:
    self.post.append(line)
```

Finally, outside the function and class, we set the script to run this MapReduce job when it is called from the command line:

```
if __name__ == '__main__':
    ExtractPosts.run()
```

Now, we can run this MapReduce job using the following shell command. Note that we are using Python 2, and not Python 3 to run this;

```
python extract_posts.py <your_data_folder>/blogs/51* --output-
  dir=<your_data_folder>/blogposts -no-output
```

The first parameter, `<your_data_folder>/blogs/51*` (just remember to change `<your_data_folder>` to the full path to your data folder), obtains a sample of the data (all files starting with 51, which is only 11 documents). We then set the output directory to a new folder, which we put in the data folder, and specify not to output the streamed data. Without the last option, the output data is shown to the command line when we run it—which isn't very helpful to us and slows down the computer quite a lot.

Run the script, and quite quickly each of the blog posts will be extracted and stored in our output folder. This script only ran on a single thread on the local computer so we didn't get a speedup at all, but we know the code runs.

We can now look in the output folder for the results. A bunch of files are created and each file contains each blog post on a separate line, preceded by the gender of the author of the blog.

Training Naive Bayes

Now that we have extracted the blog posts, we can train our Naive Bayes model on them. The intuition is that we record the probability of a word being written by a particular gender. To classify a new sample, we would multiply the probabilities and find the most likely gender.

The aim of this code is to output a file that lists each word in the corpus, along with the frequencies of that word for each gender. The output file will look something like this:

```
"'ailleurs"  {"female": 0.003205128205128205}
"'air"  {"female": 0.003205128205128205}
"'an"  {"male": 0.0030581039755351682, "female": 0.004273504273504274}
"'angoisse"  {"female": 0.003205128205128205}
"'apprendra"  {"male": 0.0013047113868622459, "female":
0.0014172668603481887}
"'attendent"  {"female": 0.00641025641025641}
"'autistic"  {"male": 0.002150537634408602}
"'auto"  {"female": 0.003205128205128205}
"'avais"  {"female": 0.00641025641025641}
"'avait"  {"female": 0.004273504273504274}
"'behind"  {"male": 0.0024390243902439024}
"'bout"  {"female": 0.002034152292059272}
```

The first value is the word and the second is a dictionary mapping the genders to the frequency of that word in that gender's writings.

Open a new file in your Python IDE or text editor. We will again need the `os` and `re` libraries, as well as `NumPy` and `MRJob` from mrjob. We also need itemgetter, as we will be sorting a dictionary:

```
import os
import re
import numpy as np
from mrjob.job import MRJob
from operator import itemgetter
```

We will also need MRStep, which outlines a step in a MapReduce job. Our previous job only had a single step, which is defined as a mapping function and then as a reducing function. This job will have three steps where we Map, Reduce, and then Map and Reduce again. The intuition is the same as the pipelines we used in earlier chapters, where the output of one step is the input to the next step:

```
from mrjob.step import MRStep
```

We then create our word search regular expression and compile it, allowing us to find word boundaries. This type of regular expression is much more powerful than the simple split we used in some previous chapters, but if you are looking for a more accurate word splitter, I recommend using NLTK as we did in *Chapter 6, Social Media Insight using Naive Bayes*:

```
word_search_re = re.compile(r"[\w']+")
```

We define a new class for our training:

```
class NaiveBayesTrainer(MRJob):
```

We define the steps of our `MapReduce` job. There are two steps. The first step will extract the word occurrence probabilities. The second step will compare the two genders and output the probabilities for each to our output file. In each MRStep, we define the mapper and reducer functions, which are class functions in this `NaiveBayesTrainer` class (we will write those functions next):

```
    def steps(self):
        return [
            MRStep(mapper=self.extract_words_mapping,
                   reducer=self.reducer_count_words),
            MRStep(reducer=self.compare_words_reducer),
            ]
```

The first function is the mapper function for the first step. The goal of this function is to take each blog post, get all the words in that post, and then note the occurrence. We want the frequencies of the words, so we will return `1 / len(all_words)`, which allows us to later sum the values for frequencies. The computation here isn't exactly correct—we need to also normalize for the number of documents. In this dataset, however, the class sizes are the same, so we can conveniently ignore this with little impact on our final version.

We also output the gender of the post's author, as we will need that later:

```
def extract_words_mapping(self, key, value):
    tokens = value.split()
    gender = eval(tokens[0])
    blog_post = eval(" ".join(tokens[1:]))
    all_words = word_search_re.findall(blog_post)
    all_words = [word.lower() for word in all_words]
        all_words = word_search_re.findall(blog_post)
        all_words = [word.lower() for word in all_words]
        for word in all_words:
            yield (gender, word), 1. / len(all_words)
```

We used `eval` in the preceding code to simplify the parsing of the blog posts from the file, for this example. This is not recommended. Instead, use a format such as JSON to properly store and parse the data from the files. A malicious use with access to the dataset can insert code into these tokens and have that code run on your server.

In the reducer for the first step, we sum the frequencies for each gender and word pair. We also change the key to be the word, rather than the combination, as this allows us to search by word when we use the final trained model (although, we still need to output the gender for later use);

```
def reducer_count_words(self, key, frequencies):
    s = sum(frequencies)
    gender, word = key
    yield word, (gender, s)
```

The final step doesn't need a mapper function, so we don't add one. The data will pass straight through as a type of `identity mapper`. The reducer, however, will combine frequencies for each gender under the given word and then output the word and frequency dictionary.

This gives us the information we needed for our Naive Bayes implementation:

```
    def compare_words_reducer(self, word, values):
        per_gender = {}
        for value in values:
            gender, s = value
            per_gender[gender] = s
        yield word, per_gender
```

Finally, we set the code to run this model when the file is run as a script;

```
if __name__ == '__main__':
    NaiveBayesTrainer.run()
```

We can then run this script. The input to this script is the output of the previous post-extractor script (we can actually have them as different steps in the same MapReduce job if you are so inclined);

```
python nb_train.py <your_data_folder>/blogposts/
  --output-dir=<your_data_folder>/models/
--no-output
```

The output directory is a folder that will store a file containing the output from this MapReduce job, which will be the probabilities we need to run our Naive Bayes classifier.

Putting it all together

We can now actually run the Naive Bayes classifier using these probabilities. We will do this in an IPython Notebook, and can go back to using Python 3 (phew!).

First, take a look at the models folder that was specified in the last MapReduce job. If the output was more than one file, we can merge the files by just appending them to each other using a command line function from within the models directory:

```
cat * > model.txt
```

If you do this, you'll need to update the following code with `model.txt` as the model filename.

Back to our Notebook, we first import some standard imports we need for our script:

```
import os
import re
import numpy as np
from collections import defaultdict
from operator import itemgetter
```

We again redefine our word search regular expression—if you were doing this in a real application, I recommend centralizing this. It is important that words are extracted in the same way for training and testing:

```
word_search_re = re.compile(r"[\w']+")
```

Next, we create the function that loads our model from a given filename:

```
def load_model(model_filename):
```

The model parameters will take the form of a dictionary of dictionaries, where the first key is a word, and the inner dictionary maps each gender to a probability. We use `defaultdicts`, which will return zero if a value isn't present;

```
    model = defaultdict(lambda: defaultdict(float))
```

We then open the model and parse each line;

```
    with open(model_filename) as inf:
        for line in inf:
```

The line is split into two sections, separated by whitespace. The first is the word itself and the second is a dictionary of probabilities. For each, we run `eval` on them to get the actual value, which was stored using `repr` in the previous code:

```
            word, values = line.split(maxsplit=1)
            word = eval(word)
            values = eval(values)
```

We then track the values to the word in our model:

```
            model[word] = values
    return model
```

Next, we load our actual model. You may need to change the model filename—it will be in the output `dir` of the last MapReduce job;

```
model_filename = os.path.join(os.path.expanduser("~"), "models",
"part-00000")
model = load_model(model_filename)
```

As an example, we can see the difference in usage of the word **i** (all words are turned into lowercase in the MapReduce jobs) between males and females:

```
model["i"]["male"], model["i"]["female"]
```

Next, we create a function that can use this model for prediction. We won't use the scikit-learn interface for this example, and just create a function instead. Our function takes the model and a document as the parameters and returns the most likely gender:

```
def nb_predict(model, document):
```

We start by creating a dictionary to map each gender to the computed probability:

```
    probabilities = defaultdict(lambda : 1)
```

We extract each of the words from the document:

```
    words = word_search_re.findall(document)
```

We then iterate over the words and find the probability for each gender in the dataset:

```
    for word in set(words):
        probabilities["male"] += np.log(model[word].get("male", 1e-
15))
        probabilities["female"] += np.log(model[word].get("female",
1e-15))
```

We then sort the genders by their value, get the highest value, and return that as our prediction:

```
    most_likely_genders = sorted(probabilities.items(),
key=itemgetter(1), reverse=True)
    return most_likely_genders[0][0]
```

It is important to note that we used `np.log` to compute the probabilities. Probabilities in Naive Bayes models are often quite small. Multiplying small values, which is necessary in many statistical values, can lead to an underflow error where the computer's precision isn't good enough and just makes the whole value 0. In this case, it would cause the likelihoods for both genders to be zero, leading to incorrect predictions.

To get around this, we use log probabilities. For two values a and b, `log(a,b)` is equal to `log(a) + log(b)`. The log of a small probability is a negative value, but a relatively large one. For instance, `log(0.00001)` is about `-11.5`. This means that rather than multiplying actual probabilities and risking an underflow error, we can sum the log probabilities and compare the values in the same way (higher numbers still indicate a higher likelihood).

One problem with using log probabilities is that they don't handle zero values well (although, neither does multiplying by zero probabilities). This is due to the fact that log(0) is undefined. In some implementations of Naive Bayes, a 1 is added to all counts to get rid of this, but there are other ways to address this. This is a simple form of smoothing of the values. In our code, we just return a very small value if the word hasn't been seen for our given gender.

Back to our prediction function, we can test this by copying a post from our dataset:

```
new_post = """ Every day should be a half day.  Took the afternoon
off to hit the dentist, and while I was out I managed to get my oil
changed, too.  Remember that business with my car dealership this
winter?  Well, consider this the epilogue.  The friendly fellas at the
Valvoline Instant Oil Change on Snelling were nice enough to notice
that my dipstick was broken, and the metal piece was too far down in
its little dipstick tube to pull out.  Looks like I'm going to need a
magnet.   Damn you, Kline Nissan, daaaaaaammmnnn yooouuuu....   Today
I let my boss know that I've submitted my Corps application.  The news
has been greeted by everyone in the company with a level of enthusiasm
that really floors me.     The back deck has finally been cleared off
by the construction company working on the place.  This company, for
anyone who's interested, consists mainly of one guy who spends his
days cursing at his crew of Spanish-speaking laborers.  Construction
of my deck began around the time Nixon was getting out of office.
"""
```

We then predict with the following code:

```
nb_predict(model, new_post)
```

The resulting prediction, male, is correct for this example. Of course, we never test a model on a single sample. We used the file starting with 51 for training this model. It wasn't many samples, so we can't expect too high of an accuracy.

The first thing we should do is train on more samples. We will test on any file that starts with a 6 or 7 and train on the rest of the files.

In the command line and in your data folder (`cd <your_data_folder>`), where the blogs folder exists, create a copy of the blogs data into a new folder.

Make a folder for our training set:

```
mkdir blogs_train
```

Move any file starting with a 6 or 7 into the test set, from the train set:

```
cp blogs/4* blogs_train/
cp blogs/8* blogs_train/
```

Then, make a folder for our test set:

```
mkdir blogs_test
```

Move any file starting with a `6` or `7` into the test set, from the train set:

```
cp blogs/6* blogs_test/
cp blogs/7* blogs_test/
```

We will rerun the blog extraction on all files in the training set. However, this is a large computation that is better suited to cloud infrastructure than our system. For this reason, we will now move the parsing job to Amazon's infrastructure.

Run the following on the command line, as you did before. The only difference is that we train on a different folder of input files. Before you run the following code, delete all files in the blog posts and models folders:

```
python extract_posts.py ~/Data/blogs_train --output-dir=/home/bob/
Data/blogposts -no-output
python nb_train.py ~/Data/blogposts/ --output-dir=/home/bob/models/
--no-output
```

The code here will take quite a bit longer to run.

We will test on any blog file in our test set. To get the files, we need to extract them. We will use the `extract_posts.py` MapReduce job, but store the files in a separate folder:

```
python extract_posts.py ~/Data/blogs_test --output-dir=/home/bob/Data/
blogposts_testing -no-output
```

Back in the IPython Notebook, we list all the outputted testing files:

```
testing_folder = os.path.join(os.path.expanduser("~"), "Data",
"blogposts_testing")
testing_filenames = []
for filename in os.listdir(testing_folder):
    testing_filenames.append(os.path.join(testing_folder, filename))
```

For each of these files, we extract the gender and document and then call the predict function. We do this in a generator, as there are a lot of documents, and we don't want to use too much memory. The generator yields the actual gender and the predicted gender:

```
def nb_predict_many(model, input_filename):
    with open(input_filename) as inf:
        # remove leading and trailing whitespace
```

```
        for line in inf:
            tokens = line.split()
            actual_gender = eval(tokens[0])
            blog_post = eval(" ".join(tokens[1:]))
            yield actual_gender, nb_predict(model, blog_post)
```

We then record the predictions and actual genders across our entire dataset. Our predictions here are either male or female. In order to use the `f1_score` function from scikit-learn, we need to turn these into ones and zeroes. In order to do that, we record a 0 if the gender is male and 1 if it is female. To do this, we use a Boolean test, seeing if the gender is female. We then convert these Boolean values to `int` using `NumPy`:

```
y_true = []
y_pred = []
for actual_gender, predicted_gender in nb_predict_many(model, testing_
filenames[0]):
    y_true.append(actual_gender == "female")
    y_pred.append(predicted_gender == "female")
y_true = np.array(y_true, dtype='int')
y_pred = np.array(y_pred, dtype='int')
```

Now, we test the quality of this result using the `F1` score in scikit-learn:

```
from sklearn.metrics import f1_score
print("f1={:.4f}".format(f1_score(y_true, y_pred, pos_label=None)))
```

The result of 0.78 is not bad. We can probably improve this by using more data, but to do that, we need to move to a more powerful infrastructure that can handle it.

Training on Amazon's EMR infrastructure

We are going to use Amazon's **Elastic Map Reduce** (**EMR**) infrastructure to run our parsing and model building jobs.

In order to do that, we first need to create a bucket in Amazon's storage cloud. To do this, open the Amazon S3 console in your web browser by going to `http;//console.aws.amazon.com/s3` and click on **Create Bucket**. Remember the name of the bucket, as we will need it later.

Right-click on the new bucket and select `Properties`. Then, change the permissions, granting everyone full access. This is not a good security practice in general, and I recommend that you change the access permissions after you complete this chapter.

Left-click the bucket to open it and click on **Create Folder**. Name the folder `blogs_train`. We are going to upload our training data to this folder for processing on the cloud.

On your computer, we are going to use Amazon's AWS CLI, a command-line interface for processing on Amazon's cloud.

To install it, use the following:

```
sudo pip2 install awscli
```

Follow the instructions at `http://docs.aws.amazon.com/cli/latest/userguide/cli-chap-getting-set-up.html` to set the credentials for this program.

We now want to upload our data to our new bucket. First, we want to create our dataset, which is all the blogs not starting with a 6 or 7. There are more graceful ways to do this copy, but none are cross-platform enough to recommend. Instead, simply copy all the files and then delete the ones that start with a 6 or 7, from the training dataset:

```
cp -R ~/Data/blogs ~/Data/blogs_train_large
rm ~/Data/blogs_train_large/6*
rm ~/Data/blogs_train_large/7*
```

Next, upload the data to your Amazon S3 bucket. Note that this will take some time and use quite a lot of upload data (several hundred megabytes). For those with slower internet connections, it may be worth doing this at a location with a faster connection;

```
 aws s3 cp  ~/Data/blogs_train_large/ s3://ch12/blogs_train_large
--recursive --exclude "*" --include "*.xml"
```

We are going to connect to Amazon's EMR using mrjob—it handles the whole thing for us; it only needs our credentials to do so. Follow the instructions at `https://pythonhosted.org/mrjob/guides/emr-quickstart.html` to setup mrjob with your Amazon credentials.

After this is done, we alter our mrjob run, only slightly, to run on Amazon EMR. We just tell mrjob to use `emr` using the `-r` switch and then set our `s3` containers as the input and output directories. Even though this will be run on Amazon's infrastructure, it will still take quite a long time to run.

```
python extract_posts.py -r emr s3://ch12gender/blogs_train_large/
--output-dir=s3://ch12/blogposts_train/ --no-output
```

```
python nb_train.py -r emr s3://ch12/blogposts_train/ --output-dir=s3://
ch12/model/ --o-output
```

You will also be charged for the usage. This will only be a few dollars, but keep this in mind if you are going to keep running the jobs or doing other jobs on bigger datasets. I ran a very large number of jobs and was charged about $20 all up. Running just these few should be less than $4. However, you can check your balance and set up pricing alerts, by going to `https://console.aws.amazon.com/billing/home`.

It isn't necessary for the `blogposts_train` and model folders to exist—they will be created by EMR. In fact, if they exist, you will get an error. If you are rerunning this, just change the names of these folders to something new, but remember to change both commands to the same names (that is, the output directory of the first command is the input directory of the second command).

If you are getting impatient, you can always stop the first job after a while and just use the training data gathered so far. I recommend leaving the job for an absolute minimum of 15 minutes and probably at least an hour. You can't stop the second job and get good results though; the second job will probably take about two to three times as long as the first job did.

You can now go back to the `s3` console and download the output model from your bucket. Saving it locally, we can go back to our IPython Notebook and use the new model. We reenter the code here—only the differences are highlighted, just to update to our new model:

```
aws_model_filename = os.path.join(os.path.expanduser("~"), "models",
"aws_model")
aws_model = load_model(aws_model_filename)
y_true = []
y_pred = []
for actual_gender, predicted_gender in nb_predict_many(aws_model,
testing_filenames[0]):
    y_true.append(actual_gender == "female")
    y_pred.append(predicted_gender == "female")
y_true = np.array(y_true, dtype='int')
y_pred = np.array(y_pred, dtype='int')
print("f1={:.4f}".format(f1_score(y_true, y_pred, pos_label=None)))
```

The result is much better with the extra data, at 0.81.

> If everything went as planned, you may want to remove the bucket from Amazon S3—you will be charged for the storage.

Summary

In this chapter, we looked at running jobs on big data. By most standards, our dataset is quite small—only a few hundred megabytes. Many industrial datasets are much bigger, so extra processing power is needed to perform the computation. In addition, the algorithms we used can be optimized for different tasks to further increase the scalability.

Our approach extracted word frequencies from blog posts, in order to predict the gender of the author of a document. We extracted the blogs and word frequencies using MapReduce-based projects in mrjob. With those extracted, we can then perform a Naive Bayes-esque computation to predict the gender of a new document.

We can use the mrjob library to test locally and then automatically set up and use Amazon's EMR cloud infrastructure. You can use other cloud infrastructure or even a custom built Amazon EMR cluster to run these MapReduce jobs, but there is a bit more tinkering needed to get them running.

Next Steps...

During the course of this book, there were lots of avenues not taken, options not presented, and subjects not fully explored. In this Appendix, I've created a collection of next steps for those wishing to undertake extra learning and progress their data mining with Python. Consider this Hero mode, the second question, of the book.

This appendix is broken up by chapter, with articles, books, and other resources for learning more about data mining. Also included are some challenges to extend the work performed in the chapter. Some of these will be small improvements; some will be quite a bit more work—I've made a note on those tasks that are noticeably more extensive than the others.

Chapter 1 – Getting Started with Data Mining

Scikit-learn tutorials

`http://scikit-learn.org/stable/tutorial/index.html`

Included in the scikit-learn documentation is a series of tutorials on data mining. The tutorials range from basic introductions to toy datasets, all the way through to comprehensive tutorials on techniques used in recent research.

The tutorials here will take quite a while to get through—they are very comprehensive—but are well worth the effort to learn.

Extending the IPython Notebook

http://ipython.org/ipython-doc/1/interactive/public_server.html

The IPython Notebook is a powerful tool. It can be extended in many ways, and one of those is to create a server to run your Notebooks, separately from your main computer. This is very useful if you use a low-power main computer, such as a small laptop, but have more powerful computers at your disposal. In addition, you can set up nodes to perform parallelized computations.More datasets are available at:

http://archive.ics.uci.edu/ml/

There are many datasets available on the Internet, from a number of different sources. These include academic, commercial, and government datasets. A collection of well-labelled datasets is available at the UCI ML library, which is one of the best options to find datasets for testing your algorithms.

Try out the OneR algorithm with some of these different datasets.

Chapter 2 – Classifying with scikit-learn Estimators

Scalability with the nearest neighbor

https://github.com/jnothman/scikit-learn/tree/pr2532

A naïve implementation of the nearest neighbor algorithm is quite slow—it checks all pairs of points to find those that are close together. Better implementations exist, with some implemented in scikit-learn. For instance, a kd-tree can be created that speeds up the algorithm (and this is already included in scikit-learn).

Another way to speed up this search is to use locality-sensitive hashing, **Locality-Sensitive Hashing (LSH)**. This is a proposed improvement for scikit-learn, and hasn't made it into the package at the time of writing. The above link gives a development branch of scikit-learn that will allow you to test out LSH on a dataset. Read through the documentation attached to this branch for details on doing this.

To install it, clone the repository and follow the instructions to install the **Bleeding Edge** code available at: `http://scikit-learn.org/stable/install.html`.

Remember to use the above repository's code, rather than the official source. I recommend you install using `virtualenv` or a virtual machine, rather than installing it directly on your computer. A great guide to `virtualenv` can be found here: `http://docs.python-guide.org/en/latest/dev/virtualenvs/`.

More complex pipelines

`http://scikit-learn.org/stable/modules/pipeline.html#featureunion-composite-feature-spaces`

The Pipelines we have used in the book follow a single stream—the output of one step is the input of another step.

Pipelines follow the transformer and estimator interfaces as well—this allows us to embed Pipelines within Pipelines. This is a useful construct for very complex models, but becomes very powerful when combined with Feature Unions, as shown in the above link.

This allows us to extract multiple types of features at a time and then combine them to form a single dataset. For more details, see the example at: `http://scikit-learn.org/stable/auto_examples/feature_stacker.html`.

Comparing classifiers

There are lots of classifiers in scikit-learn that are ready to use. The one you choose for a particular task is going to be based on a variety of factors. You can compare the f1-score to see which method is better, and you can investigate the deviation of those scores to see if that result is statistically significant.

An important factor is that they are trained and tested on the same data—that is, the test set for one classifier is the test set for all classifiers. Our use of random states allows us to ensure this is the case—an important factor for replicating experiments.

Chapter 3: Predicting Sports Winners with Decision Trees

More on pandas

http://pandas.pydata.org/pandas-docs/stable/tutorials.html

The pandas library is a great package—anything you normally write to do data loading is probably already implemented in pandas. You can learn more about it from their tutorial, linked above.

There is also a great blog post written by Chris Moffitt that overviews common tasks people do in Excel and how to do them in pandas: http://pbpython.com/excel-pandas-comp.html

You can also handle large datasets with pandas; see the answer, from user Jeff (the top answer at the time of writing), to this StackOverflow question for an extensive overview of the process: http://stackoverflow.com/questions/14262433/large-data-work-flows-using-pandas.

Another great tutorial on pandas is written by Brian Connelly: http://bconnelly.net/2013/10/summarizing-data-in-python-with-pandas/

More complex features

http://www.basketball-reference.com/teams/ORL/2014_roster_status.html

Sports teams change regularly from game to game. What is an easy win for a team can turn into a difficult game if a couple of the best players are injured. You can get the team rosters from basketball-reference as well. For example, the roster for the 2013-2014 season for the Orlando Magic is available at the above link—similar data is available for all NBA teams.

Writing code to integrate how much a team changes, and using that to add new features, can improve the model significantly. This task will take quite a bit of work, though!

Chapter 4 – Recommending Movies Using Affinity Analysis

New datasets

`http://www2.informatik.uni-freiburg.de/~cziegler/BX/`

There are many recommendation-based datasets that are worth investigating, each with its own issues. For example, the Book-Crossing dataset contains more than 278,000 users and over a million ratings. Some of these ratings are explicit (the user did give a rating), while others are more implicit. The weighting to these implicit ratings probably shouldn't be as high as for explicit ratings.

The music website `www.last.fm` has released a great dataset for music recommendation: `http://www.dtic.upf.edu/~ocelma/MusicRecommendationDataset/`.

There is also a joke recommendation dataset! See here: `http://eigentaste.berkeley.edu/dataset/`.

The Eclat algorithm

`http://www.borgelt.net/eclat.html`

The **APriori** algorithm implemented in this chapter is easily the most famous of the association rule mining graphs, but isn't necessarily the best. Eclat is a more modern algorithm that can be implemented relatively easily.

Chapter 5 – Extracting Features with Transformers

Adding noise

In this chapter, we covered *removing* noise to improve features; however, improved performance can be obtained for some datasets by *adding* noise. The reason for this is simple—it helps stop overfitting by forcing the classifier to generalize its rules a little (although too much noise will make the model too general). try implementing a Transformer that can add a given amount of noise to a dataset. Test that out on some of the datasets from UCI ML and see if it improves test-set performance.

Vowpal Wabbit

http://hunch.net/~vw/

Vowpal Wabbit is a great project, providing very fast feature extraction for text-based problems. It comes with a Python wrapper, allowing you to call it from with Python code. Test it out on large datasets, such as the one we used in *Chapter 12, Working with Big Data.*

Chapter 6 – Social Media Insight Using Naive Bayes

Spam detection

http://scikit-learn.org/stable/modules/model_evaluation.html#scoring-parameter

Using the concepts in this chapter, you can create a spam detection method that is able to view a social media post and determine whether it is spam or not. Try this out by first creating a dataset of spam/not-spam posts, implementing the text mining algorithms, and then evaluating them.

One important consideration with spam detection is the false-positive/false-negative ratio. Many people would prefer to have a couple of spam messages slip through, rather than miss out on a legitimate message because the filter was too aggressive in stopping the spam. In order to turn your method for this, you can use a Grid Search with the f1-score as the evaluation criteria. See the above link for information on how to do this.

Natural language processing and part-of-speech tagging

http://www.nltk.org/book/ch05.html

The techniques we used in this chapter were quite lightweight compared to some of the linguistic models employed in other areas. For example, part-of-speech tagging can help disambiguate word forms, allowing for higher accuracy. The book that comes with NLTK has a chapter on this, linked above. The whole book is well worth reading too.

Chapter 7 – Discovering Accounts to Follow Using Graph Mining

More complex algorithms

https://www.cs.cornell.edu/home/kleinber/link-pred.pdf

There has been extensive research on predicting links in graphs, including for social networks. For instance, David Liben-Nowell and Jon Kleinberg published a paper on this topic that would serve as a great place for more complex algorithms, linked above.

NetworkX

https://networkx.github.io/

If you are going to be using graphs and networks more, going in-depth into the NetworkX package is well worth your time—the visualization options are great and the algorithms are well implemented. Another library called SNAP is also available with Python bindings, at `http://snap.stanford.edu/snappy/index.html`.

Chapter 8 – Beating CAPTCHAs with Neural Networks

Better (worse?) CAPTCHAs

http://scikit-image.org/docs/dev/auto_examples/applications/plot_geometric.html

The CAPTCHAs we beat in this example were not as complex as those normally used today. You can create more complex variants using a number of techniques as follows:

- Applying different transformations such as the ones in scikit-image (see the link above)
- Using different colors and colors that don't translate well to graeyscale
- Adding lines or other shapes to the image: `http://scikit-image.org/docs/dev/api/skimage.draw.html`

Deeper networks

These techniques will probably fool our current implementation, so improvements will need to be made to make the method better. Try some of the deeper networks we used in *Chapter 11, Classifying Objects in Images Using Deep Learning*.

Larger networks need more data, though, so you will probably need to generate more than the few thousand samples we did in this chapter in order to get good performance. Generating these datasets is a good candidate for parallelization—lots of small tasks that can be performed independently.

Reinforcement learning

`http://pybrain.org/docs/tutorial/reinforcement-learning.html`

Reinforcement learning is gaining traction as the next big thing in data mining—although it has been around a long time! PyBrain has some reinforcement learning algorithms that are worth checking out with this dataset (and others!).

Chapter 9 – Authorship Attribution

Increasing the sample size

The Enron application we used ended up using just a portion of the overall dataset. There is lots more data available in this dataset. Increasing the number of authors will likely lead to a drop in accuracy, but it is possible to boost the accuracy further than was achieved in this chapter, using similar methods. Using a Grid Search, try different values for n-grams and different parameters for support vector machines, in order to get better performance on a larger number of authors.

Blogs dataset

The dataset used in *Chapter 12, Working with Big Data*, provides authorship-based classes (each blogger ID is a separate author). This dataset can be tested using this kind of method as well. In addition, there are the other classes of gender, age, industry, and star sign that can be tested—are authorship-based methods good for these classification tasks?

Local n-grams

`https://github.com/robertlayton/authorship_tutorials/blob/master/LNGTutorial.ipynb`

Another form of classifier is local n-gram, which involves choosing the best features per-author, not globally for the entire dataset. I wrote a tutorial on using local n-grams for authorship attribution, available at the above link.

Chapter 10 – Clustering News Articles

Evaluation

The evaluation of clustering algorithms is a difficult problem—on the one hand, we can sort of tell what good clusters look like; on the other hand, if we really know that, we should label some instances and use a supervised classifier! Much has been written on this topic. One slideshow on the topic that is a good introduction to the challenges follows:

`http://www.cs.kent.edu/~jin/DM08/ClusterValidation.pdf`

In addition, a very comprehensive (although now a little dated) paper on this topic is here: `http://web.itu.edu.tr/sgunduz/courses/verimaden/paper/validity_survey.pdf`.

The scikit-learn package does implement a number of the metrics described in those links, with an overview here: `http://scikit-learn.org/stable/modules/clustering.html#clustering-performance-evaluation`.

Using some of these, you can start evaluating which parameters need to be used for better clusterings. Using a Grid Search, we can find parameters that maximize a metric—just like in classification.

Temporal analysis

The code we developed in this chapter can be rerun over many months. By adding some tags to each cluster, you can track which topics stay active over time, getting a longitudinal viewpoint of what is being discussed in the world news.

To compare the clusters, consider a metric such as the adjusted mutual information score, which was linked to the scikit-learn documentation earlier. See how the clusters change after one month, two months, six months, and a year.

Real-time clusterings

The k-means algorithm can be iteratively trained and updated over time, rather than discrete analyses at given time frames. Cluster movement can be tracked in a number of ways—for instance, you can track which words are popular in each cluster and how much the centroids move per day. Keep the API limits in mind—you probably only need to do one check every few hours to keep your algorithm up-to-date.

Chapter 11: Classifying Objects in Images Using Deep Learning

Keras and Pylearn2

Other deep learning libraries that are worth looking at, if you are going further with deep learning in Python, are Keras and Pylearn2. They are both based on Theano and have different usages and features.

Keras can be found here: `https://github.com/fchollet/keras/`.

Pylearn2 can be found here: `http://deeplearning.net/software/pylearn2/`.

Both are not stable platforms at the time of writing, although Pylearn2 is the more stable of the two. That said, they both do what they do very well and are worth investigating for future projects.

Another library called Torch is very popular but, at the time of writing, it doesn't have python bindings (see `http://torch.ch/`).

Mahotas

Another package for image processing is Mahotas, including better and more complex image processing techniques that can help achieve better accuracy, although they may come at a high computational cost. However, many image processing tasks are good candidates for parallelization. More techniques on image classification can be found in the research literature, with this survey paper as a good start: `http://luispedro.org/software/mahotas/`.

`http://ijarcce.com/upload/january/22-A%20Survey%20on%20Image%20Classification.pdf`

Other image datasets are available at:

http://rodrigob.github.io/are_we_there_yet/build/classification_datasets_results.html

There are many datasets of images available from a number of academic and industry-based sources. The linked website lists a bunch of datasets and some of the best algorithms to use on them. Implementing some of the better algorithms will require significant amounts of custom code, but the payoff can be well worth the pain.

Chapter 12 – Working with Big Data

Courses on Hadoop

Both Yahoo and Google have great tutorials on Hadoop, which go from beginner to quite advanced levels. They don't specifically address using Python, but learning the Hadoop concepts and then applying them in Pydoop or a similar library can yield great results.

Yahoo's tutorial: https://developer.yahoo.com/hadoop/tutorial/

Google's tutorial: https://cloud.google.com/hadoop/what-is-hadoop

Pydoop

Pydoop is a python library to run Hadoop jobs—it also has a great tutorial that can be found here: http://crs4.github.io/pydoop/tutorial/index.html.

Pydoop also works with HDFS, the Hadoop File System, although you can get that functionality in mrjob as well. Pydoop will give you a bit more control over running some jobs.

Recommendation engine

Building a large recommendation engine is a good test of your Big data skills. A great blog post by Mark Litwintschik covers an engine using Apache Spark, a big data technology: http://tech.marksblogg.com/recommendation-engine-spark-python.html.

More resources

Kaggle competitions:

`www.kaggle.com/`

Kaggle runs data mining competitions regularly, often with monetary prizes. Testing your skills on Kaggle competitions is a fast and great way to learn to work with real-world data mining problems. The forums are nice and share environments—often, you will see code released for a top-10 entry during the competition!

Coursera:

`www.coursera.org`

Coursera contains many courses on data mining and data science. Many of the courses are specialized such as big data and image processing. A great general one to start with is Andrew Ng's famous course: `https://www.coursera.org/learn/machine-learning/`.

It is a bit more advanced than this book and would be a great next step for interested readers.

For neural networks, check out this course: `https://www.coursera.org/course/neuralnets`.

If you complete all of these, try out the course on probabilistic graphical models at `https://www.coursera.org/course/pgm`.

Index

A

E

F

G

H

I

J

K

L

M

N

O

P

Q

R

S

T

U

V

W

Thank you for buying

Learning Data Mining with Python

About Packt Publishing

Packt, pronounced 'packed', published its first book, *Mastering phpMyAdmin for Effective MySQL Management*, in April 2004, and subsequently continued to specialize in publishing highly focused books on specific technologies and solutions.

Our books and publications share the experiences of your fellow IT professionals in adapting and customizing today's systems, applications, and frameworks. Our solution-based books give you the knowledge and power to customize the software and technologies you're using to get the job done. Packt books are more specific and less general than the IT books you have seen in the past. Our unique business model allows us to bring you more focused information, giving you more of what you need to know, and less of what you don't.

Packt is a modern yet unique publishing company that focuses on producing quality, cutting-edge books for communities of developers, administrators, and newbies alike. For more information, please visit our website at `www.packtpub.com`.

About Packt Open Source

In 2010, Packt launched two new brands, Packt Open Source and Packt Enterprise, in order to continue its focus on specialization. This book is part of the Packt Open Source brand, home to books published on software built around open source licenses, and offering information to anybody from advanced developers to budding web designers. The Open Source brand also runs Packt's Open Source Royalty Scheme, by which Packt gives a royalty to each open source project about whose software a book is sold.

Writing for Packt

We welcome all inquiries from people who are interested in authoring. Book proposals should be sent to `author@packtpub.com`. If your book idea is still at an early stage and you would like to discuss it first before writing a formal book proposal, then please contact us; one of our commissioning editors will get in touch with you.

We're not just looking for published authors; if you have strong technical skills but no writing experience, our experienced editors can help you develop a writing career, or simply get some additional reward for your expertise.

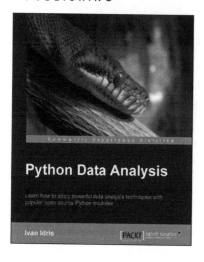

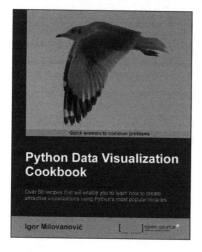

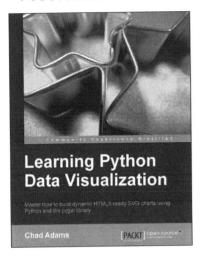

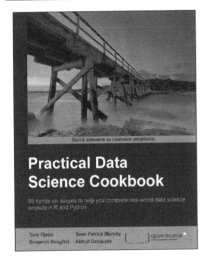

Made in the USA
Middletown, DE
29 November 2015